International Political Economy Series

Series Editor

Timothy M. Shaw, University of Massachusetts Boston, Boston, USA;
Emeritus Professor, University of London, London, UK

The global political economy is in flux as a series of cumulative crises impacts its organization and governance. The IPE series has tracked its development in both analysis and structure over the last three decades. It has always had a concentration on the global South. Now the South increasingly challenges the North as the centre of development, also reflected in a growing number of submissions and publications on indebted Eurozone economies in Southern Europe. An indispensable resource for scholars and researchers, the series examines a variety of capitalisms and connections by focusing on emerging economies, companies and sectors, debates and policies. It informs diverse policy communities as the established trans-Atlantic North declines and 'the rest', especially the BRICS, rise. NOW INDEXED ON SCOPUS!

More information about this series at
http://www.palgrave.com/gp/series/13996

Kenneth Omeje

The Failure and Feasibility of Capitalism in Africa

palgrave
macmillan

Kenneth Omeje
Bradford, UK

ISSN 2662-2483 ISSN 2662-2491 (electronic)
International Political Economy Series
ISBN 978-3-030-75169-2 ISBN 978-3-030-75170-8 (eBook)
https://doi.org/10.1007/978-3-030-75170-8

This Palgrave Macmillan imprint is published by the registered company Springer Nature Switzerland AG
The registered company address is: Gewerbestrasse 11, 6330 Cham, Switzerland

I dedicate this book to all those genuinely committed to Africa's urgent transformation, and also to my wife Ngozi and children, Rejoicing, Chibia and Ifediche for their extraordinary endurance over the Covid-19 pandemic lockdown when I spent long hours writing this book.

Foreword

Kenneth Omeje has produced a magisterial work on Africa's development, strictly speaking, the reasons for the absence of significant socioeconomic development in Africa. In the words of the author, "capitalism has failed to deliver the long-desired economic transformation and inclusive development in postcolonial Africa." In his view, this abysmal failure to trigger change is due to several dysfunctional ties rooted in the essentially non-productive forms of capitalism that tend to be dominant in most African states. Given a global system that proffers limited opportunities for growth and development in less-developing countries, the future for African economies thus seems bleak. For Omeje, part of the reasons for this stultification of growth is due to the fact that modern capitalism "inevitably and pervasively generated corrupt gains through conduct that does not transgress capitalist norms for individual's economic conduct." He warned against what he sees as the heresy that western capitalism was the harbinger of capitalism in Africa. In his view, "… capitalism was long evolving and practised in various parts of Africa alongside other pre-modern modes of production … prior to the imposition of Western colonial rule …".

The author draws attention to the parody of decolonization, whereby most African states were without economic independence, which paved the way for neocolonialism, with fiscal control of African states being determined in the old colonial capitals. With specific reference to Francophone Africa, he observed that the "refusal of monetary sovereignty means that one of the preconditions for the granting of political independence was that the French ex-colonies of Sub-Saharan Africa must maintain their ties with French colonial currency union, the franc of the French community of Africa, known as the CFA Franc …". The hijacking in 2019 of the proposed name, the "Eco," from the West African Economic Monetary Union currency by the members of the French Community of Africa (CFA), points to the extreme dependency of the Francophone African states on the ex-colonial master, France. According to Omeje, this interventionist move by the French President points to the huge benefits his country derives from "hosting" these African currencies and the loss to the African member states.

Omeje reminds his readers that the import-substitution strategy of the "Dependency Theory" era, was in reality "import reproduction" and not substitution, since it was a product-driven model, unsuitable for the domestic economies of African markets, inducing capital, engineering and marketing skills to flow from Africa to the imperialist centres.

This book, with its unique blend of sophisticated theories of development and practice, has focused our attention with much detailed insights into some of the major problems of economic and political transformation facing the African continent. It is compulsory reading for anyone interested in economic and social transformation in Africa.

March 2021

Alfred B. Zack-Williams
Professor Emeritus in Sociology
University of Central Lancashire
Preston, UK

Preface

From Adam Smith to John Maynard Keynes, from Jean-Baptiste Say to Milton Friedman, Western capitalism has had too many pundits and philosophers in every generation such that the West has no reason to fail. It is not the same with the subaltern capitalism in Africa that has historically been beset by enormous obstacles, internal and external, that have conspired to keep millions of its citizens in inexcusable poverty in the midst of plenteous potential resources. Africa needs more thinkers and epistemes of policy-relevant knowledge that can enhance an understanding of why capitalism has not delivered well in the continent, why it has failed to deliver, and what can be done to break the poor performance jinx. I volunteer in this study to write a contribution to the understanding of capitalism in Africa, my primary intellectual concern and constituency. The main purpose of this book is to explore and elucidate how and why capitalism has failed in Africa and the feasibility of turning it around.

Using a mix of empiric evidence, I argue in this book that capitalism has practically failed to deliver the long-desired economic transformation and inclusive development in postcolonial Africa. Many factors account for this abysmal performance, the most prominent being the multiple dysfunctionalities rooted in the non-productive and aberrant forms of capitalism that tend to be dominant in the African continent. For the most part, capitalism systematically dysfunctions in Africa because, as I have postulated in this research, the dominant versions of capitalism in the continent are non-productive—rentier capitalism, crony capitalism, hostage capitalism, predatory capitalism and the likes. There are corresponding governance dimensions of dysfunctional capitalism in Africa which are discussed in the study. The seemingly viable and productive forms of capitalism—mixed-economy capitalism, state capitalism and most importantly, entrepreneurial capitalism—are essentially relegated or lack the empirical feasibility for momentous transformation under the prevailing domestic and international policy frameworks and political environments. Entrepreneurial capitalism which has the greatest potential to generate growth, employment and development is practically starved and suffocated by the seemingly more dominant dysfunctional brands of capitalism in most countries. The accumulation imperatives of the dysfunctional brands of capitalism not only make a nonsense of the economics of inclusive development, but in practice divert enormous resources away from development. Personal aggrandizement of public resources and power, use of state power to promote impunity, siphoning of public funds away into overseas personal bank accounts, unseriousness with the high demands of modern governance, extreme inconsistencies and uncertainties in the policy and business environment, fetish celebration of small things and wasteful misallocation of resources are some of the defining characteristics of dysfunctional capitalism that greatly jeopardize economic transformation and development.

I am partly motivated to write this book because Africa remains by far the weakest regional link of the global economy. The effects of poor economic performance in the continent are horrendous—widespread poverty, appalling infrastructures and public service delivery, high level of youth unemployment and restiveness, vulnerability of too many hopeless young people to extremist violence and armed insurgencies, as well as high level of forced migration. The relentless wave of desperate migration of vulnerable young people from Sub-Saharan Africa across the Sahara Desert and the Mediterranean Sea to Europe is a consequence of the profound economic and governance failure in Africa.

Divided into nine chapters, this study traces and analyses the evolution of capitalism in Africa from the precolonial times through the colonial dispensation but focusing more on the postcolonial and contemporary dynamics and challenges. History is explored in this context, not necessarily to indict the past, but as a means to elucidate how structural legacies rooted in the convoluted foundations and transactions of the past have continued in a dialectical way to reproduce a nexus of institutional structures, social forces and vested interests that ultimately make capitalism to dysfunction in many African states in the contemporary dispensation. The book also interrogates the "Africa rising" debate—the controversial discourse postulating that contemporary Africa has made a substantial leap from the mire of underdevelopment and its negative governance and security correlates to the trajectory of sustainable progress. The existing literature on this subject acknowledges the growth recorded by many African countries since 2005 or thereabout as phenomenal, based on which many proponents have argued that Africa is on the path of a major economic transformation. In this study I have presented a plethora of comparative regional and international data to evaluate Africa's economic performance in a historical trajectory, and made an evidence-based analysis stressing that, beyond the smokescreen of euphoric claims and assumptions since the 2000s, capitalism has practically failed to deliver the much-desired economic transformation and development in Africa.

This volume offers an interrogative analysis of Africa's economic development policies and practices since independence and their outcomes from a comparative multi-regional perspective. I have examined among other relevant issues the political economy of Africa's relations with the West, the peculiar circumstances of French—Africa connection, China—Africa relations, as well as the regional and international circumstances that influenced the transformation of the successful East and South Asian countries from relatively poor and underdeveloped economies to high-performing capitalist economies. The lessons that Africa could learn from the Asian "economic miracles" are discussed in detail, including the potential limitations engendered by the contemporary global political economy and how Africa could constructively engage the contending forces. Learning from the experiences of the successful Asian economies, I have argued that Africa needs epicentres of big bang transformation that will sustainably engineer transgenerational growth and development with multiplier effects across many outlying economies to be able to overcome the present development challenges. Unfortunately, no country in post-independence Africa has ever come close to becoming an epicentre for such a momentous spark of regional proportion. Within the context of the prevailing highly structured global system that offers developing economies limited pathways for growth and development, this book explores the practical feasibilities for accelerated capitalist development in Africa. Significantly, the book discusses a raft of policy options that go beyond the orthodox neoliberal framework to show how to fix the nexus between political governance and economic development in Africa at both the national and regional levels in order to uplift hundreds of millions of African citizens from extreme poverty. Finally, the book adopts an unconventional approach that is subtly satirical—only in a restricted sense—but frankly discursive, interrogative and academic.

Bradford, UK Kenneth Omeje

Praise for *The Failure and Feasibility of Capitalism in Africa*

"*The Failure and Feasibility of Capitalism in Africa* offers a wide ranging and comprehensive *tour d'horizon* of the continent's historical development. Deeply critical of the 'Africa Rising' narrative, Omeje provides a compelling account of the forms, trajectories and failures of capitalist development while offering up a clear-eyed assessment of the prospects of turning around Africa's current predicaments. An urgent and provocative contribution."

—Michael Watts, *Class of 63 Professor Emeritus, University of California, Berkeley, USA*

Contents

About the Author

Kenneth Omeje is the Director of Manifold Crown Consulting Services based in Bradford, United Kingdom; a Visiting Professor at the Institute of Peace and Security Studies in Addis Ababa University, Ethiopia and an Extraordinary Professor of Development Studies at the University of South Africa (UNISA). He has previously held the positions of Senior Research Fellow in the Department of Peace Studies and International Development, University of Bradford; Senior Research Associate in the Faculty of Humanities, University of Johannesburg, South Africa; Professor of International Relations and Security Studies at the United States International University-Africa and the Georg Arnhold Visiting Professor of Sustainable Peace at the Georg Eckert Institute for International Textbook Research in Braunschweig, Germany, among others. He has about a hundred publications, including books, book chapters and articles in well-regarded journals.

Abbreviations

ACS	American Colonization Society
AD	*Anno Domini* (In the Year of the Lord)
AfCFTA	African Continental Free Trade Area
AfDB	African Development Bank
AMISOM	African Union Peacekeeping Force in Somalia
AMU	Arab Maghreb Union
APC	All Progressives Congress
APRM	African Peer Review Mechanism
ASEA	African Securities Exchanges Association
AU	African Union
AVCA	Africa Private Equity and Venture Capital Association
BCEAO	Central Bank of West African States (Acronym from French Translation)
BEAC	Bank of Central African States (Acronym from French Translation)
BRI	Belt and Road Initiative
BRICS	Brazil, Russia, India, China and South Africa
CEMAC	Central African Economic and Monetary Community
CEO	Chief Executive Officer
CFA	*Communaute francaise d'Afrique* (French Community of Africa)
CIA	Criminal Intelligence Agency
CIDCA	China International Development Cooperation Agency
CNN	Cable News Network
COMESA	Common Market for Eastern and Southern Africa
CPI	Corruption Perception Index
CVO	Covid-Organics
DoJ	Department of Justice

DPN	Democratic Party of Nigeria
DRC	Democratic Republic of Congo
EAC	East African Community
ECCAS	Economic Community of Central African States
ECOWAS	Economic Community of West African States
EFCC	Economic and Financial Crimes Commission
EITI	Extractive Industries Transparency Initiative
ENH	Empresa Nacional de Hidrocarbonetos
EPAs	Economic Partnership Agreements
EPZs	Export Processing Zones
ESA	Eastern and Southern Africa
ESP	Ecole Superieure Polytechnique
EU	European Union
FDI	Foreign Direct Investment
FFP	Fund for Peace
FOCAC	Forum on China–Africa Cooperation
FRZs	Free Trade Zones
FSI	Fragile State Index
GDP	Gross Domestic Products
GERD	Grand Ethiopian Renaissance Dam
HDI	Human Development Index
HIPC	Heavily Indebted Poor Countries
HPAEs	High Performing Asian Economies
HRW	Human Rights Watch
ICT	Information and Communications Technology
ICU	Intensive Care Unit
IDA	International Development Association
IDPs	Internally Displaced Persons
IGAD	Intergovernmental Authority on Development
ILO	International Labour Organisation
IMF	International Monetary Fund
ITC	International Trade Centre
LNG	Liquified Natural Gas
MCA	Member of County Assembly
NAB	Nigerian Agricultural Bank
NACB	Nigerian Agricultural and Cooperative Bank
NATO	North Atlantic Treaty Organisation
NBCI	Nigerian Bank for Commerce and Industry
NEITI	Nigeria Extractive Industries Transparency Initiative
NEPAD	New Partnership for Africa's Development
NGOs	Non-Governmental Organisations
NICs	Newly Industrialising Countries
NRC	National Republican Convention

NTA	Nigerian Television Authority
OAU	Organisation of African Unity
OBOR	One Belt One Road
OECD	Organisation for Economic Cooperation and Development
ONGC	Oil and Natural Gas Corporation
PDP	People's Democratic Party
PLAN	People's Liberation Army Navy
R&D	Research and Development
REC	Regional Economic Community
SABC	South African Broadcasting Corporation
SADC	Southern African Development Community
SAP	Structural Adjustment Programme
SARS	Severe Acute Respiratory Syndrome
SDG	Sustainable Development Goals
SEZ	Special Economic Zones
SMEs	Small and Medium Size Enterprises
SoEs	State Owned Enterprises
SSA	Sub-Saharan Africa
TFA	Trade Facilitation Agreement
TI	Transparency International
TJN	Tax Justice Network
TNCs	Trans-national Companies
TPLF	Tigray People's Liberation Front
UAE	United Arab Emirate
UN	United Nations
UNCTAD	United Nations Conference on Trade and Development
UNDP	United Nations Development Program
UNECA	United Nations Economic Commission for Africa
UNODC	United Nations Office on Drugs and Crime
UNSC	United Nations Security Council
USA	United States of America
USSR	Union of Soviet Socialist Republics
WAEMU	West African Economic and Monetary Union
WAMZ	West African Monetary Union Zone
WTO	World Trade Organisation
ZANU-PF	Zimbabwe African National Union—Patriotic Front

List of Boxes

List of Tables

CHAPTER 1

Capitalism and the African Context

The evolution of indigenous capitalism in Africa was profoundly interrupted and truncated by over 300 years of trans-Atlantic slave trade, followed by colonial conquest.

1.1 Introduction: The Capitalist Political Economy

This book argues that capitalism has practically failed to deliver the long-desired economic transformation and inclusive development in post-colonial Africa capable of lifting most of the citizens from poverty to the "middle class."[1] The principal factor that accounts for this failure is the prolific non-productive forms of capitalism that tend to be dominant in the African continent and their governance dimensions. In a highly structured global system that offers limited pathways for growth and development to emerging economies, the book explores the practical feasibilities for accelerated capitalist development in Africa.

Economies grow over time. The birth of capitalism from the womb of feudalism and all pre-modern forms of production was a function of growth. Capitalism is a market system of political and economic organization based on private ownership of the means of production of goods and services, and in which profit-motivated individual enterprise is considered beneficial to society. Being a market system, modern capitalism is

K. Omeje, *The Failure and Feasibility of Capitalism in Africa*, International Political Economy Series,
https://doi.org/10.1007/978-3-030-75170-8_1

also sometimes called market capitalism. Supposedly, in market capitalism, prices of goods and services, as well as wealth production, distribution and exchange are freely determined by the interplay of the forces of demand and supply. In a capitalist economy, the levers of economic growth are driven by private enterprises, which are encouraged by public policies, arguably for the good of all. Growth itself is philosophically driven by the inherent human belief, hope and quest for progress even in the midst of the worst setbacks. The Enlightenment age and industrial revolution in early modern Europe popularized the intellectual ideology of progress, but not by any means its empirical tendency and the human drive for it. In every society, people of all generations have always grappled with the quest for progress, development and growth through their various systems of livelihood and economic production and exchange. Similarly, every human society has historically made progress in their own way, and in the process have developed their own civilization and grown their economies at different times and levels (Rodney 1972). Sometimes, the process of societal progress and development for different parts of the world have suffered some internally or externally induced setbacks, such as civil wars, popular revolution, imperial invasion and conquest, as well as collective colonization, domination and exploitation. Although internal and external setbacks could temporarily arrest empirical progress as a society has always known, pursued and experienced it, the setbacks do not permanently destroy the people's collective faith and aspiration for a better future.

The assumption that progress will inevitably rebound from the ashes of any circumstantial setbacks, including setbacks arising from rebel wars and war of aggression, external domination and economic recession and depression, is insurmountably a natural tendency of mankind in all generations. Hence, the process of growth is often time empirically convoluted but the idealistic permutations and faith that underpin it are self-invigorating and indefatigable. National and global economic production have ultimately experienced growth across several generations. "In 1500, global production was about $250 billion. Today, it is around $60 trillion" (Penn 2019).

A key philosophical assumption of growth is the idea that the future will have more abundant resources than the present and it is this assumption that informs the operation of the savings, banking, credit and investment systems, which have been historically crucial in the development of capitalism (and to a lesser extent, pre-capitalist and other prevalent modes of production) in different parts of the world (Penn 2019). Economies may rise and fall, and likewise may expand or contract, as the case may be. Similarly, the absorptive capacity of investments in a certain economy could peak or may even suffer diminishing returns, but the hope that the future will have more abundant resources than the present will invariably motivate investors, economists and policymakers to embark on an endless quest for creative opportunities, alternatives and possibilities.

The greatest motivation of capitalism is individual ownership of the means of production and profit. It is also the cornerstone of capitalism. The underlying public policy assumption is that when profits are individually appropriated and owned by entrepreneurs, the same will lead to reinvestment, growth and more profit, thereby benefiting the society in diverse way, notably in commodity creation (products and services), and employment generation (labour). Loosely conceived, investible profit and finance, including repayable loans and credit facilities, capital in the hands of the capitalist are seen as being in the best interest of the public. Capital, in a larger technical sense, goes beyond money to include other valuables and measures of wealth such as properties, gold and precious gems, etc. But in the real world of capitalism, capital is literally reduced to hard cash and all the non-monetary forms of capital are convertibly measured in hard cash (Moyo 2011; Penn 2019). Another area in which capital is deemed beneficial to society is in technological development. Capitalist production relies mainly on technology and the more efficient the technology, the larger the scale of production which has the potential of leveraging market turnover and profit margin. Hence, entrepreneurial capitalists and capitalist states have vested interest in technological innovations and as a matter of fact would encourage and spearhead investments in development of new technologies to improve production and service delivery. In a nutshell, under the capitalist system growth is believed to be essentially driven by the production-related activities of the capitalists and the pillars that drive growth under the commanding leadership and entrepreneurial ingenuity of the capitalist are capital, labour and technology. Many economists have expanded the third variable, technology to what they call "total factor productivity," which according to Dambisa Moyo (2011: 8) "is a catchphrase that encompasses technological development, as well as anything not captured by the capital and labour inputs, such as culture and institutions."

In his controversial paper, Cornell University Professor of Political Philosophy and Ethics Richard W. Miller indicts modern capitalism as being inherently corrupt, but this charge of corruption seemingly goes beyond the well-known Marxian reproach of capitalist exploitation of labour and appropriation of surplus value. Miller tries to make an analytical distinction between the entrepreneurial activities of the capitalists and the underlying system of production in which they operate, "capitalism," and it is on the latter that his indictment is directed as an economic system that "inevitably and pervasively generates corrupt gains through conduct that does not transgress capitalist norms for individuals' economic conduct." Defining corruption as consisting of "deriving benefits from power over others in morally objectionable ways," Miller (2018: 31) argues that modern capitalism has two distinct features that make it a corrupt system of social production: the first is that it is fundamentally structured to generate reprehensible gains from the inferior bargaining power of most workers and, the second is that it generates similar gains from the superior political influence of those in the best economic situations. According to Miller (2018: 34), the corruption could, in principle, be ended through desirable political changes that reduce working people's inferiority in bargaining power and political power. In my view, the distinction that Miller tries to make between the capitalist and capitalism is not sustainable because the latter primarily serves the interests of the former. The capitalist employer and the capitalist state are the operative agencies that appropriate the objectionable gains derived from economic activities at the expense of the workers which Miller indicts as corrupt. It is highly debatable whether charges of corruption could be sustainably proffered exclusively on moral grounds outside the parameters of governance institutions and a legal framework as Miller tries to do. However, the important import of his paper is that without decisive intervention by a higher authority, the asymmetrical power relations inherent in capitalism could easily be used to foster the corrupt expropriation and oppression of the workers by capitalist employers.

Box 1.1 Defining Pillars of Modern Capitalism

Jahan and Mahmud (2015) have identified six defining pillars of market capitalism which include:

1. Private property ownership, both tangible and intangible assets.
2. Self-interest as a guiding principle of people's action in the pursuit of their own good.

3. Market competition for both individuals and firms, as well as for producers and consumers.
4. A market mechanism that determines price through the interaction of buyers and sellers of goods and services.
5. Freedom to choose with respect to consumption, production and investment.
6. Limited role of government to protect the rights of private citizens and maintain an orderly environment that facilitates proper functioning of markets.

Political culture and governance institutions have a key role in driving growth given the symbiotic relationship between politics and economics in the historical development of capitalism in particular, and national economies in general. The examples of how European capitalism was vigorously exported beyond national frontiers in the seventeenth and eighteenth centuries through the massive support that various European kings provided to their commercial explorers and merchants in their quest to discover and capture markets and territories abroad are pertinent illustrations of the leverage that political power confers to economic exploits. V. I. Lenin, leader of the 1917 Bolshevik revolution in Russia and the first leader of the defunct Soviet Union, argued that imperialism was a monopoly stage of capitalism, but Ali Mazrui preferred to rather describe Western imperialism as a monopoly stage of warfare in which the West assumed the duty to conquer and disarm the rest of mankind (Mazrui 1967: 30). Many of the early European explorers and merchants that undertook the risky adventures to the Americas, Africa and Asia received financial, logistical and military support from their governments which later yielded massive returns in the forms of imperial conquests, colonies, new agricultural and industrial investments, cheap slave labour, super profits, taxes, royalties and protracted imperial governance. This first-mover advantage of capitalist Europe to the uttermost parts of the earth in search of resources and markets has enabled the West to dominate the global political economy for over 400 years. The historical consequence of the Western global political economy dominance is the emergence of what political scientists have variously theorized as the world capitalist system and its contemporary concomitants such as economic globalization and institutions of global governance.

The convergence of political and economic power in the pursuit of external markets, investment opportunities and profits has not only remained a relevant pillar of international capitalism in its contemporary neoliberal expressions, but has invariably informed the politics of global hegemony in modern international history. Neoliberalism originated in the 1930s as an economic philosophy which advocated both state intervention and free markets (seeking to provide a middle path between the perceived failure of classical economics in the 1930s and a Marxist approach); however, this original meaning of neoliberalism has been lost (George 1999; Pettinger 2018). In contemporary history, neoliberalism is a term commonly used to describe free-market economics, with emphasis on policies associated with free trade, privatization, price deregulation, a reduced size of government and flexible labour markets, as well as more increasingly, policies of austerity and attempts to reduce budget deficits—usually by cutting government spending on social programmes (Pettinger 2018). Neoliberal ideologies have indeed continued to mutate, evolve and adapt to various domestic conditions across the world. Since the end of World War II, Western governments and institutions under America's internationalist hegemony have been the leading proponents of neoliberalism around the world—in its economic, political and sociocultural dimensions.

During the Cold War, the arms race and ideological struggle for global hegemony between the two world powers, USA and the defunct Soviet Union, were premised on the unstinted mobilization and deployment of the economic and political power of either side on a worldwide scale. Bereft of the advantages of the worldwide market investments and super profits which was the bulwark of the American capitalist system, the communist-oriented ex-Soviet Union proved to be no match to the USA. The Americans decisively won the Cold War and both the Soviet Union and the international communist system fell apart, thereby ending the bipolar politics of the Cold War era.

Box 1.2 Debate on the Successor to the Cold War Bipolarity
International Relations experts are still debating the successor to the Cold War bipolarity and what the prevailing global security structure looks like. The concept of polarity is informed by the neorealist assumption that power defined in terms of military and similar harder capabilities is the

driving force behind international relations and that the most powerful actors in the international system are states (Buzan 2018: 148). In his 1990 triumphalist manifesto, the famous American neorealist and *Washington Post* ex-columnist Charles Krauthammer declared the emergence of "The Unipolar Moment" with the end of the Cold War in which "the centre of world power is an unchallenged superpower, the United States, attended by its Western allies."[2]

Samuel Huntington (1999: 36) argued that the post-Cold War era is "a uni-multipolar world," "a strange hybrid with one superpower and several major powers," in which the interplay of power and culture in the various regions of the world will make it difficult for America to play the role of the world policeman amid the contending regional powers. "The settlement of key international issues," Huntington (1999: 36) further argues, "requires action by the single superpower but always with some combination of other major states; the single superpower can, however, veto action on key issues by combinations of other states."

Sounding a note of caution to the triumphalist US foreign policy intelligentsia and protagonists of the unipolar moment at the end of the Cold War, the then head of the US Central Intelligence Agency, James Woolsey (1993), likened the post-Cold War global security order to the West, having slain the dragon (of Soviet threat), but now living in a jungle full of poisonous snakes.[3]

Narayanappa Janardhan (2018), among other scholars, have postulated that the present global security structure is a "uni-tripolar order" or simply "a tripolor world order" in which USA, Russia and China are at the helm of world affairs, however, the USA is *primus inter pares*. The European Union is occasionally featured as a separate power bloc in some of the tripolar and multipolar world order analyses (cf. Donette 2012; *McCormick* 2012; Buraga 2016). China is more frequently featured as a contending pole of power. Barry Buzan (2018: 147) contends that the international system is probably faced with the possibility of a bizarre scenario of "a world with no superpowers, only great and regional ones."

Having for the most part pursued a pragmatic brand of communism outside the orbit of the Soviet Union during the Cold War, and commenced an ambitious reformist agenda before the Cold War ended, China was able to survive the collapse of the communist bloc and bounce back stronger on the global stage. The Chinese market-oriented economic reform spearheaded by Deng Xiaoping in 1979 laid the foundation for the emergence of China as a global power by copying the functional advantages of the Western growth model, encouraging foreign trade and investment through joint ventures, and retaining the perceived strength of the communist model—centralized control of political and economic governance. Using this unique experimental model of state capitalism in which the state is the leading investor in the domestic and international market, tempered with regulated support and facilitation of private enterprises, the Chinese were able to achieve a quantum leap from a low-income Third World economy to an upper-middle income country and the world's second largest economy in less than 30 years. The level of resource-intensive manufacturing and exports achieved by China, as well as the proportion of its nationals that have been lifted from poverty within a few decades is unprecedented in human history. Since China began to open up and reform its economy in 1979, GDP growth has averaged almost 10% a year, and more than 850 million people have been lifted out of poverty (World Bank 2020). Some more conservative estimates put the Chinese economic growth rate at about 7.5% average (Moyo 2018). Remarkably, the number of people lifted out of poverty in China since the inception of their economic reform is significantly more than the population of Europe (Europe's current population is about 747 million). The Chinese poverty rate dropped radically from 88.3% in 1981 (roughly 870 million people) to less than 3% (about 5.51 million) by the end of 2019 (Gupta 2020). Contrast the figures with the nearly 18.5 million Americans that live in "deep poverty," the US Census Bureau's version of extreme poverty.[4] In late November 2020, China announced that it has eliminated extreme poverty nationwide, thereby meeting the Chinese Communist Party's policy of poverty eradication and reducing the level of income inequality in the country. To achieve this milestone claimed by the government, state officials certified that the last nine Chinese counties to scale over the poverty threshold based on a matrix of indicators that include income, health, education, shelter and other human needs, are now poverty-free (Areddy 2020). All the nine counties are located in the mountainous province of Guizhou in southwest China.

1.2 Capitalism in the African Context: A Historical Perspective

Capitalism was differently conceived in the womb of pre-modern modes of production—notably feudalism, communalism, commercialism and artisanism and birthed in various sociological formations in different parts of the world. In his "Introduction" to Max Weber's timeless classic *The Protestant Ethics and the Spirit of Capitalism* (1905), Anthony Giddens made the following striking remarks:

> Capitalism thus defined, in the shape of mercantile operations, for instance, has existed in various forms of society: in Babylon and Ancient Egypt, China, India and mediaeval Europe. But only in the West, and in relatively recent times, has capitalistic activity become associated with the rational organisation of formally free labour. By 'rational organisation' of labour here Weber means its routinised, calculated administration within continuously functioning enterprises. (Giddens 1992: x–xi)

Ancient Egypt[5] is the only African country mentioned by Giddens in his examples of where pre-modern capitalism existed, but it suffices to say that the rest of Africa was not an exception. African political, economic, sociocultural and technological achievements in the pre-modern world have been well-researched and documented (Rodney 1972; Diop 1978; Zeleza 1996). Notable among these documented facts are the great achievements of ancient Egypt in literacy, numeracy, medicine, engineering, architecture and political philosophy dating back to about five thousand years, well before the Arab invasion of North Africa that started in the seventh century and the European contact with Sub-Saharan Africa of the late fifteenth century. The most outstanding of these achievements is the ancient pyramid of Giza that comprised over two million blocks of stone, many of immense size and weight, and which has a base of 230 meters and rises to a height of 146 meters (Mark 2016). The Giza pyramid and many others like it still standing in Egypt were believed to have been built as tombs of eternal value for the ancient Egyptian royals. Indeed, early in the fifth century A.D., when the renowned Christian theologian Saint Augustine was the Bishop of Hippo Regius in today's Algeria, North Africa was as much a centre of Christianity as Italy or Greece, and an integral part of the Greco-Roman civilization (Kaplan 2016). Apart from pre-Arabized North Africa:

> Some of the world's other great civilizations, such as Kush, Axum, Mali, and Great Zimbabwe, flourished in Africa in the years before 1500. In this early period Africans participated in extensive international trading networks and in trans-oceanic travel. Certainly, some African states had established important trading relations with India, China and other parts of Asia long before these were disrupted by European intervention.[6]

One of the irrefutable evidence of the strength of the civilization that existed in precolonial Africa is the innumerable cultural artefacts and treasures looted from various African kingdoms during imperial conquest and colonial rule, a large number of which are still exhibited in the various Europeans museums as monuments of imperial glory and wonder. If this continued exhibition of stolen cultural artefacts is not "the audacity of theft," then I don't have a better phraseology for it. Colonial Asia and the defunct Ottoman empire were also looted. The looted African treasures include exotic fabrics and customs, assorted jewelries, bronze sculptures, golden crowns and works, historic carvings and paintings, and so forth (Lime 2018; Maclean 2018). These looted treasures are not only displayed in European public museums, but some are in renowned universities and other dignified places. In colonial and early post-colonial history, the pillaged African treasures were oftentimes auctioned publicly in European cities and open markets where they were purchased by the highest bidders, which was how some of the famous universities, curators and art collectors acquired them. Since the end of colonial rule, many Africans and non-Africans alike have campaigned for the repatriation of these stolen treasures of inestimable values to their places of origin but with limited success. Africa was indeed part of pre-modern civilization, which laid the foundation for the evolution of capitalism as much as other parts of the world.

One of the fallacies found in the literature on the development of capitalism in Africa and other postcolonial regions is the assumption that capitalism is a Western invention that was spread to transitional societies through the imposition of colonial rule (cf. Sender and Smith 1986; Blaut 1989). Colonialism did not originate capitalism in Africa but rather introduced a peculiar brand of capitalism that primarily aimed to enhance the development of Europe at the expense and disadvantage of Africa. Capitalism, as Moghalu (2014) and Ayittey (2018) have aptly pointed out, was not alien to Africa as several analysts that have portrayed precolonial Africa as entirely rooted in communal modes of production have erroneously argued. Communalism, peasantry, bonded labour production systems rooted in slavery and semi-feudal formations, and capitalism—all had indigenous foundations in precolonial Africa. The history of communalism in Africa dates to immemorial antiquity. Communalism has not only existed in Africa as an economic system, but most importantly, it has provided a social culture of solidarity, collaborative help, as well as wealth transfer and redistribution. In this sense, communal practices were a social culture that cut across the entire spectrum of economic production irrespective of the mode. It is pertinent to mention that diverse operating modes—peasantry, bonded labour systems, entrepreneurship and indigenous open-market capitalism—characterized Africa's economic history prior to European contact. The diverse modes of production were not successive in a Marxian evolutionary sense but coexistent in several African political communities. Market-oriented production, compensation of some sort and in some cases profit-sharing among members of the producing unit (household, extended family network, joint venture partnerships, etc.) were practices that characterized the various production systems. Production for local and distant markets was rife. The African open-market transaction system has existed since precolonial history, both daily and periodic markets—two-daily, four-daily, weekly, etc. (Ayittey 2018). Furthermore, the different modes of production largely coexisted in a rather complementary and sometimes contradictory form; however, "peasant capitalism" which according to George Ayittey (2018) was based on clan or extended family agrarian production and profit-sharing seemed to be the most prevalent economic structure in precolonial Africa. The concept of "peasant capitalism" enunciated by George Ayittey is still a contested one.

1.3 Indigenous Capitalism, Trans-Atlantic Slave Trade, and the First Scramble for Africa

Clearly, capitalism was long evolving and practiced in various parts of Africa alongside other pre-modern modes of production and transaction prior to the official imposition of Western colonial rule on the continent in the later part of the nineteenth century. Research on African precolonial economic history has shown that capitalist production and market system were already discernible in Africa both before and during the trans-Atlantic slave trade, albeit it was not the dominant system (Jerven 2016). Indigenous capitalist production and market transactions in precolonial Africa were predominantly driven by kinship-centred agrarian producers and farmers, handicraft fabricators and inventors, gold- and black-smiths, livestock breeders and commercial pastoralists, fishermen, cloth weavers, wine brewers, assorted partnership ventures, cottage industry entrepreneurs, as well as wholesale and retail merchants, including market women. However, the developing indigenous markets in most cases faced institutional constraints due mainly to the centralized governance institutions operated by most indigenous empires and political communities. Cottage industrialists, agrarian producers and other emerging entrepreneurs sold their products in local and distant markets by barter and diverse commonly accepted currencies (e.g., cowries, precious stones, metallic coins, etc.). Alluding to the immense variety and complexity of monetary systems in precolonial and early colonial Africa, Alison Quiggen remarked with a smack of ethnographic sarcasm, that the Congo River Basin was characterized by a "jungle of currencies" (Guyer 2004: 32). Market forces had not effectively developed due largely to some institutional constraints related to traditional status, class, gender and other socio-culturally determined limitations. "Formal" credit, financial institutions and capital markets were practically non-existent, but informal credit systems thrived (Austin 2009). Some of the "informal" precolonial credit systems, which still exist in contemporary Africa include rotating credit associations and kinship-based micro-finance initiatives. I have used the distinction between formal and informal credit systems with great caution. Findings from diverse studies on financial practices carried out by many economic anthropologists across the global North and South have long pointed to the futility of such a binary which some mainstream scholars had previously exploited to impose a hierarchy of values on the two categories (cf. Zeleza 1996; Guyer 2018; Musaraj and Small 2018: 5). The functional relativism of formal and informal economies, as well as their complex interconnectedness in many parts of the world over time have made any dichotomous distinction between the two categories untenable.

The evolution of indigenous capitalism was profoundly interrupted and truncated by over 300 years of trans-Atlantic slave trade, followed by colonial conquest. Trans-Atlantic slave trade marked the first "scramble for Africa" in which millions of African people were carted away from the continent to the "new world," specifically the American continent. European imperial agents and colonizers had conquered and established largescale production outposts and exploitable colonies largely centered on plantation agriculture in the Americas. The quest for cheap and massive labour to work on the established plantations and facilities in the Americas necessitated the trans-Atlantic slave trade which also ignited intense rivalry between the British, Portuguese, Dutch, French and other European slave dealers in Africa. Many Western historians and African American scholars have over the years debated the nature and extent of European and African agencies in the actual capture of slaves from the continent, with some apportioning blames of varied proportions on either side. I will not dabble into this circular argument, a controversial but diversionary discourse that was brilliantly researched and arguably settled by the famous Caribbean political historian Walter Rodney in his 1972 seminal study, *How Europe Underdeveloped Africa*. European slave dealers conscripted their African victims by direct kidnapping, trickery, capture and most of all, by threatening African chiefs and community leaders with conscription of themselves and their households if they did not produce those to be taken into captivity and enslavement (see also, Jalata 2016). This persistent pressure, made credible by the occasional conscription of recalcitrant chiefs and royal households, instigated continuous inter-community raiding and warfare among chiefdoms competing to capture and deliver citizens of rival communities to the brutally armed and waiting slave masters and ships.

The consequences of the centuries of externally induced human trade on the African economy, security and development have been well-researched and documented by political economists and historians (Rodney 1972; Ake 1981; Jerven 2016). Africa was systematically robbed of its labour force—the critical mass of people of the most productive age cluster required to engineer and sustain development at home—for the development of the Western world. As coalesced by Lewis:

> Depopulation and a continuing fear of captivity made economic and agricultural development almost impossible throughout much of Western Africa. A large percentage of the people taken captive were *young men and women of childbearing ages, to a lesser extent* (reworded with my emphasis). The European slavers usually left behind persons who were elderly, disabled, or otherwise dependent - groups who were least able to contribute to the economic health of their societies. (Lewis, n.d.)

As a result of the trans-Atlantic slave trade, Sub-Saharan Africa immeasurably stagnated for at least over the last three hundred years of precolonial history while the beneficiary Western world made accelerated progress with the help of African labour.

African slave labour contributed significantly to the industrial revolution and the industrialization of Europe (Rodney 1972). Regarding the contribution of slave-driven production to the industrialization of Europe, economists like Steven Langdon, Archibald Ritter and Yiagadeesen Samy have made the following conservative submission:

> British economic historians have identified the rising trade in slave produced products as a central factor in Britain's industrial revolution; re-exports of these items to Europe rose threefold over 1750–1790, and added to the high direct profit from slaving in the gathering together of capital that came to support industrialization. (Langdon et al. 2018: 22)

According to the famous British economic historian and Essex University's professor of sociology, Robin Blackburn:

> Slave-owning planters, and merchants who dealt in slaves and slave produce, were among the richest people in 18th-century Britain. Profits from these activities helped to endow All Souls College, Oxford, with a splendid library, to build a score of banks, including Barclays, and to finance the experiments of James Watt, inventor of the first really efficient steam engine. Liverpool merchant bankers, heavily involved in the slave-based trades, extended vital credit to the early cotton manufacturers of its Lancashire hinterland. West Indian planters built stately homes - some, ridiculously extravagant dwellings such as William Beckford's Fonthill - and furthered the modernisation of British agriculture by 'improving' their estates. Others invested in canals. And, of course, many spent their ill-gotten gains on gambling, prize fights and riotous living. (Blackburn 2011)

As Blackburn further reports:

> The plantations were themselves by-products of a new economic system. Plantation slavery thrived, thanks to a consumer revolution that took place in Britain and the Netherlands in the 17th century. In these countries, consumer markets widened as farmers and manufacturers hired wage workers as the best way to expand output and sales. … In his famous 1944 book 'Capitalism and Slavery', the Trinidadian scholar Eric Williams argued that profits from slavery "fertilised" many branches of the metropolitan economy and set the scene for England's industrial revolution. (Blackburn 2011)

Due to the trans-Atlantic slave economy, scattered parts of Sub-Saharan Africa were introduced to the Western money economy earlier than colonial rule. Outpost European agents and frontier captors stationed at coastal slave reception and evacuation fortresses were paid in cash (various European currencies) while the local middlemen, including some of the African chiefs were paid some custom fee, and in many cases, offered gifts. The European and American slave merchants offered a wide range of gifts and goods to the African middlemen in exchange for slaves and the list include Indian cottons and other exotic textile materials, Brazilian tobacco, brassware from Aachen, New England rum, glass from Venice and Bohemia, and Muskets and gunpowder, which viciously fueled the slave raiding wars (Tempest 2019). Some commentators have described the entire process as triangular trade in which arms, textiles and wine were shipped from Europe to Africa, slaves from Africa to the Americas, with sugar, coffee and other products shipped from the Americas to Europe (Lewis, n.d.). Generally, the slave economy engendered various forms of Western currencies and exchange commodities which coexisted with African indigenous currencies for many generations prior to colonial conquest.

1.4 Frontier Capitalism of Colonial Africa: The Second Scramble for Africa

Europe's quest for exploitable colonies sparked off the second scramble for Africa that culminated in the historic Berlin Conference of 1884–1885 in which Africa was balkanized into colonizable parts by leading Western imperial powers, as it were, leaders that knew little about Africa's complex political structures and geodemographic configurations. The Berlin Conference was convened by the German Chancellor Otto von Bismarck to provide an opportunity to the various imperial powers of the West to settle their scramble for Africa and avert the risk of waging major armed conflicts in their contested colonial frontiers on the continent. Fifteen imperial powers attended the Conference namely: Germany, France, Italy, Great Britain, Belgium, Denmark, Portugal, Russia, Spain, Austria-Hungary, Sweden, Norway, Netherlands, Turkey and USA (Langdon et al. 2018: 26). Africa already had many established nations, kingdoms and empire states in the 1800s (e.g., Egypt, Mali, Ethiopia, Somalia, Buganda, Ghana, Dahomey, etc.) but ironically none of them was invited to the Conference. Africa was shared out by the various European powers at the Conference whose imperial spheres of influence were already strongly asserted in some of the territories they secured at the roundtable. With the exception of Ethiopia and Liberia the rest of Africa was effectively colonized. Under the leadership of Emperor Menelik II, Ethiopia defeated imperial Italy at the Battle of Adowa in 1896 to assert their independence and resist being colonized. Like the Ethiopians, most African kingdoms and nations resisted colonization but were not as fortunate and powerful as pre-colonial Ethiopia. Africans were militarily defeated in their initial attempts to resist colonization by the superior fire power of the Europeans. Anti-colonial theorists and activists like Frantz Fanon (1961) argued in the heydays of decolonization that because colonialism was practically imposed and maintained by the instrumentality of military violence, the colonized subjects were justified to use organized violence to resist it and regain their sovereignties. In addition to military conquest, many African kings and chiefs were lured and tricked into signing away their kingdoms and territories as protectorates of various European powers through dubious treaties that will not pass tests of legality in any serious court of justice regardless of the underlying jurisprudence.

Liberia on the other hand was a creation of a private philanthropic association, the American Colonization Society (ACS) that acquired a track of land in the present-day Monrovia and its environs in December 1821 for the resettlement of freed Black slaves from America (Guannu 2009: 21). Thousands of slaves were repatriated to this ACS-governed settlement or colony, both those that voluntarily accepted the offer and those pressured to emigrate. The new settlement which was later named Liberia was declared independent on 26 July 1847 by ACS with US government's subsequent recognition. The independence of Liberia was respected by the Berlin Conference. The countries that benefited from the imperial balkanization of Africa in Berlin were Britain, France, Spain, Belgium, Portugal, Germany and Italy. A vast majority of the colonial territories went to France and Britain. The Germans were to later lose all their African colonies following their defeat in World War I, while the Italians similarly lost theirs after their World War II defeat. All the lost territories of Germany and Italy were handed over to the British, French and Belgians as international trust territories under the authorization mandate of the defunct League of Nations and later, the United Nations.

The driving purpose of colonialism was economic—to produce agricultural products (the colonial cash crops) and extract mineral resources needed as raw materials by the nascent industrial factories and manufacturing companies in Europe, most of which were offshoots of the industrial revolution. Among the required raw materials were cocoa, cotton, tea, coffee beans, groundnuts, palm oil, copper, manganese, iron ore, bauxite, coal, gold and diamond, etc. Missionary activities and Christianization remarkably followed colonial conquest in many parts of Africa, and in some places preceded the arrival of the colonizers (e.g. the Boer settler in Southern Africa, among others). The missionaries were interested in conversion of Africans from indigenous religious practices to Christianity, albeit there were some of the early missionaries that abetted the trans-Atlantic slave trade, the brutal conquest of Africans and land grabbing. Minimal proselytization and conversion occurred in parts of Africa where Islam already had a stronghold. European missionaries pioneered and promoted Western education and social service delivery in many communities, especially schools and healthcare. It is pertinent to point out that prior to the arrival of Western missionaries in Africa and the Boer settlers in South Africa, Christianity already flourished in some parts of Africa north of the equator dating back to the first century AD—e.g. the Coptic Orthodox Church of Alexandria. From its inception in the fourth century AD, the Ethiopian Orthodox Church was part of the Coptic Church of Alexandria until its administrative separation in 1959.

The impact of Western market capitalism on African economies can be most appropriately captured by the Marxian dictum that all societies and people make their own history, albeit not under conditions of their own choosing (Guyer 2004: 5). Following colonial conquest, the development of African productive forces, including the systemic evolution of indigenous capitalism was systematically arrested, supplanted and replaced by the imperatives of Western market capitalism. The conquest of Africa and what Claude Ake (1981) aptly described as the "disarticulation of its economies" did not of course start with the imposition of colonial rule in the late 1800s.

Africa was historically integrated into the orbit of the Western capitalist economy as a peripheral appendage. The peripheral and extraverted model of capitalism imposed on Africa was unskilled labour-intensive and as such did not encourage the development of the continent's productive forces, especially human capital and production technologies. The comparatively more innovative aspect of the production chain, high-value industrial manufacturing, was carried out in the Western homelands of the colonizers using African cash crops and mineral resources as raw materials (e.g., cotton, cocoa, palm oil, groundnut, timber, copper, gold, aluminium ore, etc.). The concentration of export-oriented manufacturing in Europe had far-reaching multiplier effects. It catalyzed and accelerated the development of Western productive forces, skilled jobs, specialized education and training, and top-edge value chain services, including marketing, international trade and financial services. Ultimately, the colonial conquest and exploitation of Africa and the rest of the global South contributed to an inexorable deepening of the innovative and highly productive forms of capitalism that had emerged in Europe following the industrial revolution of the late eighteenth and nineteenth centuries (notably entrepreneurial capitalism) and the creation of surplus wealth for the benefit of the underprivileged classes. The globalization of trade during the colonial era provided an additional impetus to entrepreneurial capitalism in the West through unlimited control of the conquered colonial markets and arbitrary determination of the terms of trade, including the prices of raw material imports and finished goods exports. Africa exported relatively cheap raw materials and imported and consumed more expensive manufactured goods. This logic of the paradigm of international trade engendered by the colonial order has not changed in many significant ways in contemporary history.

While entrepreneurial capitalism flourished in imperial Europe and the West in general, in colonial Africa a different dysfunctional pattern occurred. The lopsided dichotomy in the international division of labour intrinsic to colonialism imposed upon Africa "a frontier-type of capitalism organised around enclaves, especially mining enclaves" (Mbembe 2016). Executed with enormous coercion, the colonizers' frontier capitalism in Africa essentially disrupted and unravelled sections of the precolonial economic systems. Apart from lacking the innovative genius known to be the hallmark of mainstream capitalism, the frontier capitalism foisted on colonial Africa was not fundamentally designed for the benefit and development of Africa, but for the service and benefit of imperial Europe. From an African perspective, frontier capitalism was capitalism for Africa's underdevelopment. The extensive damage unleashed on Africa by the colonizers' frontier capitalism has been well-researched and documented in the literature on African political economy (cf. Rodney 1972; Mbembe 2001; Amin 2011).

Led by many passionate and charismatic nationalists who were part of the emerging new African elite, Africans fought the scourge of colonial oppression for many decades. The nationalist leaders that led the decolonization struggles were largely educated in the colonizers' schools and the West. The struggle for the liberation of Africa was intensified to African advantage after the World War II when the major colonial powers had suffered extensive economic, financial, political, military and moral devastation. The morale of the Africans on the other hand was boosted by the gallantry of their returnee servicemen who fought alongside the European colonizers in many fronts during the World War and felt more convinced that with the adequate weapons and resources, they would prevail in the decolonization struggles. Under the emerging Cold War climate, weapons and resources were increasingly made available from the Eastern bloc to support the liberation struggles. The colonizers were forced to accentuate the process of political participation by making more concessions to African representation in the undemocratic governance apparatuses they had started rolling out in different countries even before World War II. Voting rights, electoral representation and party politics were systematically introduced and increased in many countries to appease the decolonization movements and nationalist leaders. African liberation struggles were violent in some countries, but less violent in others.

Some of the most violent liberation struggles occurred in "settler colonies." Settler colonies were a distinct type of colonies in which the colonizers "came to stay" and therefore devised and pursued policy strategies aimed at replacement of indigenous populations with an invasive settler community that, over time, develops a distinctive identity and sovereignty (Veracini 2015). Robert Young (2001: 17) uses the term "dominion colonies" to describe the same phenomenon—defining them as "colonies predominantly established as dominions for the purpose or forms of settlement: e.g., British North America, Australia and New Zealand, diverse Portuguese colonies—Brazil, Angola, Mozambique, etc." Land expropriation for industrial farming and mining was colossal and brutal in settler or dominion colonies, and likewise forced labour and "systematic extermination and/or displacement of indigenous populations," which Young described as "geographical violence" (Young 2001: 17). Availability of extensive land and favourable climatic conditions for farming and settlement, among other things, were the major factors for the establishment of settler colonies. The major settler colonies in Africa were South Africa, Angola, Mozambique, Southern and Northern Rhodesia (Zimbabwe and Zambia), South West Africa (Namibia) and Kenya. Settlers from Holland, Britain, Germany, and Portugal colonized these areas.[7] With the exception of Kenya that regained its independence in 1963 through an eight year long violent rebellion against the British settler colonizers led the ethnic-Kikuyu-dominated *Mau Mau* warriors, the liberation of the rest of the settler colonies occurred much later, between the 1970s and 1990s.

Another major type of European colonies in Africa were the dependency colonies. These were colonies established as dependencies for economic exploitation without a view to largescale and permanent settlement: e.g., most of the colonies in the high humidity tropics. Dependency colonies were mostly governed using such ideologies as the British direct and indirect rule, French assimilation theory and direct imposition of metropolitan culture, which was practiced by all colonial powers. Scholars like Jean-Francois Bayart et al. (1999) have argued that because a few European officials were involved in administering the vast colonial territories, all the colonial powers actually adopted a combination of direct and indirect rule even if some like the French and the Portuguese did not frame theirs in a pivotal policy as the British did.

In general, colonial rule was scarcely interested in Africa's economic and national development, beyond resource extraction for European advantage. Economic growth was essentially driven by the few commodities that the colonizers needed for their factories and economies overseas. Europe was scarcely interested in setting up manufacturing plants and industries in Africa to help Africans add value to the natural resources they produced. Colonial infrastructures like roads and railways were limited to the natural resource extraction centres and also linking these centres to the seaports for evacuation of products. Hence, transport and communication infrastructures "tended to connect colonies to the European center, and not to each other — at independence one could make a direct call to Paris from Francophone Africa, but it was impossible to find a train that would travel from Ghana to the Ivory Coast *next door*" (Cooper, n.d.). Educational infrastructures were grossly inadequate and Western education was for the most part tailored to service the purpose of colonialism—to produce the necessary manpower required in colonial service—clerks, interpreters, civil servants, teachers, technicians, domestic servants and most importantly, military and police personnel. It is some of these educated Africans that ultimately formed the vanguard of the African decolonization or liberation struggles.

It is important to mention that the primary focus of the African liberation struggles was on political independence. There was little consideration about economic independence and how to deal with the deeply entrenched Western interests rooted in frontier capitalism, which was the mainstay of the colonial economies. Most nationalist leaders and pan-Africanists who recognized the economic dimension of African liberation simply believed that once political independence is regained and

Africans are on the driving seat of national politics, then the economic question could be easily addressed. In the popular liberation mantra of Kwame Nkrumah during the struggle for Ghana's independence, he rallied Ghanaians to "Seek ye first the political kingdom and all else shall be added unto you" (Bonsu 2016). Nkrumah's slogan was a mimicry of a famous biblical dictum of Jesus Christ about the utmost need of prioritizing and advancing God's heavenly kingdom on earth, which will ultimately attract all other benefits. After their long-drawn-out liberation struggles, most African leaders secured the political kingdom at independence, but the economic kingdom remained farfetched, and in several cases, completely elusive. The embedded structures of frontier capitalism were difficult to dismantle principally because of deadly opposition from the West and the self-aggrandizing interests of the postcolonial governing elites. The African postcolonial elites had to devise pragmatic ways of tinkering with the economic status quo to foist their own wealth accumulation interests on the structures of frontier capitalism (see Sect. 5.1). The resultant effect was neocolonial capitalism and its aftermaths, manifested in its various convoluted forms. As Moghalu (2014: 17) rightly argued, the philosophical ideology or worldview of the African independence struggles was narrowly limited to political freedom and attached insufficient importance to the economic imperatives of freedom. As is often taught in basic undergraduate modules in many Business Schools: "He who fails to plan is planning to fail." The economics of independence was largely left unplanned or in some cases misplanned, and the catastrophic results were almost evident within the first two decades of independence—a litany of failed economies, which inadvertently conspired with diverse exogenous forces to trigger a montage of failed states.

Summary Points

1. Capitalism is a market system of political and economic organization based on private ownership of the means of production of goods and services, and in which profit-motivated individual enterprise is considered beneficial to society.
2. Capitalism has failed to deliver the long-desired economic transformation and inclusive development in postcolonial Africa. The principal reason for this failure is because of the dysfunctional nature of the dominant forms of capitalism practiced in the continent.

3. Capitalism has both national and international dimensions. The dominant version of international capitalism is linked to neoliberalism, which as an economic philosophy has had varied meanings since it first emerged in Europe in the 1930s.
4. Since the end of World War II, Western governments and institutions under America's internationalist hegemony have been the leading proponents of neoliberalism around the world—in its economic, political and sociocultural dimensions.
5. China has embraced and promoted an internationalist model of state capitalism following the market-oriented economic reforms pioneered by Premier Deng Xiaoping in 1979.
6. Contrary to the widespread assumption in sections of the international political economy literature, colonialism did not originate capitalism in Africa. Capitalism was long evolving and practiced in various parts of Africa alongside other pre-modern modes of production and transaction prior to the official imposition of Western colonial rule on the continent in the later part of the nineteenth century. However, colonialism introduced a peculiar brand of capitalism, frontier capitalism, that primarily aimed to enhance the development of Europe at the expense and disadvantage of Africa.
7. The evolution of indigenous capitalism was profoundly interrupted and truncated by the over 300 years of trans-Atlantic slave trade, followed by colonial conquest.
8. The primary focus of the African liberation struggles was on political independence with the result that economic independence was largely overlooked and compromised.
9. The African postcolonial governing elites devised various pragmatic ways of twisting the economic status quo to foist their own wealth accumulation interests on the structures of frontier capitalism, thereby transforming it to neocolonial capitalism and its various convoluted aftermaths.

Discussion Questions

1. What are the underlying public policy assumptions that justify individual ownership of the means of production and appropriation of profits in a capitalist system?

2. Why does Richard W. Miller indict modern capitalism as being inherently corrupt? Do you agree with his indictment? Explain your position.
3. What are the defining features and differences between "the first scramble for Africa" and "the second scramble for Africa"?
4. How did the "world capitalist system" emerge?
5. From an international political economy perspective, why did the ex-Soviet Union and international communist bloc lose the Cold War to the US-led Western bloc?
6. How would you characterize the nature of African indigenous capitalism prior to colonial conquest?
7. Describe the nature of frontier capitalism in Africa during the colonial era?
8. What are the similarities and differences between "settler colonies" and "dependency colonies" in Africa?

Notes

1. The "middle class" is highly contested category. In the African context, the middle class has been defined by the African Development Bank (AfDB) as those with a per capita daily consumption level of \$2–\$20 [further sub-categorised into "floating class" with a consumption level of \$2–\$4 per day; "lower middle class" with a consumption level of \$4–\$10 per day, and "upper middle class" with a consumption level of \$10–\$20 per day] (AfDB 2011: 2). The AfDB's threefold conception of the African middle class is similar to the threefold classification of the middle class in the US based on income levels by the US News and World Report. In the US classification, the middle class comprises "the working class, lower middle class and upper middle class" (see Livingstone 2015).
2. Charles Krauthammer (1990/1991) "The Unipolar Moment", *Foreign Affairs: America and the World*; quoted in Charles Krauthammer (2002/2003) "The Unipolar Moment Revisited", *The National Interest*, Winter: 5.
3. James Woolsey (1993) "Testimony to Senate Hearing", Washington, DC, February. Quoted in Paul Rogers (2002) "The United Nations and the Promotion of Peace", *Medicine, Conflict and Survival*, no. 18, p. 116.
4. The US Census Bureau defines deep poverty as those living in a household with a total cash income below 50% of the American poverty threshold. See US Census Bureau (2018, 2019).

5. Geographically, the ancient Egyptian empire at the peak of its civilization extended to vast parts of the present-day Sudan and limited parts of Libya and the Middle East. See Joshua K. Mark (2017) "Egyptian Empire", September 25, https://www.ancient.eu/Egyptian_Empire/.
6. See, Black History 365 – "Africa before Transatlantic Enslavement", 16 June 2020, https://www.blackhistorymonth.org.uk/article/section/history-of-slavery/africa-before-transatlantic-enslavement/.
7. Taken from the following source: https://is.mendelu.cz/eknihovna/opory/zobraz_cast.pl?cast=61459. See also: Mahmood Mamdani (1997) *Citizen and Subject: Contemporary Africa and the Legacy of Late Colonialism*. Princeton: Princeton University Press.

References

AfDB. 2011. The Middle of the Pyramid: Dynamics of the Middle Class in Africa. Africa Development Bank (AfDB) Market Brief, April 20. https://www.afdb.org/fileadmin/uploads/afdb/Documents/Publications/The%20Middle%20of%20the%20Pyramid_The%20Middle%20of%20the%20Pyramid.pdf.

Ake, Claude. 1981. *A Political Economy of Africa*. Lagos: Longman.

Amin, Samir. 2011. *Maldevelopment: Anatomy of a Global Failure*, 2nd ed. Oxford: Pambazuka Press.

Areddy, T. James. 2020. China Says It Has Met Its Deadline of Eliminating Poverty. *The Wall Street Journal* (WSJ), November 23. https://www.wsj.com/articles/china-says-it-has-met-its-deadline-of-eliminating-poverty-11606164540.

Austin, Gareth. 2009. Factor Markets in Nieboer Conditions: Pre-colonial West Africa, c.1500-c.1900. *Continuity and Change*, 24 (1), 23–53.

Ayittey, George. 2018. Indigenous African Free-Market Liberalism. September. https://yafopportunities.org/pdf/INDIGENOUS-AFRICAN-FREE.pdf.

Bayart, S., Stephen Ellis Jean-Francois, and Beatrice Hibou. 1999. *Criminalisation of the State in Africa*. Oxford: James Currey Publishers.

Blackburn, Robin. 2011. Enslavement and Industrialisation. BBC History, February 12. http://www.bbc.co.uk/history/british/abolition/industrialisation_article_01.shtml.

Blaut, J. Morris. 1989. Colonialism and the Rise of Capitalism. *Science & Society* 53 (3): 260–296.

Bonsu, Paa Kwesi. 2016. Seek Ye First the Political Kingdom. December 2. https://www.modernghana.com/news/740576/seek-ye-first-the-political-kingdom.html.

Buraga, Manoj Babu. 2016. India, China and the EU in a Multipolar World Order: A Perception. *European Academic Research* 4: 5806–5817.

Buzan, Barry. 2018. Polarity. In *Security Studies: An Introduction*, ed. Paul D. Williams and Matt MacDonald, 147–160. London: Routledge.

Cooper, Ryan. n.d. Why African Independence Was Such a Disaster. *This Week*. https://theweek.com/articles/574386/why-african-independence-such-disaster.

Diop, C.A. 1978. *Black Africa: The Economic and Cultural Basis for a Federated State*. Westport, CT: Lawrence Hill & Co.

Fanon, Frantz. 1961. *The Wretched of the Earth, trans Constance Farrington*. London: Penguin Books.

Francis, David. 2006. *Uniting Africa: Building Regional Peace and Security Systems*. Aldershot: Ashgate.

George, Susan. 1999. A Short History of Neoliberalism, March 24. https://www.tni.org/en/article/short-history-neoliberalism.

Giddens, Anthony. 1992. "Introduction" to Max Weber's Book. In *The Protestant Ethics and the Spirit of Capitalism,* First published 1930 and trans. Talcott Parsons. London: Routledge.

Guannu, Saye Joseph. 2009. The Political History of Liberia and the Civil War. In *War to Peace Transition: Conflict Intervention and Peacebuilding in Liberia*, ed. Kenneth Omeje, 19–40. Lanham, MD: University Press of America.

Gupta, Rachana. 2020. China on Target to Eliminate Extreme Poverty by 2020, January 21. http://www.china.org.cn/opinion/2020-01/21/content_75636612.htm.

Guyer, I. Jane. 2004. *Marginal Gains: Monetary Transactions in Atlantic Africa*. Chicago: The University of Chicago Press.

Guyer, I. Jane. 2018. Value and Wealth: What Do Value and Wealth Do? 'Life' Goes on, Whatever 'Life' Is. In *Money at the Margins: Global Perspectives on Technology, Financial Inclusion and Design*, ed. Bill Maurer, Smoki Musaraj, and Ivan Small, 87–90. New York: Berghahn.

Huntington, P. Samuel. 1999. The Lonely Superpower. *Foreign Affairs* 78 (2): 35–49.

Jalata, Asafa. 2016. Colonial Terrorism and the Incorporation of Africa into the Capitalist World System. In *Phases of Terrorism in the Age of Globalization*. New York: Palgrave Macmillan. https://doi.org/10.1057/9781137552341_6.

Jahan, Sarwat, and Ahmed Saber Mahmud. 2015. What Is Capitalism?. *Finance and Development* 52 (2) (June). https://www.imf.org/external/pubs/ft/fandd/2015/06/basics.htm.

Janardhan, Narayanappa. 2018. Is China Forging a New Tripolar World Order? *The Diplomat*, April 25. https://thediplomat.com/2018/04/is-china-forging-a-new-tripolar-world-order/.

Jerven, Morten. 2016. Capitalism in Precolonial Africa: A Review. *African Economic History Working Paper Series No. 27*. Norwegian University of Life Science. https://www.aehnetwork.org/wp-content/uploads/2016/06/AEHN-WP-27.pdf.

Kaplan, D. Robert. 2016. How Islam Created Europe. *The Atlantic*, May. https://www.theatlantic.com/magazine/archive/2016/05/how-islam-created-europe/476388/.

Karbo, Tony. 2018. Introduction: Towards a New Pax Africana. In Tony Karbo and Virk Kudrat (eds.), *The Palgrave Handbook of Peacebuilding in Africa*, 3–28. New York: Palgrave Macmillan.

Langdon, Steven, Archibald R.M. Ritter, and Yiagadeesen Samy. 2018. *African Economic Development*. London: Routledge.

Lewis, Thomas. n.d. Trans-Atlantic Slave Trade. https://www.britannica.com/topic/transatlantic-slave-trade#info-article-history.

Lime, Ashley. 2018. A Guide to Africa's Looted Treasures. BBC Africa, November 23. https://www.bbc.co.uk/news/world-africa-45406557.

Livingstone, Amy. 2015. What Is Considered Middle Class in America? – Definition, Income Range and Jobs. https://www.moneycrashers.com/middle-class-america-definition-income-range-jobs/.

Maclean, Ruth. 2018. Bronzes to Benin, Gold to Ghana … Museums under Fire on Looted Art. *The Guardian*, December 2. https://www.theguardian.com/culture/2018/dec/02/british-museums-pressure-give-back–looted-african-art-treasures.

Mark, J. Joshua. 2016. Great Pyramids of Giza, December 19, 2020. *Ancient History Encyclopedia*. https://www.ancient.eu/Great_Pyramid_of_Giza/.

Mazrui, Ali. 1967. Towards a Concept of *Pax Africana*. Chapter from Ali Mazrui's Book, *Towards a Pax Africana: A Study of Ideology and Ambition*. Chicago: University of Chicago Press. Reprinted in, Karbo, Tony, and Virk Kudrat (eds.). 2018. *The Palgrave Handbook of Peacebuilding in Africa*, 29–44. New York: Palgrave Macmillan.

Mbembe, Achille. 2001. *On the Postcolony*. Berkeley: University of California Press.

Mbembe, Achille. 2016. Africa in the New Century, June. https://africasacountry.com/2016/06/africa-in-the-new-century/.

McCormick, John. 2012. The European Union: A Different Kind of Beast. In *Multipolarity in the 21st Century: A New World Order*, ed. Murray Donette and Brown David. London: Routledge.

Miller, W. Richard. 2018. Is Capitalism Corrupt? *Social Philosophy and Policy* 35 (2): 31–53.

Moghalu, C. Kingsley. 2014. *Emerging Africa: How Global Economy's 'Last Frontier' Can Prosper and Matter*. London: Penguin Books.

Moyo, Dambisa. 2011. *How the West Was Lost: Fifty Years of Economic Folly and the Stark Choices Ahead*. New York: Penguin Books.

Moyo Dambisa, 2018. *Edge of Chaos: Why Democracy is Failing to Deliver Economic Growth and How to Fix It*. London: Little Brown.

Donette, Murray. 2012. Introduction. In *Multipolarity in the 21st Century: A New World Order*, ed. Murray Donette and Brown David. London: Routledge.

Musaraj, Smoki, and Ivan Small. 2018. Introduction: Money and Finance at the Margins. In *Money at the Margins: Global Perspectives on Technology, Financial Inclusion and Design*, ed. Bill Maurer, Smoki Musaraj, and Ivan Small, 1–18. New York: Berghahn.

Penn, Amanda. 2019. History of Capitalism: A Comprehensive Guide. *Shortform*, November 13. https://www.shortform.com/blog/history-of-capitalism/.

Pettinger, Tejvan. 2018. Neo-Liberalism: Examples and Criticisms, January 25. https://www.economicshelp.org/blog/20688/concepts/neoliberalism/.

Rodney, Walter. 1972. *How Europe Underdeveloped Africa*. London: Bogle-L'Ouverture Publication.

Sender, John, and Sheila Smith. 1986. *The Development of Capitalism in Africa*. London: Methuen.

Tempest, Stephen. 2019. What Did Europeans Offer the Africans in the Slave Trade? January 7. https://www.quora.com/What-did-Europeans-offer-the-Africans-in-the-slave-trade.

US Census Bureau. 2018. What Is the Current Poverty Rate in the United States? October 15. https://poverty.ucdavis.edu/faq/what-current-poverty-rate-united-states.

US Census Bureau. 2019. Income and Poverty in the United States: 2018, September 17. https://www.census.gov/library/publications/2019/demo/p60-266.html.

Veracini, Lorenzo. 2015. *The Settler Colonial Present*. London: Palgrave Macmillan. https://globalsocialtheory.org/concepts/settler-colonialism/.

World Bank. 2020. The World Bank in China. The World Bank, April 23. https://www.worldbank.org/en/country/china/overview.

Young, J.C. Robert. 2001. *Postcolonialism: An Historical Introduction*. Malden, MA: Blackwell Publishing.

Zeleza, Paul Tiyambe. 1996. *A Modern Economic History of Africa*, vol. 1. Dakar: CODESRIA Books.

CHAPTER 2

The Postcolonial State: From Frontier Capitalism to Neocolonial Capitalism

Taking advantage of state power, the governing elites in the African postcolonial states have substantially tinkered with the frontier capitalism inherited from the colonial era, to mainstream their accumulation interests in the economy without due regard to citizens' wellbeing and national development.

2.1 Political Decolonization and Neocolonial Capitalism

Most countries of Africa were colonized by different imperial states of Europe between the 1880s and 1960s before they regained their independence, but only political independence. The political decolonization of Africa was achieved through nationalist struggles, which took various forms in different colonies; some more violent than others. Among the typically colonized African countries, the Arab countries of North Africa (Egypt, Algeria, Libya, Morocco, and Tunisia) obtained independence comparatively earlier than the Sub-Saharan African countries. Their political independence occurred between 1922 and 1956. Sudan and Mauritania which claim to be Arab countries but without Arab demographic majorities regained their independence in 1956 and 1961

K. Omeje, *The Failure and Feasibility of Capitalism in Africa*, International Political Economy Series,
https://doi.org/10.1007/978-3-030-75170-8_2

respectively. Ghana, which regained its political independence in 1957 was the first to be decolonized in Sub-Saharan Africa.

1960, popularly known as "The Year of Africa," was the most decisive year of African decolonization. It was the year in which the largest number of African countries, 17 of them, regained their self-rule. The colonial state gave way to a distinct form of postcolonial state, as colonialism was replaced by what many pan-Africanists, statesmen and political thinkers depicted as neocolonialism. Neocolonialism was a term used to describe the new form of colonialism that emerged in Africa and other regions of the global South in which political independence was perceived to be a superficial phenomenon devoid of economic independence. The neocolonial arrangements were largely seen as deliberate arrangements in which the colonizers worked through the political processes that formally terminated colonial rule to inaugurate protégé regimes in the former colonies that maintained preponderant loyalty to the ex-colonial powers in the metropole and protected the latter's economic and strategic interests in the new independent states (Rodney 1972). Neocolonialism was deeply undergirded by a distinct form of capitalism, neocolonial capitalism, which is peripheral to the international capitalist system created by the lopsided division of labour between the European imperial powers and the economies of their dependent colonies during the colonial era.

Under the neocolonial economic order (neocolonial capitalism), African economies were dominated by monopoly mining and commercial companies of Western origin, most of which had been in operation since the colonial era, thereby continuing the dependency of the African economies on the West. Kwame Nkrumah (1965), Ghana's foremost nationalist and post-independence leader, published a highly influential study explaining the stranglehold and dynamics of "neocolonialism" (read: "neocolonial capitalism") in Africa, which he called "the last stage of imperialism." As an ardent pan-Africanist, Nkrumah advocated for Africa's unification and the formation of an all-inclusive federalist or unionist government. This in his view would end the balkanisation of Africa into many small states under diverse spheres of influence by foreign powers, especially in the light of the Cold War politics. "Africa must unite," Nkrumah's ideological rhetoric for the ultimate unification of the continent into a coherent independent federation was his remedy for neocolonialism, a remedy he also considered a *sine qua non* for transforming the continent into a respectable sovereign entity with strong bargaining power in the international system. Nkrumah was the foremost leader in the struggle for Ghana's independence. With independence secured from Britain in 1957, Nkrumah went on to effectively support different liberations struggles for the decolonization of the rest of the continent stressing that Ghana's independence was meaningless unless it is linked up with the total liberation of the African continent. Nkrumah proposed the establishment of an African high command to spearhead the liberation struggles to free the African continent and to coordinate regional security efforts (Karbo 2018: 17).

Writing in 1967, the renowned Kenyan professor of political science Ali Mazrui coined the concept of *Pax-Africana* to elaborate on Nkrumah's vision for an African high command as the military security wing of a "united states of Africa," effective for both decolonization and maintenance of peace and security. Because Mazrui was writing at a time when Nkrumah's vision for a political unification of Africa had collapsed, he was not concerned with political unification in *Pax-Africana* but with an African-led collective security arrangement to solve the problems of armed conflicts and instability in any part of the continent as a way to guarantee African independence, and prevent external military intervention of all sorts, which almost invariably promote non-African interests. Mazrui agrees with Nkrumah on the dictum that "peace in any part of Africa could only be assured under the supervising eye of the rest of the continent," what Mazrui called "the principle of continental jurisdiction" (Mazrui 1967: 35 & 37). Unlike *Pax-Romana*, *Pax-Britannica* and other imperial military complexes before it, Mazrui argues that the envisioned *Pax-Africana* has no extra-continental ambition of imposing peace on other states.

In the context of the Cold War politics, Nkrumah as head of state and a leading proponent of pan-Africanism tried to assert himself as non-aligned even though his fiery rhetorics were considered unsettling in the West and largely interpreted as pro-communist. Nkrumah's government was later overthrown in a military coup in 1966, a coup that was allegedly backed by the American CIA (Francis 2006: 17).

Besides Nkrumah, left-leaning critics of neocolonialism in the Cold War years such as the famous Egyptian professor of political economy Samir Amin (1973, 1976) advocated that the newly independent states should "delink" from the exploitative international capitalist system and pursue a socialist path to development. Amilca Cabral, the leader of the national liberation struggle in Guinea-Bissau espoused clearcut ideological views and strategies of using "the national liberation struggle as revolution" against colonialism and all its legacies, including "the complete liberation of the national productive forces" from neocolonial domination to unleash the development potential of the African state and people (Cabral 1979:134). The French Caribbean pan-Africanist and naturalized Algerian philosopher of decolonization struggles Frantz Fanon (1961) propounded a similar theory of revolutionary break with the colonial past in all its political, social, cultural and economic ramifications. Like Ernesto "Che" Guevara, the famous Argentine Marxist revolutionary and proponent of revolution by guerrilla warfare, Cabral and Fanon formulated detailed strategies of how to mobilize grassroots populations for guerrilla insurgencies to liberate the African colonial state and the postcolony from the forces of imperialist domination and neocolonial capitalism. Radical views of these sorts aimed against the legacies of colonialism and neocolonialism, not only gained tremendous traction among African intellectuals, social activists and statesmen between the late 1950s and 1980s, but also fed into the Cold War politics of that era. The concept of neocolonialism has come under vigorous attack from many African political economists of diverse intellectual orientations, a critique that has been well addressed in literature and therefore will not engage my attention in this book (cf. Lazarus 1999; Zeleza 2006; Omeje 2015).

It is important to remark that the frontier capitalism of the colonial era did not succeed in obliterating all the precolonial modes of production in Africa, ostensibly because of the inexorable resistance mounted by the Africans on the one hand, and the limited governance capacity of the colonialists on the other hand. Hence, when most of the African countries regained their independence in the 1960s, they inherited varied levels of disarticulated economies comprising the Western-imposed system of frontier capitalism and the survivors of the precolonial economic structures, especially the most widespread system of "peasant capitalism." The combination of frontier capitalism and indigenous capitalism obtainable in post-colonial Africa is an aberrant departure from the manufacturing-oriented mainstream capitalism that has historically developed and flourished in the West. Taking advantage of state power, the governing elites in the African postcolonial states have devised diverse mechanisms to enthrone and advance their interests in the aberrant economic systems they inherited from the colonial era in which frontier capitalism impregnated with Western accumulation interests is dominant. In the process of tinkering with the inherited frontier capitalism to mainstream their accumulation interests, the governing African postcolonial elites have succeeded in proliferating diverse contraptions and aberrations of capitalism that have conspired to impede the development of genuine brand(s) of capitalism suitable for African social structures. This observation is developed and examined in greater depth in Chapter 5.

2.2 The Convoluted Legacies of Colonialism and the Economies of the Postcolonial States

Some of the devastating impacts of colonialism on African economies have already been highlighted in the preceding chapter. In this chapter, I wish to highlight two convoluted legacies in Africa's colonial history that seem to stand out in the economies of the postcolonial states. The first is the argument that Nkrumah and many critics of neocolonialism have made: that the proliferation of many small neocolonial economies in Africa, which are a creation of the infamous Berlin Conference, and reinforced by the diverse colonial legacies is inimical to development. Postcolonial Africa is made up of 54 sovereign states,[1] and with the exception of Eritrea and South Sudan that successfully separated from Ethiopia and Sudan following protracted armed conflicts, the rest were all states inherited from Western colonial rule. Evidently, some of the core reasons for the secession of Eritrea and South Sudan are all rooted in the social contradictions inherent in the colonial histories of their former sovereign unions.

To be sure, the artificiality of the African states and the territorial smallness of many of them are bad enough, but they are not as devastating as the neocolonial nature of their small economies. While the former made the African countries divided against themselves to the advantage of the outside world, the latter dedicated them to producing unprocessed primary commodities for external markets. There are many territorially small countries in the world that have excelled in economic performance, but they were not essentially founded as frontier economies for producing and exporting non-value adding commodities to the international market. There are of course a few exceptions to this observation, especially among the Asian postcolonial states—e.g., Singapore (which was originally part of postcolonial Malaysia). A plethora of studies has been published over the decades about how reliance on primary commodity exports has greatly disadvantaged African economies, exposing them to intermittent structural crises, too often externally induced, including balance of payment crisis. These crises have often been aggravated or preceded by a catalogue of resource misallocation, mismanagement and prebendal graft.

Africa entered the 2000 millennium as a heavily beleaguered continent marked by a postcolonial history of massive governance and development deficits. Decades of states' policy failures and prebendal plunder in several low-performing neocolonial economies that are overly dependent on production and export of primary commodities exposed them to erratic balance of payment deficits, rising external borrowing and debt crisis, skewed and unsustainable development, massive youth unemployment, high poverty levels and ultimately armed rebellion and civil wars. In its worst post-independence economic crisis of the 1980s and 1990s, the vulnerably dependent African economies were left exposed and devastated. The embryonic light manufacturing sector, partly propped up by the widespread government policies of import-substitution industrialization was heavily battered. At the early stage of the economic crisis in mid-1980, about 23% of African manufacturing industries had ceased production and a further 57% were functioning at less than 70% of nominal capacity—below their break-even point (Mytelka 1989: 77). Things got worse over the next two decades and the situation was evidently exacerbated by the inappropriate therapy of Structural Adjustment Programme (SAP) foisted on most countries of Sub-Saharan Africa by the World Bank and IMF, working in concert with the Africa's major creditors, notably the leading European central banks and the US Department of Treasury. SAP involved loan packages that prioritized debt repayment and liberalization of the economy by the already highly indebted poor countries over their longstanding social development obligations to their citizens such as funding of health care, education, agriculture and so forth (Cilliers 2021: 27). It also whittled the state's involvement in the economy, replacing it with the agenda of foreign capital and unrestrained dominance of the private sector.

The African economic crisis of the 1980s and 1990s was the most devastating expression of the structural impediments associated with small economies founded on primary commodity exports. The ill-fated SAP therapy placed emphasis on stringent credit financing that attracted conditionalities, such as huge debt service obligations, currency devaluation, dismantling of state's social development obligations, privatization of public enterprises and massive deregulation of the economy (Dibua 2006;

Moghalu 2014). The unbearable external debt overhang and debt service obligations associated with the SAP regime bankrupted African economies and ruptured their political systems.

Nkrumah's visionary efforts to end the proliferation of small neocolonial economies (some of which are practically unviable), favoured in varied measures by member states of the minority Casablanca Group of post-independence pan-Africanism collapsed in 1963. The Casablanca Group was the radical bloc that more or less had a shared vision of pan-Africanism regarding the need for a political unification of Africa in the run up to the formation of the continental body, the Organisation of Africa Unity (OAU), in 1963. The Casablanca Group[2] comprised countries like Egypt, Guinea, Mali, Morocco and Algeria. The alternate group that canvassed an opposite vision of African unity was the Monrovia Group. The latter preferred a cooperative association of self-governing African states that would respect the territorial integrity and sovereignty of one another. The Monrovia Group had 17 member states which included countries like Liberia, Nigeria, Cameroun, Senegal, Ethiopia, among others.[3] The debate was between an immediate political unification of Africa and a gradualist approach to African unity that will not compromise the hard-earned sovereignty of member states. The debate was won by the Monrovia Group. Consequently, the two Groups united to form the regional body OAU on 1 May 1963 based on the vision of the majority bloc, the Monrovia Group. The OAU was renamed and transformed into the African Union (AU) in 2002. Sixty years after independence, the unviability of most of the African economies has even become more pronounced. I will later return to this point.

The second issue in Africa's colonial history that tends to stand out in the economies of the postcolonial states is the emergence and dominance of a largely unproductive and parasitic governing elite that sees access to state power as a means of self-aggrandizement. There was a density of literature on this subject during the Cold War era, most of them from Marxist scholars, including prominent theorists like Samir Amin (1969), Claude Ake (1978), Terisa Turner (1981), among several others. These scholars were strictly post-Marxist in the sense that they tried to tweak and adapt the mainstream Marxist theory to the African and Third Word context. The argument of Marxist intellectuals can be summarized as follows. Under a capitalist system where the means of production are privately owned, the dominant class is the capitalist class who own and control the means of production. The state is controlled by the capitalists and the various policies of the state fundamentally serve their interests, especially the economic, development and foreign policies, as the case may be. In Marxist terminology the capitalist class is known as the bourgeoisie and this wealthy investment and property-owning class is contrasted with the subject classes comprising the working class or proletariat, artisans and smallscale farmers, etc. The two classes, the dominant capitalist class and the subject classes have contradictory material interests which inadvertently pitch them against each other in inexorable class struggles that might result in an anti-capitalist revolution (a revolution that the West was able to avert through ingenious pro-working class welfare reforms at home and export of capital to transitional economies for colonial and neocolonial exploitation). The analysis comprised in the classical Marxist model essentially applies to a proper capitalist state and economy where the means of production are controlled by a productive capitalist class, such as the type of capitalism that developed in the West. The analysis does not strictly apply to frontier capitalism of the colonial order discussed in Sect. 1.4 in Chapter 1 of this book.

Under frontier capitalism of the colonial order, the dominant frontier capitalist class comprised the colonizers who owned and controlled the means of production, especially the pillars of the cash crop economy, mining industries, banks and trading companies. Most importantly, the colonizers instituted and controlled the entire colonial state apparatuses which, according to Mbembe (2001: 32–35), enabled them to exercise sovereignty with violence and impunity. Compliance to colonial decrees and the imperatives of colonial economic exploitation was brutally enforced on the "natives"[4] who comprised the bulk of the subject classes in a Marxist sense.

When most of the African countries regained political independence, the control of the colonial state apparatuses was essentially the effective change that occurred. The levers of frontier capitalism for the most part remained unchanged. The nationalist leaders, most of whom practically had no economic and financial resources in a capitalist senses were given political power which had been designed for perpetuating the inherited structures of frontier capitalism to the advantage of West. Using various policy devices and programmatic interventions, such as indigenization of foreign enterprises to boost domestic equity participation, creation of industrial and agricultural development banks to provide soft credits to potential local investors, import-substitution industrialization, land tenure reforms to consolidate state expropriation for the benefit of largescale private investors, etc., the post-independence governing elites tried frantically to get a foothold on their expatriate-dominated national economies. The enactment and implementation of some of these reform policies were met with stiff external and local oppositions, in some cases resulting in coups d'etat and political instability. However, it is these efforts aimed at reformation of the inherited frontier capitalism which yielded mixed results that by and large enabled Africa's transition to neocolonial capitalism. Given the continued dominance of primary commodity exports and with little or no industrial manufacturing, neocolonial capitalism is by no means as productive as mainstream capitalism. In fact, it is deformed contraption in which the African state managers and local businessmen and middlemen too often play the second fiddle to the more influential external forces, but certainly not in all countries and circumstances. In the heydays of Marxist scholarship (during the Cold War), proponents used various adjectival qualifiers to input inauthenticity to the African bourgeoisie—"lumpen," "petty" and "comprador"[5] (e.g., comprador bourgeoisie). Analytically, these concepts have become largely outmoded.

Not having a strong economic base, the dominant neocolonial capitalists and governing elites in Africa have taken advantage of their weak political and governance institutions at home to institutionalize impunity as a culture of governance and accumulation, resulting in extreme forms of abuse of public office, corruption, and persecution of genuine opposition. Renowned American political scientist Richard Joseph (1987) has used the concept of prebendalism[6] to theorize this phenomenon while Daniel Bach (2011) has creatively applied the familiar theory of neopatrimonialism[7] to elucidate the same. Most significantly, in the course of the persistent tinkering with frontier and neocolonial capitalism, the African governing elites have proliferated various dysfunctional versions of capitalism that are in a large sense essentially antithetical to growth and development. This is the subject of Chapter 6 of this book.

With the neoliberal West having won the Cold War and subsequently promoting competitive neoliberal democracies in Africa many of the Marxist scholars, including the African Marxists became converted to the dominant neoliberal ideology, while others pragmatically retooled their analytical lenses to remain relevant in the neoliberal age. Consequently, Marxist-oriented scholarship has taken a nosedive in Africa and in most parts of the world since the end of the Cold War. The apparent decline in Marxist-oriented scholarship seems to have created an unconscious or implicit assumption that the nature and character of the African governing elites did suddenly change with the end of the Cold War and the subsequent transplantation and proliferation of multi-party democracies in the continent. This seems to be far from the reality! The African governing elites have not fundamentally been transformed and their accumulation patterns and tendencies are still for the most part subversive of authentic capitalist development in Africa almost as much as during the Cold War. In fact, in straggling countries like Zimbabwe, Guinea-Bissau, and Equatorial Guinea, as well as in war-affected states like Sudan, Libya, Burundi, South Sudan, Chad and Somalia, the accumulation patterns of the governing elites and other powerful agents have from all indications become more virulent in the post-Cold War dispensation relative to the Cold War era. These countries are all among the most corrupt and most fragile states in the world following all the reports of the Transparency International (TI) "Corruption Perception Index" (CPI) and/or the Fund for Peace (FFP) "Fragile State Index" (FSI) in recent years.[8] Furthermore, as Moghalu (2014: 371) has aptly illustrated, despite being officially independent, several African countries still take political, economic and even military guidance and protection from previous colonial powers.

Table 2.1 presents snapshots of the top ten African and Asian nominal GDPs in 1960 and 2019 and their per capita incomes.

It is clear from the statistical table that the largest economies in Asia were far ahead of their African counterparts in 1960 when the vast majority of the African countries became independent. With a combined GDP of $141.06 billion, the top three largest economies in Asia—China, Japan and India—had a GDP level that was just about $10 billion more than the GDP of Sub-Saharan Africa ($131.49 billion) in 1960.[9] Going by 2018 figures, however, the GDP of each of these three Asian economies—China ($13.61 trillion), Japan ($4.97 trillion) and India ($2.72 trillion)—is larger than the GDP of the entire 54 countries in Africa ($2.5 trillion).[10]

Countries like Bangladesh, Iran, Korea, Pakistan, Thailand and Philippines to a lesser extent were at GDP levels comparable to the top four African economies in 1960 (South Africa, Nigeria, DRC and Algeria). In terms of per capita, the Asian countries were averagely better off but the gaps were nowhere close to the mindboggling gaps in contemporary history as could be clearly discerned from Table 2.2. The structure of

Table 2.1 Top ten African and Asian economies by nominal GDP and per capita in 1960

African countries	*GDP (billion)*	*Per capita*	*Asian countries*	*GDP (billion)*	*Per capita*
South Africa	$7.56	$2,191	China	$59.72	$567
Nigeria	$4.20	$567	Japan	$44.31	$2,954
DRC	$3.36	$489	India	$37.03	$766
Algeria	$2.72	$1,723	Turkey	$14.00	$1,662
Morocco	$2.04	$815	Philippines	$6.68	$1,133
Sudan	$1.31	$709	Bangladesh	$4.27	$952
Ghana	$1.22	$894	Iran	$4.20	$2,946
Zimbabwe	$1.05	$989	Korea	$3.96	$904
Senegal	$1.00	$1,047	Pakistan	$3.71	$638
Kenya	$0.79	$659	Thailand	$2.76	$943

Source Compiled from the listed sources: World Bank (2020) "GDP in Sub-Saharan Africa," 1 April 2020. https://addictedtodata.com/gdp-in-sub-saharan-africa/; see also: CEPR (2005) "Per Capita GDP Growth, 1960-2000," https://cepr.net/documents/publications/econ_growth_2005_11_27_table_1.htm; https://tradingeconomics.com/sudan/gdp

Table 2.2 GDP Disparities between Asian Economies at comparable GDP levels with Africa in 1960, and their African counterparts (2019 figures)

Asian countries	*GDP (billion)*	*Per capita*	*Africa countries*	*GDP (billion)*	*Per capita*
South Korea	$1,629.53	$31,430.6	Nigeria	$446.54	$2,222.00
Indonesia	$1,111.71	$4,163.80	South Africa	$358.84	$6,100.40
Saudi Arabia	$ 779.289	$22,865.20	Egypt	$302.26	
Taiwan (Province of China)	586.104	$24,827.90	Algeria	$ 172.78	$3,980.10
Thailand	$529.18	$7,792.00	Morocco	$ 119.04	$3,046.60
Iran	$ 458.50		Kenya	$ 98.60	$1,997.60
United Arab Emirate (UAE)	$ 405.771	$37,749.90	Ghana	$ 67.08	$2,223.40
Israel	$ 387.72	$42,823.30	DRC	$ 48.99	$500.60
Philippines	$330.91	$3,294.50	Sudan	$ 30.87	$714.30
Bangladesh	$317.47	$1,905.70	Senegal	$ 23.94	$1,427.90
Pakistan	$ 284.21	$1,388.20	Zimbabwe	$12.82	$860.00

Source Compiled from the listed sources: Statistics Times (2020) "List of Asian Countries by GDP", February 12, https://statisticstimes.com/economy/asian-countries-by-gdp.php; Statistics Times (2020) "List of African Countries GDP," February 24, http://statisticstimes.com/economy/african-countries-by-gdp.php. http://statisticstimes.com/economy/asian-countries-by-gdp-per-capita.php. http://statisticstimes.com/economy/african-countries-by-gdp-per-capita.php

exports from the highly performing economies of Asia has also changed radically from primary commodities in the early 1960s to high-tech industrial products in contemporary time. In 1962, South Korea exported mostly raw materials like fish, rice, iron ore and unprocessed silk while today it boasts of a well-diversified export portfolio that includes electronics, cars, ships and other high-end machinery (Cilliers 2021: 34). Similarly, there are many other Asian countries not included in the above table of 10 because their 1960 GDP levels were significantly below that of Thailand (the No 10 in the list), whose GDP levels were comparable to the African top 10 in 1960. These Asian countries include Indonesia, Taiwan, Saudi Arabia and United Arab Emirate. It may suffice to take a snapshot of the 2019 GDP levels of only the above 10 Asian countries at comparable levels of GDP with Africa in 1960, and the largest African economies (both in 2019 and 1960). From a political economy perspective, there is the need for caution regarding this comparison because of the too many distortion variables. Notable among the variables is that whereas the majority of African countries were just starting the journey of self-rule in 1960, most of the Asian countries in Table 2.2 had already been self-governing over a much longer time with the exception of Bangladesh that seceded from Pakistan in 1971 (with the help of India), and United Arab Emirate that regained its independence from Britain in December 1971. Self-rule has significant implications for a people's capacity to engineer and sustain growth and development, especially in taking forward the level of development of a country's productive forces at the moment of achieving self-rule. From the standpoint of political and economic development, many Sub-Saharan African countries like Guinea, Guinea-Bissau, Mozambique, Central African Republic, Burundi, Rwanda, Malawi, Niger, Chad, Mali, etc., literally achieved self-rule from ground zero. In fact, most of the Francophone and Lusophone countries in Africa for want of appropriate terminology were literally "over-colonized" frontiers of what some African Marxist used to describe as "surrogate capitalism" during the Cold War. A Country like South Africa and the Chinese province of Hong Kong that regained their sovereignties in the 1990s did so at significantly high levels of development of their productive forces, which is the clearest illustration of the difference I am trying to point out. However, South Africa was comparatively more disadvantaged than Hong Kong in terms of human capital development because of the protracted and systematic exclusion that the apartheid regime inflicted on the majority Black population which created huge gaps in education and social wellbeing between the Whites, Coloured and Blacks.

At a more intellectual level, it is pertinent to sound another note of caution and this concerns the reliability of the 1960 macroeconomic data, generated or extrapolated from a dispensation in history when some of the countries concerned were still colonial entities or new independent states with little or no capacity to generate their own data. In fact, even today many postcolonial states still lack the capacity to generate their own national planning and development data with the result that international development agencies generate and apply irresistible statistical data on them. I do not wish to comment on the politics of generating statistical data in international development, a phenomenon that has been insightfully analysed by a publication like *Enough is Enough: Dear Mr Camdessus ... Open Letter of Resignation to the Managing Director of the International Monetary Fund* written by the Senior IMF economist from Granada, Davidson L. Budhoo. Having heeded the notes of caution, let us now examine the empirical data (Table 2.2).

The disparities are quite glaring as Table 2.2 indicates. Africa's largest GDP state Nigeria is exceedingly surpassed by the top six Asian countries in the above GDP league table. In fact, what is most remarkable is that Nigeria and South Africa, the two largest African economies in 1960 (and also in 2019) had larger GDPs than the top six Asian countries that have presently surpassed them—South Korea, Indonesia, Saudi Arabia, Taiwan (Province of China), Thailand and Iran. Presently, Nigeria has the world's largest number of people living below poverty line based on the World Poverty Clock estimates, about 94 million people (*The Guardian* 2019). Nigeria overtook India to achieve this parlous record notwithstanding that the country's population is only about one-sixth of India's 1.35 billion people.

Box 2.1 A Case Study of the Decline of Zimbabwe

It is noteworthy that Zimbabwe, which though still a colonial state in 1960 had one of Africa's 10 largest GDPs is today in complete tatters. Postcolonial Zimbabwe was destroyed by a combination of prolonged Western sanctions spearheaded by the UK government and the disastrous political and economic policy blunders of the ZANU-PF regime, including extreme mismanagement, ruthless dictatorship and prebendal corruption. The Western sanctions were imposed on Zimbabwe (mostly on top state officials and big businesses) for forcibly taking back large expanses of farmlands expropriated during colonial rule by the minority White settlers. Subsequently, the economy collapsed, forcing millions of Zimbabweans into economic refuge abroad, most of them in neighbouring South Africa but with a large number migrating to the West. Astronomical rise in inflation destroyed the purchasing power of the local currency (the Zimbabwean Dollar) prompting the government to stop printing it and to adopt the US Dollar and South African Rand as national currencies. In mid-November 2008, during the height of the country's inflation crisis, Zimbabwe recorded a monthly inflation rate of 79.6 billion%; the country's inflation rate has remained one of the highest in the world since the early 2000s, only second to Venezuela in May 2020.[11] There is persistence of acute shortage of essential commodities, high cost of living and high rate of unemployment in Zimbabwe. The government reintroduced the Zimbabwean Dollar in 2019, ten years after it was suspended, but there is little confidence in the currency as a means of transaction among Zimbabweans.

Despite the exit and demise of Robert Mugabe, the Zimbabwean maximum leader, "the United States and the European Union (EU) have both maintained sanctions, citing a lack of progress in democratic and human rights reforms, as well as restrictions on press freedoms" (BBC News, 25 October 2019). However, the real sticking point seems to be the destroyed infrastructures and seized farmlands of the White settlers. Since assuming office in November 2017, Mugabe's successor and former embattled vice president, Emmerson Mnangagwa, has not been able to steer the country out of the woods. In fact, the levels of inflation, insecurity, corruption, unemployment and restiveness tend to be worsening.

In August 2020, the Zimbabwean government launched a compensation scheme of $3.5 billion to pay off for the destroyed and confiscated infrastructures of local White farmers and subsequently offered to return their farmlands seized violently under the controversial government's expropriation programme between 2000 and 2001 (BBC News, 2 September 2020). These government's conciliatory measures are expected to pave the way for the lifting of Western sanctions on Zimbabwe and hopefully end the economic quandary and extreme hardship of the preceding two decades.

2.3 Explanations for the Rise of the Asian Economies and the African Context

Several explanations have been proffered about the rise of the Asian economies, some of them focusing on an analysis of the different waves of industrialization that have transformed these previously low-performing agrarian economies into major regional and international manufacturing hubs. In 1960, as we have seen, some of the highly successful Asian economies were at comparable levels with many African economies. Three waves of growth and industrialization have been associated with the modern Asian economies. The first wave of industrialization that benefitted South Korea, Singapore, Taiwan and Hong Kong was mainly triggered by the rapid growth in post-war Japan (backstopped by American aid) which had risen from the ruins of World War II to become the world's second largest economy by 1970. Challenged with seeking new territories and opportunities for cheap labour and low-cost production beginning from the 1960s, the growing Japanese Trans-national Companies (TNCs) who were producing for the regional and global markets chose to expand their manufacturing and production factories into the neighbouring East Asian countries, culminating in the first generation of "Newly Industrialising Countries" (NICs) in the post-World War II era. By a massive knock-on effect many local firms developed in the host countries, often described as Asian Tigers, that progressively opened their economies to Japanese TNCs and other capitalist investors, especially American TNCs. Within a few years, these local firms and SMEs (small and medium enterprises), some of which started as family-based businesses (e.g., the South Korean Chaebols—Samsung, LG Corporation, Daewoo, Hyundai, etc.), grew to become global conglomerates and the national brand of their "developmental capitalism," the model of capitalism characteristic of "the developmental state." Without delving into the contending theories of developmentalism as a contemporary path to capitalist development among emerging economies, it suffices to say that developmental capitalism combines moderate and effective state intervention in production and distribution of wealth to ensure sustainable growth, with financial stability (Bresser-Pereira 2018).

It is important to note that the Asian Tigers were not just passive recipients of the Japanese largesse and assorted foreign direct investments. They had some strategic advantages and also undertook proactive reforms that worked to the mutual benefits of all parties. These strategic advantages and proactive reforms of the host Asian Tigers largely include:

- Infrastructural investments leading to well-developed level of infrastructures and their progressive expansion—e.g., roads, railways, ports, power, schools and hospitals.
- Relatively well-educated population with the required technical skills, achieved through investments in education and upgrading standards.
- Cultural traditions and worldviews that place great values on education, hardwork, achievement and the collective good, supported by massive state-assisted transition from education and skills training to work.
- Taking advantage of geostrategic assets, especially in the case of Singapore, which is situated between the Indian and Pacific Ocean, and has one of the largest deep-water harbours in the world, facilitating trade on a global scale.
- Government support to local firms and SMEs (e.g., by offering venture capital, low-interest rates on bank loans, import restriction using high taxes to stimulate local production, funding of research & development related to high-tech products).
- Less rigid laws and regulations on labour, taxation and pollution relative to the home countries of TNCs, conducing to more profitable operations (i.e., low-cost manufacture with cheap labour) (adapted from Weebly, n.d.).[12]

Ostensibly, the most critical driving force for the transformation of the four Asian Tigers and the subsequent countries that benefited from the second and third waves of industrialization in the Asian region is the role of political leaderships with a sound vision for industrialization, institutional and governance reforms, as well as the political will and discipline to implement well-set-out policy measures. The most impactful policy interventions and strategies from the examples of the Asian NICs are usually those with relatively longer-term perspectives. This is where the pattern of neoliberal democracies practices in many African countries characterized by periodic elections (every 4 or 5 years as the case may be), populist programmes that can easily appease the voters and discontinuities in strategic policies and pro-industrialization projects can be a major setback.

Most Asian countries had the advantage of strong centralized states with limited or no democratic credentials (from a neoliberal perspective) during the foundational years of their strategic reforms and take-off. China under Deng Xiaoping, Singapore under Lew Kuan Yew, Indonesia under Mohamed Suharto and Malaysia under Mahathir Mohamad are just some of the several examples (Moghalu 2014: 327).

Rapid increases in wage levels and cost of production in the East Asian NICs coupled with attractive economic climates elsewhere in the region partly contributed to the second wave of industrialization. As such, Japanese and Western TNCs expanded FDIs to the neighbouring South Asian economies of Malaysia and Thailand in the 1970s and 1980s leading to the sprouting of many labour-intensive manufacturing industries. Special economic zones (SEZs) backed with market-friendly policy reforms were created by the governments with the object of attracting high-tech investments from the booming economies in East Asia and beyond. By 1990, Malaysia had achieved a per capita income of $2,300 and Thailand a per capita income of $1,400 which put them squarely in the middle-level range among world economies (Stubbs 2018:18). In 1993, the World Bank coined the term "High Performing Asian Economies" (HPAEs) to describe the stupendous growth and human development levels recorded by eight Asian countries from 1965 to 1990, that was just before China and India joined the trailblazers in a big way. The eight HPAEs are Hong Kong, Indonesia, Japan, Malaysia, the Republic of Korea, Singapore, Taiwan (China) and Thailand (World Bank 1993).

With the market-oriented reforms embarked upon by Deng Xiaoping from 1979, China laid the foundation to benefit from the competition for industrialization among the many Asian economies. China and India subsequently emerged as targets for FDI by TNCs (as third phase of NICs) and since 1990, both countries have shown rapid growth.[13] Tax incentives and SEZs were introduced to encourage foreign companies to invest in the economies. China imitated some of the economic reform policies that helped the East Asian Tigers to industrialize while maintaining its Communist political ideology as a defining philosophy of governance, human development and collective identity. The benefits of the drive for growth have been immense in China which is today the world's second largest economy, and in India, to a lesser extent.

India, the world's seventh largest economy, has remained proactive in its quest to attract FDIs and promote export-oriented growth. As part of its pro-growth reforms, India has between 2000 and 2018 established about 223 operational SEZs, which are geographic regions with more liberal regulations than the rest of the country, and aimed to attract FDIs, create employment opportunities, develop infrastructure and facilitate transfer of technology and access to global markets through export promotion (WEDC 2020). The broad category of Indian SEZs encompasses several more specific zone types, such as free trade zones (FTZs), export processing zones (EPZs), free zones, industrial estates, free ports and urban enterprise zones (WEDC 2020). Investments in India's SEZs have increased over the last decade, rising from $590 million in 2006 to $69.3 billion in 2018 (WEDC 2020). With a strong advantage of highly skilled professionals, cheap labour and the Commonwealth English language heritage, India has excelled greatly in the service sector with many Western companies outsourcing telecommunication and IT-related works, among others, to Indian firms and subsidiaries. The service sector is the largest sector of the Indian economy, contributing about 54.3% to the country's GDP in 2018, up from about 40% in 1980.[14] India moved about 270 million of its citizens out of poverty between 2005 and 2018, reducing the total number of people living below poverty line to 75 million or about 5.5% of the population, which is highly significant (OpIndia 2018). India's current population is about 1.35 billion.

Explaining why the Asian economies were able to grow so rapidly, the renowned American economist Mark Skousen pointed out that:

> First, the *High Performing Asian economies (HPAEs)* are largely market-friendly, avoiding wage-price controls and excessive regulation of business. Second, they encourage macroeconomic stability (avoiding high levels of inflation and budget deficits), limit government activism, and discourage social welfare schemes. Third, they offer stable and secure financial and legal systems. Fourth, they promote high levels of saving and capital investment rather than high consumption spending. Fifth, many East Asian nations offer tax holidays for export-oriented businesses and impose few (if any) taxes on investments. Sixth, they are open to global technology and foreign capital.[15]

Offering one of the most well-conceptualized analysis of the Asian economic miracles, the British-Canadian political economist, Professor Richard Stubbs provides contending theoretical explanations that may not be mutually exclusive. The five theoretical perspectives discussed by Stubbs are worth summarizing as follows:

First, *neoclassical economic explanations* – Proponents argue that the East and Southeast Asian economies excelled because of their greater adherence to market-oriented policies, highlighting important features like capital formation – the development of physical and human capital or resources within the economy – and efficient allocation of resources; the remarkable savings rates of the successful economies; stable and effective exchange rates; the ability to attract foreign investments; the promotion of the export of manufactured goods; the supply of a well-educated and skilled labour force; the effective use of new technologies; and the need for a competent, stable and non-interventionist government.

Second, *statist explanations* – Statists emphasized the pervasive role of a strong state – the capitalist "developmental state" – in driving economic policies, notably by not only deciding on the overall economic strategy to be adopted, but also intervening to plan and execute most aspects of economic policies, from the allocation of capital to the emasculation of labour. It is argued that while the Asian developmental states were committed to private property and the market, they intervened in the economy by way of a small group of elite bureaucrats to guide and promote economic development.

Third, *cultural explanations* – In attempting to show why all the successful Asian economies came from the same part of the world, proponents of the cultural perspective emphasized the impact of culture on political and economic institutions and development. Analysts stressed the crucial role played by value systems characteristic of Confucianism (sometimes combined with elements of Buddhism) such as obligations and loyalty to the family as the basic social unit, obedience to legitimate authority and the high value placed on education, duty, hardwork and self-discipline in the rapid and sustained development of the "miracle" economies.

Fourth, *Japan-centered explanations* – This explanation has two strands. The first is that even though Japanese colonial occupation of South Korea and Taiwan was hash and repressive, it was during this period that the foundation of their later economic success was laid, including a strong centralised bureaucratic state, increased agricultural productivity, the development of an industrial sector (heavy industries and processing of agricultural products) and a clearly defined class structure. The second strand is that Japan served as the engine for growth and the model for successful development to its regional neighbours, pouring substantial amount of aid and FDIs into their economies – South Korea from the late 1960s, Taiwan and Hong Kong in the 1970s, and later, Singapore, Malaysia, Thailand, and ultimately China.

> Fifth, *American-hegemony explanations* – Countering the arguments of dependency theory and other leftist theories that essentially saw the world capitalist system from a center – periphery perspective, proponents of the American hegemony explanations argue that in the context of the geography of the Cold War, America used its dominant military and economic power to support Japan, South Korea and Taiwan, injecting enormous capital into the region through various types of aid, FDIs and increased trade. (Stubbs 2018: 3–14)

Stubbs' final submission is that while each perspective has its strengths and weaknesses, contrary to the seemingly dominant neoclassical and statist explanations, the politics of war, "hot" wars and the Cold War, is a more superior explanation for the rise of the East and Southeast Asian economies. As the Americans sought to retain their dominant position, the author argues, they strategically offered massive and uplifting military and economic assistance to the original seven highly successful Asian economies during the Cold War (Japan, South Korea, Taiwan, Hong Kong, Singapore, Malaysia and Thailand) "as part of a crescent of containment in the battle against communism" (Stubbs 2018: 3–14). This is a quintessentially "post-Tillian argument"[16] and a *realpolitik* discourse.

I do not intend to critique the fine-grained analysis and unapologetic submission of Stubbs. What is of foremost importance to me as an Africanist explaining and analysing the failure and feasibility of capitalism in Africa is that the politics of "Cold War capitalism" did not benefit Africa as it did to the Asian economies. If anything, it proliferated vicious wars and armed conflicts that ruined Africa's growth and development—from DRC and Angola to Mozambique, Sudan, Liberia and so forth. The Cold War politics led to the assassination and overthrow of several visionary leaders in Africa, propped up and sustained a litany of corrupt dictators that destroyed their countries in cahoots with their powerful foreign allies, and ultimately produced diverse proxy wars that were fought with weapons and aid provided by foreign allies while all the war actors looted the abundant natural resources of the war-torn states. Secondly, the Cold War has come and gone, and may never be replicated, at least not in the predictable future, and as such a Cold War-oriented model and path to capitalist development is ruled out for Africa. Hence, while the highly successful Asian countries benefited from the Cold War in many ways and largely managed to avoid "hot" wars, African states with their interlocking land borders were battered and setback by internal armed conflicts and spillover externalities from the implosion of neighbouring states.

At the turn of the last century, Sub-Saharan Africa's twenty years economic and political crisis of the 1980s and 1990s had generated over two dozen armed conflicts of varied intensities which prompted the London-based magazine *The Economist* to portray Africa in its May 2000 edition as "The Hopeless Continent." The latter was the controversial title of the magazine's cover story. Despite the apparent hopelessness of the African long-drawn-out crisis, many African intellectuals, policy practitioners and statesmen were visibly offended by this pessimistic castigation of the continent as "the hopeless continent."

One of the most exciting debates in African political economy since the past decade or a little longer is the discourse of "Africa rising." The contending subject of the debate is the claim by proponents that contemporary Africa has made a substantial leap from the longstanding thrall of underdevelopment and its negative governance and security correlates to the trajectory of sustainable progress. Guns have been silenced in most of the war-torn countries of the 1980s and 1990s such as Liberia, Sierra Leone, Cote d'Ivoire, Angola, Mozambique, Uganda, Southern Senegal and Rwanda; political repression and state-sponsored terror have waned; democracy has replaced many dictatorships, and the infrastructural conditions for economic take-off, growth and development seem to be taking shape in many countries. For the few countries and subnational territories where armed conflicts have not been completely exterminated such as northern Mali, South Sudan, Libya, Darfur-Sudan, Eastern Congo, and Somalia there has been significant de-escalation of hostilities relative to the peak years of war.

In a radical reversal of its May 2000 cynical cover story, *The Economist* magazine in the December 2011 edition carried a bullish cover page story about Africa titled "The Hopeful Continent: Africa Rising," a narrative that chronicled the fast-moving positive changes of the preceding decade. According to this later edition of *The Economist* (2011):

> After decades of slow growth, Africa has a real chance to follow in the footsteps of Asia. ... Over the past decade six of the world's ten fastest-growing countries were African. In eight of the past ten years, Africa has grown faster than East Asia, including Japan. ... The commodities boom is partly responsible. In 2000-08 around a quarter of Africa's growth came from higher revenues from natural resources. ... But the growth also has a lot to do with the manufacturing and service economies that African countries are beginning to develop.

Besides the significant decline in wars, improvement in governance and commodity boom, "Africa rising" has also been associated with "China rising," notably the increased trade, investment and infrastructure development partnerships between many African countries and a rising China that required massive supply of natural resources from the continent for its economic transformation. According to IMF data, between 2008 and 2017, a number of African countries such as Ethiopia, Rwanda, Ghana, Tanzania, Mozambique, DRC, Zambia, Uganda, Niger and Burkina Faso recorded an average annual GDP growth rate of between 5.6 and 10%, with Ethiopia recording an impressive growth rate of roughly 10%, making it the world's second fastest-growing economy over the 10 years period (Global Finance 2018). Is continental Africa finally witnessing what the famous American post-war economist W. W. Rostow called the "preconditions for take-off" or probably his actual "take-off of self-sustaining economic growth?" In what specific empirical forms and ways have Africa recorded the highly publicized rising progress or take-off? What are the local, regional and international factors that have enabled Africa to rise and to what extent are African states and institutions in command of these variables?

I and several colleagues have addressed the contested issue of "Africa rising" in a recent book I edited titled: *The Governance, Security and Development Nexus: Africa Rising* (2020).[17] I will not therefore venture into the debate *in extenso*. I can only remark that export of non-value-added primary commodities can hardly produce or sustain the type of growth and multi-faceted development that powered the sustainable rise of the East and South Asian economies, and almost wiping off extreme poverty (or reducing it to insignificant levels) in many of the countries. This point even becomes stronger when placed against the backdrop of the seemingly dominant paradigms of dysfunctional governance and capitalism in Africa that ruin development. This is not the first experience of commodity boom-driven growth in Africa. It happened in late colonial history when Africa had a boom in the export of cash crops (cocoa, palm oil, cotton, groundnuts, etc.) and at different intervals of the post-independence era when the demand and prices of oil, gold, diamond, and copper have appreciated significantly in the international market. Solid minerals also had dispensations of demand-driven boom in colonial history. None of the previous commodity booms was able to trigger the much-needed technology and industrialization-oriented development in Africa. The commodity boom (copper, gold, diamond, oil and agricultural produce) responsible for Africa's recent economic recovery and resurgence, most decisively the oil boom, have all practically ended. There has also been a systematic decline in the demand of many African primary commodity exports due to a slowdown in growth among major economies that import Africa's natural resources long before the onset of the Covid-19 pandemic that has dealt an added blow to the global economy and its weakest links.

2.4 The Counternarrative about Failed Capitalism in Africa

I am not oblivious of the fact that many critics and neoliberal apologists will attempt to counter my argument that capitalism has failed in postcolonial Africa by advancing some of the best examples of the performing economies in Africa, such as Ethiopia that has been the world's second fastest-growing economy for 10 years, South Africa that has the most industrialized economy on the continent—thanks to the obnoxious apartheid regime, Botswana that has had a relatively well-managed economy and functional democracy since independence, the Indian Ocean island of Seychelles that has higher income per capita than some EU countries like Croatia, Poland and Romania, and perhaps the big factor Nigeria that has Africa's largest GDP.

Let me make some brief comments about these intriguing cases starting with Ethiopia. By courtesy of the developmental state model of capitalism the country has pursued for almost 30 years, Ethiopia has recorded an impressive economic growth rate of roughly 10% for many years, making it the fastest-growing economy in Africa and the second fastest in the world for over the 10 years preceding the Covid-19 pandemic (AfDB 2018; Laniran 2020). However, Ethiopia is still considerably a small economy. With a population of over 100 million people Ethiopia's 2019 GDP is about $91.17 billion which is less than one-third of the 2019 GDP of Malaysia ($365.30 billion) that has a population of 32.34 million.[18] In 1960 Malaysia had a GDP of $234.94 million, over three times below the GDP of several Sub-Sahara African countries, including DRC, Sudan, Zimbabwe, Ghana, Senegal and Kenya (see Table 2.1). Per capita income level in Ethiopia is about $953.20 but public sector wage level in the country is one of the lowest in Africa. The country's Human Development Index (i.e., life expectancy at birth, expected and mean years of schooling, and Gross National Income per capita) has not been impressive. Ethiopia's HDI ranking is the 17th global worst case in 2019 (UNDP 2019). Youth unemployment is estimated at nearly 27%, and there is a low literacy rate of 68% among the youth (USAID 2017; AfDB 2018). Unemployment and poverty levels are exacerbated by youth-led communal violence, often resulting in massive displacement of people. Statistics released by Reliefweb indicate that as of January 2020, roughly 1.78 million people have been displaced across different parts of Ethiopia, of which 70% are displaced due to violent conflicts, especially in pastoral areas (USAID 2020). An additional significant measure of human displacement has been reported from the Tigray region where thousands of people have crossed into neighbouring Sudan following the armed hostilities that erupted in November 2020 in what the Ethiopian government described as "law enforcement action" against "a criminal clique within the dominant party in the region, the Tigray People's Liberation Front (TPLF)" (BBC News 25 October 2020). The relationship between the TPLF-controlled regional government and the federal government sharply deteriorated under the first two and half years of Prime Minister Abiy Ahmed's regime, culminating in a predictable standoff and military solution. It is highly debatable whether the military solution was avoidable or not. Hence, even though Ethiopia has made remarkable economic progress, the country remains one of the most developmentally challenged in Africa.

South Africa is the most industrialized economy in the continent and has the second largest GDP (about $358.839 in 2019), and a per capita income of about $6,100.4, the sixth highest in Africa.[19] But South Africa is one of the most unequal countries in the world and structural poverty is one of the major underpinnings of high crime rate and violence in the country. In the first quarter of 2020, South Africa's high unemployment rate stood at 30% and is likely to rise further in the short-run due to the adverse toll of the Covid-19 pandemic on the economy (*The Economist*, 18 July 2020). One of the enduring legacies of apartheid in South Africa is that about top 1% of South Africans own 70.9% of the country's wealth while the bottom 60% only controls 7% of the country's assets; poverty remains concentrated in previously disadvantaged areas, such as the former homelands (*Sunday Times* 2018). South Africa is struggling with a massive problem of structural poverty inherited from its apartheid past and barely has enough to deal with it. However, being the only economy in Sub-Saharan Africa that is relatively large and industrialized, South Africa has been inundated with economic migrants from Zimbabwe, Nigeria, Somalia, and many other broken and straggling countries in the region. Xenophobic attacks and violence by several downtrodden and hopeless South African youths, which can hardly be justified by any reasonable stretch of the imagination, have been part of the backlash of the influx of immigrants to South Africa. By analogy, one of the greatest tragedies of household poverty in Sub-Saharan Africa is that once one manages by desperate struggles to lift his head above the poverty line, he becomes the hope and benefactor of all other members of the family still trapped in poverty and he is obliged to help. They all look up to him for provision of food, education, healthcare—practically everything—and some may relocate permanently to his home for their daily bread. Overwhelmed by the enormous needs, the helper could easily be pulled back permanently to poverty or if he is lucky, he might end up swinging up and down across the poverty line for the rest of his life. It is this African sociological reality that Richard Dowden (2008: 441) pictured vividly in Nigeria in his anecdote about why despite the extreme privation of the masses against the ostentatious opulence of the wealthy few, Nigeria has failed to collapse or disintegrate many years ago as several analysts had predicted. According to Dowden:

> The secret lies in the layers of millions upon millions of networks, personal ties, family links, ethnic loyalties … and scores of other unrecorded, informally organised bonds of trusts that make things happen. Forget the government, the formal structures. What makes Nigeria work is a matrix of social, political, and economic connections that ensure most people get food and shelter. (Dowden 2008: 441)

Donald Duke, the two-times governor of Cross River State in Nigeria described this structural dependency of the poor on the "rich" in Nigeria as "a goodwill economy" (The Africa Report, 16 July 2018). The Nigerian and African diaspora in general are major players in this goodwill economy through their enormous remittances.

In a large sense, Dowden's observation about how many get food and shelter in Nigeria is true for almost every part of Sub-Saharan Africa. Some social analysts have attributed the endemic nature of corruption in the public sphere in many African states to the pressure that this social fabric places on the public office holder who is informally obligated to provide for a recycling concentric of the poor in his family, kindred, clan and so forth. Not having the personal means to meet the sprawling expectations, the public officer is tempted to dip his hands into the public till. There are certainly many legitimate and constructive ways to solve the problem of mass poverty.

From my analogy of household poverty in Africa, South Africa is like that sole household member that is perceived to have gotten his head just above the poverty line and therefore has the obligation to help others, especially when all others had rallied behind them and made huge sacrifices to help them overcome apartheid in the spirit of African brotherhood.

Box 2.2 Seychelles and Botswana: Examples of Well-Managed African Economies

Seychelles and Botswana have small economies and populations, but they are not poor countries. The two countries deserve some credit for how they have steered their economies since independence. Botswana has a GDP of $18.690 billion, per capita of $7,859.20 and a population of about 2.35 million. Seychelles has a GDP of $1.64 billion and per capita of $ 17,052.20 (the highest in Africa in 2019), and a population of 98,342 people, one of the smallest in the world. Poverty level in Seychelles is minimal. With less than a hundred thousand people, Seychelles is the equivalent of a small town such as Kontangora or Kuje in Nigeria. Botswana is a diamond-rich country and one of the few African countries that has made substantial progress in value chain development in their natural resource economy. Value chain development in Botswana's diamond economy is divided into three sectors—upstream (prospecting, mining and processing), midstream (sorting, valuation and sale of rough diamond) and downstream (cutting, polishing and the sale of polished jewellery, and diamond-support services) (Botswana Daily News, 19 December 2019). Value chain in the upstream and midstream sectors is highly advanced while that the downstream sector has grown remarkably since the diamond multinational De Beers' relocation of the sales activities of Diamond Trading Company International from London to Botswana in 2013, and the setting of the Diamond Trading Company Botswana to promote growth in the sale component of the value chain in Botswana (Botswana Daily News, 19 December 2019). Skills and technological development in the diamond industry have continued to grow and likewise the diamond support services such as allied industries to the three-tier diamond streams, hotels and catering, banking and insurance, transportation and marketing, tourism, etc. Thousands of jobs have been created. However, youth unemployment and rural poverty levels in Botswana are relatively high. Youth unemployment level in Botswana is about 20.7% and rural poverty is dispersed, and in some community clusters it is as high as 46% (Thomas 2017; World Bank 2020). As small economies with small populations, Seychelles and Botswana barely have enough for themselves.

I do not want to talk about Nigeria, Africa's largest economy and most populous country. Between the second quarter and last quarter of 2020, unemployment rate in Nigeria rose from 27% to 33.3%, and further evidence suggests that more than half of the country's labour force is unemployed or underemployed, making it one of the highest global records (Olurounbi 2021). Nigeria spends 50% of the country's revenue on servicing its rising external debt, as against the average of 17% external debt servicing spent by countries in West Africa (Punch, 11 June 2020). Most disastrously, Nigeria is the country with the highest rate of extreme poverty in the world. That says it all.

In a 2019 published report, Kristofer Hamel et al. described Africa as "the last frontier in the fight against extreme poverty." About one in three Africans presently live below the global poverty line, and most of the 43 countries in the world with the highest poverty rates are fragile or conflict-affected situations (FCS) in Sub-Saharan Africa (Hamel et al. 2019; World Bank 2020). Among the world's three least developed regions, the UNDP 2018 global Human Development Index (HDI)[20] report shows that South Asia has had the fastest-growing HDI value over 1990–2017, at 45.3%, followed by East Asia and the Pacific at 41.8%, while Sub-Saharan Africa lags behind with 34.9% (UNDP 2018: 2). As Jakkie Cilliers (2020: 4) coalesced Africa's contemporary development performance from a global perspective: "Of 31 low-income countries around the world, 24 are in Africa. The continent has 21 of the 47 low-middle-income countries globally and only eight out of 60 upper-middle-income countries. Of 80 high-income countries, only one is in Africa, the island state of Seychelles." This is not a report card that warrants any applause. In another more telling publication, Cilliers summarized Africa's marginal position in the global economy from a comparative regional perspective as follows:

> In 1960 Africa accounted for 3% of the global economy. Sixty years later, that share has *only* increased to 4% despite the fact that Africa's share in the global population almost doubled from 9 to 17%. Compare this to East Asia and the Pacific, a region that increased its share of global economic output from about 11% in 1960 to more than 30% today. East Asia's share of the global population, on the other hand, has shrunk from 34 to 30% during this period pointing to its much more productive economies. (Cilliers 2021: 13–14)

Capitalism is fundamentally about capitalists doing business to make profits and grow the economy. Responsible governance will help a thriving capitalist economy to ensure that the benefits of doing good business are somehow felt by the entire society. The World Bank compiles a Doing Business index of about 190 countries and ranks them on a set of 10 indicators that cover different aspects of the business cycle such as: starting a business, dealing with construction permits, getting electricity, registering property, getting credit, protecting minority investors, paying taxes, trading across borders, enforcing contracts and resolving insolvency (World Bank 2018, 2019). The 2018 and 2019 doing business reports indicate that 7 of the 10 countries with the most cumbersome record of doing business are in Africa, and they are: Somali, Eritrea, Libya, South Sudan, DRC, Central African Republic and Chad. The only non-African countries in the bottom 10 over the two years are Venezuela, Yemen and Haiti/Timor-Leste.

Despite the economic growth hype associated with Africa rising narrative, Africa's share of world trade is a minute 2.4%, with less than 5% of FDI flows (Moghalu 2014: 6; WTO 2018: 78). According to global investment trends published by UNCTAD in 2018, Africa has disproportionately continued to receive the least FDI flows among the developing regions—declining from $58.1 billion in 2008 to $42 billion in 2017, which represents a paltry share when compared to the 2017 FDI flows of $476 billion to the developing economies of Asia and the FDI flows of $151 billion to Latin America and the Caribbean (UNCTAD 2018: 4 & 38). The top FDI host economies in Africa in 2017 are Egypt, Nigeria, Ghana and Mozambique, Ethiopia and Morocco—most of them, commodity-exporting economies. The AfDB's 2019 Africa Economic Outlook shows that Africa's gross government debt-to-GDP ratio reached 53% in 2017, and out of 52 countries, 16 (including Algeria, Botswana, Burkina Faso and Mali) have a debt-to-GDP ratio below 40% while six (Cape Verde, Congo, Egypt, Eritrea, Mozambique, Sudan) have debt ratios above 100% (World Economic Forum 2019). Worst of all, Africa's growth remains insufficient to make a dent on unemployment and poverty as the continent is not meeting the desired imperative for the benefits of growth to be shared by everyone, particularly by providing its growing populations with good jobs and social protection (World Economic Forum 2019). There is therefore the need to complement the GDP-driven growth model with a constructive model of inclusive development.

I argue that Africa needs epicentres of "big bang" transformation in its overall political economy that will sustainably engineer transgenerational growth and development with multiplier effects across many outlying economies to be able to overcome the present development challenges. No country in post-independence Africa has ever come close to becoming an epicentre for such a momentous spark of regional proportion. Countries with the potential of generating the African "big bang" (akin to the Asian big bang successively generated by Japan and China) have practically wasted the limited opportunities that political independence offered—Sub-Saharan African countries like Nigeria and DRC. Worse still, post-independence Nigeria and DRC have incubated and fostered some of the most dysfunctional versions of capitalism widespread in Africa. My argument about the evident failure of the big African states and economies has been brilliantly analysed in a 2006 publication edited by Christopher Clapham titled *Big African States*. The book is a narrative of the relative dysfunctionalities of the big African states in terms of political and economic development against all expectations that they would not only perform well but ultimately be a positive influence on the entire region. The big states studied by Clapham et al. are Angola, DRC, Ethiopia, Nigeria, South Africa, Sudan.

Small economies with small populations that do not command tremendous "big bang" or "big push" potential are the countries that have instead shown reasonable promise, but their best may just barely be enough to feed themselves—countries like Seychelles, Mauritius, Botswana and Cape Verde. The north African countries with all their obfuscating political structures and governance challenges have relatively performed better than Sub-Saharan Africa, but none has had enough economic power to generate a regional momentum. With all the potentials held by their country, the political elites in post-Apartheid South Africa have not shown that they learnt any lessons from all the costly mistakes made by the rest of post-colonial Africa who started the journey of national development some years and decades earlier.

Summary Points

1. From a political economy perspective, the independence of most African countries was a ceding of political sovereignty devoid of economic independence.
2. The frontier capitalism of the colonial era failed to obliterate all the precolonial modes of production in Africa, ostensibly because of the inexorable resistance mounted by the Africans on the one hand, and the limited governance capacity of the colonialists, on the other hand.
3. The African "neocolonial economies" have suffered enormous structural disadvantages arising mainly from their over-reliance on primary commodity exports, aggravated by problems of widespread resource misallocation, mismanagement and prebendal graft.
4. African economies have been greatly out-performed by the economies of many Asian and Middle Eastern countries they were at the same or comparable levels of development with in the early 1960s. Prominent among these Asian countries are South Korea, Indonesia, Thailand, Saudi Arabia, Taiwan (Province of China) and United Arab Emirate.
5. The high-performing East and South Asian market economies have gone through three waves of growth and industrialization between the 1960s and 1990s, principally induced by FDI from Japan and the West. The Asian countries were not just passive recipients of FDI but embarked on massive structural and market-oriented reforms.
6. Over the decades that many Asian economies were on the rise, most African economies were battered by structural crises associated with revenue decline from their primary commodity exports. This triggered extreme balance of payment deficits forcing most countries to adopt the World Bank/IMF Structural Adjustment Programmes (SAP) intervention therapy. SAP ultimately compounded the economic crises resulting in political turmoil and series of armed conflicts, civil wars and state collapse in Sub-Saharan Africa between the 1980s and 1990s.

7. The early years of the new millennium came with a ray of hope for many African economies due to a boom in commodity prices and increase in external revenues leading to a narrative that African economies were on a growth trajectory otherwise known as "Africa rising" in the regional political economy literature. The commodity boom behind the "Africa rising" narrative lasted for about a decade, from 2005 to 2015.

Discussion Questions

1. What are the main features of neocolonialism in Africa?
2. Is the term "neocolonialism" still a useful concept?
3. What are the connotations of the concept of *Pax-Africana* originally coined by Ali Mazrui in 1967?
4. Is *Pax-Africana* still a useful concept today?
5. How did the World Bank/IMF Structural Adjustment Programmes (SAP) impact the economies of Sub-Saharan African countries?
6. Discuss the defining features of the three waves of industrialization among the leading East and South Asian economies between the 1960s and 1990s?
7. What do you understand by the term "Africa rising" and what are its key features?

Notes

1. This number (54 sovereign states) excludes the Sahrawi Arab Democratic Republic (SADR), a quasi-state with disputed sovereignty but which is recognized by the African Union as a state. Morocco regards SADR as part of its territory and still controls about 80% of its territory.
2. Casablanca is the capital of Morocco and the Group was named after the preparatory meeting for African unity convened by King Mohammed V of Morocco in January 1961.
3. Monrovia is the capital of Liberia and the Monrovia Group was named after a Monrovia Conference of 8–12 May 1961, hosted by President William Tubman.
4. The "natives" were broadly the colonized, but the concept was used in a racist and derogatory sense. Colonial rule thrived on a racial and

cultural dichotomy between the colonizers and "natives". Intrinsic to this dichotomy was the colonizers' denigration of the natives' modes of social organization as primitive, and the use of brute force in the self-imposed mission to civilize the natives. Every colonial authority had to come up with policies and conventions on how to deal with the native question (see Mamdani 1996: 4). One of the most prevalent policies was the promotion of separate settlement and development schemes for natives and European settlers in colonial urban centres. In some countries, the policy was extended to local indigenes and migrants from other ethno-cultural groups. "Indirect rule" using native authorities and traditional institutions was another famous policy.

5. See Ake (1987) and Turner (1981).
6. Richard Joseph (1987) propounded the theory of prebendalism to describe the sense of entitlement among public office holders in Africa who feel they have a right to use public revenues under their charge for their own personal benefits and also to benefit their kins and loyalists. He used the theory to draw an analogy with similar practices and tendencies exhibited by many Catholic priests appointed overseers of parishes in mediaeval Europe.
7. Neopatrimonialism is a post-Weberian concept originally coined by Eisenstadt (1973) to describe the confusion observable in many developing countries between the public and private spheres; between public office and the office holder in a state that is at least formally endowed with the Weberian modern legal-bureaucratic institutions. However, beyond the façade of the public bureaucratic institutions, the day-to-day running of state affairs, including the formulation and implementation of government policies, are conducted through informal clientelist networks (often rooted in clannish, ethno-cultural and other primordial tendencies) ultimately linked to a few powerful state office holders. See Bach (2011) for the classification and retheorising of neopatrimonialism in African politics.
8. Compiled from the following sources: TI (2018) Corruption Perception Index 2018. Transparency International (TI), https://www.transparency.org/cpi2018. TI (2019) Corruption Perception Index 2019. Transparency International (TI), https://www.transparency.org/cpi2019. FFP (2018) Fragile States Index 2018 – Annual report, 24 April. Fund For Peace (FFP), http://fundforpeace.org/fsi/2018/04/24/fragile-states-index-2018-annual-report/. FFP (2019) Fragile States Index 2019 – Annual report, 10 April. Fund For Peace (FFP), https://fundforpeace.org/2019/04/10/fragile-states-index-2019/.
9. Sources: Euler Hermes (2020) "Sub-Saharan Africa GDP Per Capita from 1960 to 2018", 27 January, https://opendata.eulerhermes.com/explore/dataset/gdp-1960-2017/information/?disjunctive.country_name&refine.country_name=Sub-Saharan+Africa&dataChart=eyJxdWVya

WVzIjpbeyJjaGFydHMiOlt7InR5cGUiOiJzcGxpbmUiLCJmdW5jIjoiU1VNIiwieUF4aXMiOiJnZHBfcGVyX2NhcGl0YV9jdXJyZW50X3VzIiwic2NpZW50aWZpY0Rpc3BsYXkiOnRydWUsImNvbG9yIjoiIzFEMzc2MiJ9XSwieEF4aXMiOiJ5ZWFyIiwibWF4cG9pbnRzIjpudWxsLCJzb3J0IjoiIiwidGltZXNjYWxlIjoieWVhciIsImNvbmZpZyI6eyJkYXRhc2V0IjoiZ2RwLTE5NjAtMjAxNyIsIm9wdGlvbnMiOnsiZGlzanVuY3RpdmUuY291bnRyeV9uYW1lIjp0cnVlLCJyZWZpbmUuY291bnRyeV9uYW1lIjoiU3ViLVNhaGFyYW4gQWZyaWNhIn19fV0sInRpbWVzY2FsZSI6IiIsImRpc3BsYXlMZWdlbmQiOnRydWUsImFsaWduTW9udGgiOnRydWV9. See also: https://knoema.com/jesoqmb/historical-gdp-per-capita-by-country-statistics-from-the-world-bank-1960-2018. I could not compute the 1960 GDP of the entire Africa for lack of documented data on three North African countries – Egypt, Libya and Tunisia.

10. Ibid., references to the sources in note 9. See also: AU (2019), Kiersz (2019), and Thomas and Bhasker (2018).
11. Reem Abdellatif (2019) "These Countries Have the Highest Inflation Rates in the World", Al Arabiya Business Economy, 11 September, https://english.alarabiya.net/en/business/economy/2019/09/11/These-countries-have-the-highest-inflation-rates-in-the-world; See also: World Population Review (2020) "Inflation Rate by Country 2020", https://worldpopulationreview.com/country-rankings/inflation-rate-by-country.
12. These six key points are adapted and modified from: Weebly (n.d.) "The Asian Tigers", http://developmentandglobalisation.weebly.com/the-asian-tigers.html.
13. Ibid., reference to note 12.
14. See *Statistics Times* (2019) "Sector-wide Contribution to the GDP of India", 8 February 2019, https://statisticstimes.com/economy/sectorwise-gdp-contribution-of-india.php.
15. *High Performing Asian economies (HPAEs)* is my emphasis. See: Mark Skousen (1996) "How Real Is the Asian Economic Miracle?" 1 July, https://fee.org/articles/how-real-is-the-asian-economic-miracle/.
16. This is an allusion to the theory of the American sociologist Charles Tilly that "wars make states". Based on the historical experience of Europe, Tilly argues that the modern states in their institutional, territorial and functional terms were violently created by the activity of war-making, and that a symbiotic relationship exists between capital accumulation, state-making and war-making. See: Charles Tilly (1992) *Coercion, Capital, and European States, AD 990–1992*, Malden, MA: Basil Blackwell.
17. Kenneth Omeje, ed. (2020) *The Governance, Security and Development Nexus: Africa Rising*. New York: Palgrave Macmillan. The preceding two paragraphs before this citation were adapted from my Chapter 1 in this edited volume.

18. *Statistics Times* (24 February 2020) "List of African countries by GDP", http://statisticstimes.com/economy/african-countries-by-gdp.php; *Statistics Times* (24 February 2020) "List of Asian countries by GDP", http://statisticstimes.com/economy/asian-countries-by-gdp.php.
19. Ibid., reference to note 18. See also: *Statistics Times* (24 February 2020) "List of African countries by GDP Per Capita", http://statisticstimes.com/economy/african-countries-by-gdp-per-capita.php
20. The UNDP's HDI is a measurement of national achievements in health, education and income.

References

AfDB. 2018. 2018 Country Policy and Institutional Assessment: CPIA Questionnaire. Africa Development Bank (AfDB), July. https://cpia.afdb.org/documents/public/cpia2018-questionnaire-en.pdf.

Ake, Claude. 1978. *Revolutionary Pressures in Africa*. London: Zed Books.

Amin, Samir. 1969. *The Class struggle in Africa*: Cambridge Mass.: African Research Group.

Amin, Samir. 1973. *Neo-Colonialism in West Africa*. Harmondsworth: Penguin Books.

Amin, Samir. 1976. *Unequal Development: An Essay on the Social Formations of Peripheral Capitalism*. New York: Monthly Review Press.

AU. 2019. African Continental Free Trade Area. African Union Documentary, January 28. https://www.bing.com/videos/search?q=africa+continental+free+trade+areadocumentary&&view=detail&mid=7EE60C60564E73FF59 1B7EE60C60564E73FF591B&&FORM=VRDGAR.

Bach, C. Daniel. 2011. Patrimonialism and Neopatrimonialism: Comparative Trajectories and Readings. *Commonwealth and Comparative Politics* 49 (3): 275–294.

BBC News. 2019. Zimbabwe Sanctions: Who Is Being Targeted? 25 October. https://www.bbc.co.uk/news/world-africa-50169598.

BBC News. 2020. Zimbabwe to Return Land Seized from Foreign Farmers, September 2. https://www.bbc.co.uk/news/world-africa-53988788.

BBC News. 2020. Ethiopia's Tigray Crisis: Fears of Ethnic Profiling Stalk Conflict, November 25. https://www.bbc.co.uk/news/world-africa-55043373.

Botswana Daily News. 2019. Botswana's Diamond Industry Value Chain Developed, December 19. http://www.dailynews.gov.bw/news-details.php?nid=53584.

Bresser-Pereira, Carlos Luiz. 2018. The Two Forms of Capitalism: Developmentalism and Economic Liberalism, February 9, Doc Research Institute,

Berlin. https://doc-research.org/2018/02/the-two-forms-of-capitalism-developmentalism-and-economic-liberalism/.

Budhoo, L. Davidson. 1990. *Enough Is Enough: Dear Mr. Camdessus–Open Letter of Resignation to the Managing Director of the International Monetary Fund*. New York: New Horizons Press.

Cabral, Amilcar. 1979. *Unity and Struggle: Speeches and Writings*. London: Heinemann.

Clapham, Christopher (ed.). 2006. *Big African States*. Johannesburg: Wits University Press.

Cilliers, Jakkie. 2020. *Africa First! Igniting a Growth Revolution*. Policy Brief 146, June. Institute for Security Studies (ISS), Pretoria, South Africa.

Cilliers, Jakkie. 2021. *The Future of Africa: Challenges and Opportunities*. Cham, Switzerland: Palgrave Macmillan.

Dibua, I. Jeremiah. 2006. *Modernization and the Crisis of Development in Africa*. Aldershot: Ashgate.

Dowden, Richard. 2008. *Africa: Altered States, Ordinary Miracles*. London: Portobello Books.

Fanon, Frantz. 1961. *The Wretched of the Earth, trans Constance Farrington*. London: Penguin Books.

Francis, J. David. 2006. *Uniting Africa: Building Regional Peace and Security Systems*. Aldershot: Ashgate.

Global Finance. 2018. Countries with Highest GDP Growth 2017, November 12. https://www.gfmag.com/global-data/economic-data/countries-highest-gdp-growth-2017.

Hamel, Kristofer, Baldwin Tong, and Martin Hofer. 2019. Poverty in Africa Is now Falling but not Fast Enough, Brookings Policy Report, April 28. https://www.brookings.edu/blog/future-development/2019/03/28/poverty-in-africa-is-now-falling-but-not-fast-enough/.

Joseph, Richard. 1987. *Democracy and Prebendal Politics in Nigeria: The Rise and Fall of the Second Republic*. Cambridge: Cambridge University Press.

Karbo, Tony. 2018. Introduction: Towards a New Pax Africana. In Tony Karbo and Virk Kudrat (eds.), *The Palgrave Handbook of Peacebuilding in Africa*, 3–28. Cham: Palgrave Macmillan.

Kiersz, Andy. 2019. This Map Shows that Each US State Is Basically Its Own Country. *Business Insider*, March 29. https://www.businessinsider.com/state-vs-country-gdp-map-2019-3?r=US&IR=T.

Laniran, J. Tope. 2020. Interrogating the Political Economy of Africa Rising: Who Are the African Tigers? In *The Governance, Security and Development Nexus: Africa Rising*, ed. Kenneth Omeje, 31–56. New York: Palgrave Macmillan.

Mazrui, A. Ali. 1967. Towards a Concept of Pax-Africana. Reproduced in Tony Karbo and Kudrat Virk (eds.). 2018. *The Palgrave Handbook of Peacebuilding in Africa*, 29–44. Cham: Palgrave Macmillan.

Mamdani, Mahmood. 1996. *Citizen and Subject: Contemporary Africa in the era of Late Colonialism*. Oxford: James Currey.

Mbembe, Achille. 2001. *On the Postcolony*. Berkeley: University of California Press.

Moghalu, C. Kingsley. 2014. *Emerging Africa: How Global Economy's 'Last Frontier' Can Prosper and Matter*. London: Penguin Books.

Moyo, Dambisa. 2011. *How the West Was Lost: Fifty Years of Economic Folly and the Stark Choices Ahead*. New York: Penguin Books.

Moyo, Dambisa. 2013. *Winner Take All: China's Race for Resources and What It Means for Us*. London: Penguin Books.

Mytelka, Krieger Lynn. 1989. The Unfulfilled Promise of African Industrialization. *African Studies Review* 33 (3): 77–138.

Nkrumah, Kwame. 1965. *Neo-Colonialism: The Last Stage of Imperialism*. London: Thomas Nelson and Sons.

Lazarus, Neil. 1999. *Nationalism and Cultural Practice in the Postcolonial World*. New York: Cambridge University Press.

Olurounbi, Ruth. 2021. Nigeria Unemployment Rate Rises to 33%, Second Highest on Global List, March 15. Bloomberg. https://www.bloomberg.com/news/articles/2021-03-15/nigeria-unemployment-rate-rises-to-second-highest-on-global-list.

Omeje, Kenneth. 2015. Debating Postcoloniality in Africa. In *The Crises of Postcoloniality in Africa*, ed. Kenneth Omeje, 1–27. Dakar: CODESRIA Books.

OpIndia. 2018. India's Success in Eliminating Poverty Has Been Even Greater Than Many Believed. News Report, July 5. https://www.opindia.com/2018/07/indias-success-in-eliminating-poverty-has-been-even-greater-than-many-believed/.

Punch. 2020. Debt Servicing Gulps over 50% of Nigeria's Revenue – AfDB, June 11. https://punchng.com/debt-servicing-gulps-over-50-of-nigerias-revenue-afdb/#:~:text=It%20said%2C%20%E2%80%9CCape%20Verde%20had%20the%20highest%20external,cent%2C%20followed%20by%20Nigeria%20at%20128%20per%20cent.

Rodney, Walter. 1972. *How Europe Underdeveloped Africa*. London: Bogle-L'Ouverture Publication.

Sunday Times. 2018. SA Most Unequal Country in World: Poverty Shows Apartheid's Enduring Legacy.

Stubbs, Richard. 2018. *Rethinking Asia's Economic Miracles: The Political Economy of War, Prosperity and Crisis*, 2nd ed. London: Red Globe Press.

The Africa Report. 2018. NIGERIA: "We are Pushing the Population to the Brink - Donald Duke, July 16. https://www.theafricareport.com/583/nigeria-we-are-pushing-the-population-to-the-brink-donald-duke/.

The Economist. 2011. The Hopeful Continent: Africa Rising, December 3. https://www.economist.com/leaders/2011/12/03/africa-rising.

The Economist. 2020. Measuring the Poverty: Pandemic Covid-19 Has Throttled South Africa's Economy, July 18. https://www.economist.com/middle-east-and-africa/2020/07/18/covid-19-has-throttled-south-africas-economy.

The Guardian. 2019. 94 m Nigerians Currently Live Below Poverty Line – Oxfam, October 7. https://guardian.ng/news/94m-nigerians-currently-live-below-poverty-line-oxfam/.

Thomas, Jeanine. 2017. *Causes of Poverty in Botswana*, September 23. https://borgenproject.org/causes-of-poverty-in-botswana/.

Thomas, Tanya, and Utpal Bhasker. 2018. Narendra Modi at AIIB: With $2.8 trillion Size, Indian Economy Is the 7th Largest in the World, June 26. https://www.livemint.com/Politics/7lAcbOsQ36d1KIl8GcY3wM/Narendra-Modi-at-AIIB-With-28-trillion-size-Indian-econo.html.

Turner, Terisa. 1981. Multinational Corporations and the Nigerian State. *Review of African Political Economy* 3 (5): 63–79.

UNCTAD. 2018. World Investment Report 2018: Investment and New Industrial Policies. Geneva: United Nations. https://unctad.org/en/PublicationsLibrary/wir2018_en.pdf.

UNDP. 2018. Human Development Indices and Indicators 2018 Statistical Update. UNDP. http://hdr.undp.org/sites/default/files/2018_summary_human_development_statistical_update_en.pdf.

UNDP. 2019. Human Development Index 2019. UNDP Human Development Report Office; http://hdr.undp.org/en/content/2019-human-development-index-ranking.

USAID. 2017. Developing Ethiopia's Youth, July, USAID. https://www.usaid.gov/sites/default/files/documents/1860/Fact_Sheet_Developing_Ethiopias_Youth_Jul_2017.pdf.

USAID. 2020. Desert Locust, High Food Prices, and Conflict Threatens Household Food Security Across the Country, USAID, January 31. https://reliefweb.int/sites/reliefweb.int/files/resources/Ethiopia%20-%20Key%20Message%20Update_%20Fri%2C%202020-01-31.pdf.

WEDC. 2020. India's Special Economic Zones Boost Foreign Investments. Wisconsin Economic Development Corporation. https://wedc.org/export/market-intelligence/posts/indias-special-economic-zones-boost-foreign-investment/.

World Bank. 1993. The East Asian Miracle: Economic Growth and Public Policy: Main Report. https://documents.worldbank.org/en/publication/documents-reports/documentdetail/975081468244550798/main-report.

World Bank. 2018. Doing Business: Training and Reforms. The World Bank. http://www.doingbusiness.org/content/dam/doingBusiness/media/Annual-Reports/English/DB2019-report_web-version.pdf.

World Bank. 2019. Doing Business: Training and Reforms. The World Bank. https://www.doingbusiness.org/en/rankings.

World Bank. 2020. Poverty. The World Bank, April 16. https://www.worldbank.org/en/topic/poverty/overview.

World Economic Forum. 2019. How Africa Can Secure Its Long-Term Economic Growth, September 4. https://www.weforum.org/agenda/2019/09/how-africa-can-secure-its-long-term-economic-growth/.

WTO. 2018. *World Trade Statistical Review 2018*. World Trade Organisation (WTO). https://www.wto.org/english/res_e/statis_e/wts2018_e/wts2018_e.pdf.

Zeleza, T. Paul. 2006. The Troubled Encounter between Postcolonialism and African History. *Journal of the Canadian Historical Association*, New Series, 17 (2): 89–129. http://www.erudit.org/revue/JCHA/2006/v17/n2/016592ar.pdf. Website accessed on 19 June 2020.

CHAPTER 3

The "French–Africa Connection" and the Refusal to Decolonize

Without Africa, France will have no history in the 21st century.[1]—*Former French President François Mitterrand*

3.1 Contextualising the "Connection"

The French–Africa Connection is the title of an Al Jazeera television three-part documentary that chronicles the complex history of France's colonial and postcolonial relationships with the African countries under its neocolonial orbit loosely known as "Françafrique."[2] Al Jazeera has on repeated occasions broadcast the series since it was premiered in August 2013 and the three-part series is available online.

> *The French - African Connection* is a brutal and nefarious tale of corruption; massacres; dictators supported and progressive leaders murdered; weapons-smuggling; cloak-and-dagger secret services; and spectacular military operations. The series includes interviews with former oil barons; investigating judges into corruption scandals; former French ambassadors to African states; former French secret services; African presidents; and Francois Mitterand's son. (Al Jazeera 2013)

Remarkably, Al Jazeera's *French–African Connection* depicts Françafrique at its best and its worst. At its best Françafrique works for the benefit of

K. Omeje, *The Failure and Feasibility of Capitalism in Africa*, International Political Economy Series,
https://doi.org/10.1007/978-3-030-75170-8_3

France and the protégé leaders governing its former African colonies. At its worst, it wrecks the African masses and the few "rebellious" African leaders that occasionally dared to assert Africa's genuine interests. Either way, Françafrique is a win–win for France.

The origin of the term Françafrique (originally France-Afrique) is a somewhat contested one but many analysts believe that it was the first Ivorian President Félix Houphouët-Boigny that introduced the expression "La Françafrique" in 1955 to define the wish of some members of the African elite to maintain special relations with France after their independence (Korkmaz 2019). As a privileged Ivorian nationalist leader that rose to the rank of becoming a parliamentarian and Cabinet Minister in France while still campaigning for Ivorian self-rule in his country—thanks to the French Assimilation policy—Houphouët-Boigny must have been well-meaning about La Françafrique. The proposal was an acquiescence to the paternal responsibility of France to help its African ex-colonies to gradually stand on their feet, while the enfant postcolonial states, on their part, continue to maintain full allegiance to their master. Houphouët-Boigny was a finished product of the French colonial ideology of Assimilation which encouraged Africans to literally shed their Africanness and aspire to become French by a multifaceted process of sociocultural evolution. Special colonial education for the native people imbued with a well-crafted civilizing mission, as well as proven evidence of compliance were the principal yardsticks of Assimilation. Assimilation made Frenchness and allegiance to France highly attractive to the educated African elites, who were also conferred putative French citizenships and branded the *Évolué* (literally, the "evolved" in French). In postcolonial Francophone Africa, the structural legacy and mentality of Frenchness and allegiance to France among the educated middle class and privileged elites have remained a powerful weapon of neocoloniality. However, the tide seems to be presently changing due to the growing awareness of the twists and disservice of Françafrique.

There are different dimensions of Françafrique—the sociocultural, educational, geopolitical, military and economic dimensions—some of which have been arguably credited with considerable benefits. The supposed benefits include technical cooperation and FDIs. But fundamentally, Françafrique is a pact of neocolonization with all its ambiguities, intrigues and shenanigans. The French economic historian and founder of the NGO *Survie* François-Xavier Verschave is famous for using the term Françafrique in his 1998 book *La Françafrique* as a parody "to denounce the clientelistic dimension of France's Africa policy and the high levels of corruption that accompanied Franco-African relations" (Erforth 2020: 14).

A key defining characteristic of Françafrique as an instrument of maintaining France's neocolonial domination of the political economies of its former colonies on the continent is secrecy. Françafrique is shrouded in sundry deals, diplomatic briefs and corporate business transactions hammered out and often operated in secrecy. For the uninitiated, including most investigative journalists and academic researchers of my constituency—the more you look the less you see! The famous British journalist and African correspondent Richard Dowden described the duplicity and clandestine politics of France in Africa in the following terms:

> The French remained directly engaged with Africa after their colonies became independent. They officially handed over administrative control in formal flag-raising ceremonies, but not all their officials left their former territories. France held together a shadow empire in Africa to gain votes at the UN, but mainly to project its own self-image as a world power. The shadow empire was run secretly through shady deals and clandestine networks. For fourteen years formally – and many more years informally – it was run by Jacques Foccart, a secret service agent known as Monsieur Afrique, who headed the *réseaux*, a network of informants and enforcers based on a system of the French Resistance. From 1960 almost until he died in 1997, Foccart made sure that no government changed hands in Francophone Africa without his say-so. In his memoirs he admitted to murdering one opposition leader. They were almost certainly many more. (Dowden 2008: 59–60)

In his book titled *Contemporary French Security Policy in Africa*, Benedikt Erforth (2020) provides insightful detail on how the strategic calculation to remain a great power during the Cold War when in reality it was no longer one, influenced the French to pursue a strong paternalistic foreign and security policy in Africa characterized by projection of political, economic and cultural power over its former colonies. Despite the end of the Cold War, the French do not seem to have abandoned this foreign policy predilection. Erforth argues that *Operation Serval* launched in January 2013 to safeguard the sovereignty of Mali from the advancing northern rebel forces with extremist Islamist agendas, and *Operation*

Sangaris launched a year later to curb sectarian violence in the war-torn Central African Republic are among the contemporary evidence of France's projection of hard power in Francophone Africa (Erforth 2020: 1–2). With northern Mali recovered from the rebel insurgents that hitherto overran it, France launched *Operation Barkhane* in August 2014 to replace *Operation Serval* and with a wider anti-insurgency, counter-terrorism mandate that covers the entire Sahel. *Operation Barkhane* is a sprawling military deployment with about 4,500 French soldiers covering the entire Sahel and coordinating counter-terrorism engagements with five Sahelian countries known as the G5 Sahel—Mali, Chad, Burkina Faso, Niger and Mauritania. The concealed goal of *Operation Barkhane* and other military solutions backed by the West in the Sahel and Maghreb regions of Africa is the security of Europe. It is common-knowledge that since the NATO-backed military destruction of Libya and assassination of President Muammar Gaddafi in 2011, fortress Europe has witnessed an unprecedented wave of trans-Mediterranean migration originating from some of the most fragile countries in Sub-Saharan Africa and the Arab world. Given the fact that the Sahelian belt of West Africa almost entirely consists of ex-French colonies, France is leading the EU in the quest to fix its perceived security breaches in the Sahel. As the French President Emmanuel Macron summarized this imperial governance mission in the virtual summit of leaders of the G5 Sahel in February 2021: "We are there because we have a shared destiny with the Sahel. If the Sahel falls into the hands of terrorism, Africa will gradually fall into the hands of Islamist terrorists, and Europe will live with the consequences of this tragedy very clearly. So, I think it is our duty to be by your side" (Tidey 2021). The pervading anxiety among European leaders, conservative voters and right-wing activists is that the post-Arab Spring rise in trans-Sahara, trans-Mediterranean migration not only risks compromising the high levels of comfort prevalent in the welfare states of Europe but also increases their vulnerability to terrorist infiltration and attacks.

The Senegalese novelist Boubacar Boris Diop (2018) writes that Françafrique "perfectly illustrates France's dogged refusal to decolonise" and strings of connectedness in which "the African president thus 'elected' … knew what was expected of him: to put the resources of his country at France's disposal and routinely vote alongside the latter at the UN." Compliance with the economic and political imperatives of Françafrique guarantees regime protection to the African political elites in former French colonies regardless of their human rights records and how much money they siphon from their countries to private bank accounts in continental Europe.

3.2 Independence Without Monetary Sovereignty

In Chapter 2, I have discussed the point that the decolonization of most African states was without economic independence, culminating in neocolonial capitalism. This is common knowledge. In the peculiar case of 12 ex-French colonies in Sub-Saharan Africa, neocolonial capitalism had an added twist—the refusal or denial of monetary sovereignty. Refusal of monetary sovereignty means that one of the preconditions for the granting of political independence was that the French ex-colonies of Sub-Saharan Africa must maintain their ties with the French colonial currency union, the Franc of the French Community of Africa known as CFA Franc for short. "CFA initially stood for *Colonies francaises d'Afrique* (French Colonies of Africa) and then later became *Communaute francaise d'Afrique* (French Community of Africa)."[3] The new currency was created for French colonies in December 1945 to principally help shore up the French economy ridden with high inflation and weakened currency after World War II by fostering the integration of the colonial economies controlled by France, peg the direct convertibility of the CFA currencies to the metropolitan French Franc, and ultimately bolster the export trade of France. Comparatively, inflation was significantly lower in the cash crop export economies colonized by France during World War II and the early post-war years.

Post-independence CFA union has 14 countries split into two currency zones and operating under two monetary institutions beholden to France—West African Economic and Monetary Union (WAEMU) and Central African Economic and Monetary Community (CEMAC). WAEMU comprises eight West African countries—Benin, Burkina Faso, Côte d'Ivoire, Mali, Niger, Senegal, Togo and Guinea-Bissau. Guinea-Bissau, an ex-Portuguese colony is the only country in WAEMU that is not an ex-French colony. Guinea and Mali, two former French West African colonies pulled out of the French Franc after independence, but Mali later rejoined the currency union in 1984. CEMAC is made up of six Central African countries namely Cameroon, Central African Republic, Republic of the Congo, Gabon, Chad and Equatorial Guinea. Equatorial Guinea, a former Spanish colony is the only country in CEMAC that is not an ex-French colony. All the north African countries—Morocco,

Tunisia and Algeria ditched their various Francs after independence. Comoros, an ex-French colony made up of a network of islands in the Indian Ocean joined the CFA Franc zone in 1997 while the nearby island of Madagascar left the zone in 1973. The two subsisting neocolonial Francs in West and Central Africa were designed to be directly convertible to the French Franc, and later the Euro (when France abolished the Franc to join the European Currency Union), but they are not inter-convertible, and similarly there is hardly any significant trade between the two Franc zones.

According to the Senegalese development economist Ndongo Samba Sylla, the CFA has four negotiated statutory pillars authorized by France:

> Firstly, a fixed rate of exchange with the Euro (and previously the French franc) set at 1 Euro = 655.957 CFA Francs. Secondly, a French guarantee of the unlimited convertibility of CFA Francs into Euros. Thirdly, a centralisation of foreign exchange reserves. Since 2005, the two central banks – the Central Bank of West African States (BCEAO) and the Bank of Central African States (BEAC) – have been required to deposit 50% of their foreign exchange reserves in a special French Treasury "operating account." Immediately following independence, this figure stood at 100% (and from 1973 to 2005, at 65%). This arrangement is a *quid pro quo* for the French "guarantee" of convertibility. The accords stipulate that foreign exchange reserves must exceed money in circulation by a margin of 20%. Before the fall in oil prices, the money supply coverage rate (the ratio of foreign exchange reserves to money in circulation) consistently approached 100%, implying in theory that Africans could dispense with the French "guarantee." The final pillar of the CFA Franc is the principle of free capital transfer within the Franc zone. (Sylla 2017)

On 21st December 2019, the eight WAEMU states that use the CFA Franc in West Africa emerged from a summit in Abidjan, Cote d'Ivoire and announced a new plan to replace their CFA Franc widely regarded as a Françafrique neocolonial currency with an independent currency to be called the Eco. Two things made this surprising announcement quite puzzling. The first is that the French President Emmanuel Macron attended the Abidjan summit where this decision was reached and stood side by side with the Ivorian President Alassane Ouattara as he addressed a press conference to make the announcement. Why was the French President present at the meeting? Evidently, the promulgated plan to replace the CFA Franc with Eco had the full backing and blessing of France. The second puzzle about the currency replacement plan is that the name of the new currency adopted by the WAEMU summit "Eco" is the same as the currency that the 15-member ECOWAS regional bloc has been negotiating to adopt as common currency with effect from 2020, but later postponed to 2027 due to the logistical impact of the Covid-19 pandemic. In making the announcement, President Ouattara extended an invitation to the rest of the ECOWAS countries, the Anglophone bloc and Guinea to join the proposed Eco which "will still be pegged to the Euro and backed by the French Central Bank" (The Africa Report, 17 January 2020).

The negotiation for Eco had been ongoing among the ECOWAS states for decades with an ambivalent participation from the Francophone bloc who strongly maintain allegiance to France and their existing monetary union but occasionally romanticize the idea of a wider ECOWAS monetary union. France has repeatedly undermined the ECOWAS economic integration project as a way of protecting its market and economic interests in Francophone West Africa from Nigeria's encroachment. Nigeria is by far the largest economy in West Africa and the regional hegemon, accounting for more than half of the region's GDP. Among other things, France and the Francophone bloc are concerned that Nigeria could dominate monetary policies to its market advantage in a joint currency union. The ECOWAS single currency roadmap had been planned in phases to accommodate the differences between the Anglophone and Francophone blocs, the former will kickstart it and then the latter will join in due course. According to the ECOWAS single currency roadmap, the second monetary zone of the mainly Anglophone bloc was scheduled to be launched in 2015 but to be eventually merged with the CFA bloc by 2020 to form a common currency.[4] The currency was first planned to be introduced in 2003 but this process has been repeatedly delayed to ensure effective coordination between fiscal and monetary policies in the ECOWAS region.[5] Specifically, the failure of member states to meet some key macroeconomic convergence criteria set by ECOWAS have been responsible for the repeated postponement of the launch of the West African monetary union. There are four primary and six secondary convergence criteria.

The primary convergence criteria include: Budget Deficit/GDP ratio (excluding grants) of less or equal to 4%; Inflation rate of less or equal to 5%; Central Bank Financing of Budget Deficit of less or equal to 10% of previous year's Tax Revenue, as well as Gross External Reserves of greater than or equal to six months of imports cover (Nwachukwu 2020).

The secondary convergence criteria adopted by ECOWAS as conditions for the launch of the West African Monetary Union Zone (WAMZ) are: Prohibition of new arrears and liquidation of all outstanding ones; Tax Receipts/GDP ratio of greater or equal to 20%; Salary Mass/Total Tax Receipts ratio of greater or equal to 35%; Public Investments financed from internal resources/Tax Receipts ratio of greater or equal to 20%; Positive Real Interest Rates; and Real Exchange Rate Stability (Nwachukwu 2020). Most ECOWAS countries have not fulfilled the convergence criteria they have set for themselves. There have been marked inconsistencies in meeting the criteria such that one country could meet it in one year but fail over the next two years—one step forward, two steps backward. Apparently, it is only Togo that has met the criteria in the preceding two years. Hence, the currency union's take-off postponement continues, probably *ad infinitum*!

The December 2019 WAEMU summit that adopted Eco as replacement currency for the Francophone bloc was convened a few months ahead of an ECOWAS summit to determine the preparedness of the regional body for the introduction of their common currency Eco. The Francophone bloc has reversed the ECOWAS roadmap and jumped the gun. Apparently, a pre-emptive or subversive action had been executed—a monetary *coup d'etat*—and France is not innocent of the plot. What is the likely game plan of France? It is twofold—to disorganize the ECOWAS common currency plan by a Francophone subversive hijack or to bring the entire West African region into Francosphere—the monetary and economic orbit of France. The latter is a tall order and therefore less likely than the former. The Nigerian President Mohammadu Buhari had these unkind words to describe the entire saga:

> We cannot ridicule ourselves by entering a union to disintegrate, potentially no sooner than we enter it. ... We must proceed with caution and comply with the agreed process of reaching our collective goal while treating each other with utmost respect. Without these, our ambitions for a strategic Monetary Union as an ECOWAS bloc could very well be in serious jeopardy. (Momoh 2020)

There is enormous controversy about the relevance of preserving a neocolonial currency tied to France and pegged to the Euro like the

CFA Franc. Proponents among other things argue that the CFA Franc shields the Francophone user economies from undue inflation and fiscal instability. It is further argued that the major driver of growth in Francophone countries like Cote d'Ivoire has been high investment because of low interest rates which come from a stable currency guaranteed by France (Dewast 2019). Sometimes, proponents make allusion to Guinea, a Francophone country that pulled out of the CFA Franc after its independence but has had worse economic performance characterized by high levels of inflation, poor fiscal planning and instability, low FDI, as well as gross indiscipline in economic and political governance.[6]

I will not be diverted to the circular argument of measuring and comparing degrees of failure with regard to the performance of the CFA Franc economies. In an examination where 40% is the minimum pass mark, the candidate that scored 35% and the one that scored 15% both failed. My primary argument in this book is that capitalism has failed in postcolonial Africa, which includes the CFA Franc zones. So, it is not a question of whether Burkina Faso has done better than Guinea. Afterall, the North African countries of Morocco, Algeria and Tunisia that did equally ditch their different colonial Francs after independence have comparatively performed better than the CFA Franc countries of Sub-Saharan Africa in virtually all indicators of growth and development.

Critics on the other hand argue that the CFA Franc hinders the economic development of the user states because in exchange for the guarantees provided by the French treasury, African countries channel more money to France than they receive in aid (Konkobo 2017). It is further argued that the African countries have no say in deciding key monetary policies agreed to by European countries, which are members of the Eurozone (Konkobo 2017).

Box 3.1 CFA Franc: The Controversial Common Currency in Francophone Africa

The CFA Franc was introduced by France as a common currency for its colonies in 1945 and the French have preserved the currency since then, making it one of the oldest surviving currency unions in the world. Originally introduced to help mitigate inflation, boost international trade and shore up the French economy by integrating the more resilient colonial economies with the metropolitan French Franc in the aftermath of World War II, the perpetuation of the CFA Franc in contemporary Africa generates enormous controversy. Many critics see it as a testament to the

French refusal to decolonize its ex-colonies and a violation of their monetary sovereignty. Al Jazeera broadcaster captures the loss of monetary sovereignty under the CFA Franc regime in the following terms:

> The CFA Franc limits monetary sovereignty. France guarantees the value of the CFA Franc, and in return, the countries that use it are required to keep 50% of their foreign exchange reserves with the French treasury. Because the exchange rate between the CFA Franc and Euro is fixed, the central banks of the two CFA Franc zones need to follow the monetary policies of the European Central Bank (ECB) in order to maintain the peg. Put simply, the ECB effectively sets interest rates for countries that use the CFA Franc. (Al Jazeera 2019)

The CFA Franc is likely to remain a highly divisive and controversial currency in Africa as long as it remains tied to France because of the deep-rooted and growing sentiments against the perceived exploitative activities of the neocolonial and neo-imperial powers in Africa.

Evidently, the greatest problem with CFA Franc is the compromising of monetary sovereignty under seemingly dubious circumstances. In the CFA Franc zones, sovereignty concerning monetary and exchange rate policies, interest rates and foreign reserves have been inimically compromised and parceled out to France and the European Union in such a way that no forward-thinking capitalist economy or indeed any other economy for that matter, will be able to achieve its full potential. The CFA Franc encourages massive capital outflow and France holds a *de facto* veto on the boards of the two central banks within the CFA Franc zone (Sylla 2017).

Ultimately, the CFA Franc regime hinders planning, export competitiveness, growth and development among the user states. From the standpoint of regional economic and market integration in Africa under the auspicious of the "regional economic communities" (RECs) or the continental African Union, CFA Franc is a throwback to neocolonial domination and obstructionism.

3.3 Vociferous Narratives About the French–Africa Connection

There has been extensive hullabaloo about the French–Africa connection in recent years. Critics of the perceived French domination, exploitation and manipulation of its ex-African colonies have become louder in exposing what they perceive to be the atrocities of France, demanding that "enough is enough." In a large sense, these vociferous narratives are advocacy-oriented. They principally aim to inform, conscientize and inspire Africans at home and in the diaspora about the sources of the African predicaments and what they can do about it. Advocacy is positive and necessary for desired change, but it has to be evidence-based and constructive. France has come under heavy lampoon and indictment by the vociferous advocacy-oriented narratives that tend to be growing by the day.

There are different reasons why the vociferous public rebuke of France cannot be ignored in this book, especially when I have devoted a chapter to the subject of French relationships with its ex-colonies in Africa. The first reason why the loud narratives cannot be ignored is because increasingly they are championed by highly influential and respected African voices, especially many in the diaspora community. Secondly, the issues canvassed in the narratives have ignited debates and seminars in many institutions of learning about the French legacy and their continued role in Africa. Thirdly, the largely ungoverned online media which has become the greatest platform for political discourses in this high-tech age is awash with unverified news, narratives and reports about Françafrique. Because Françafrique, especially the financial and economic dimensions of it, is largely shrouded in secrecy, one does not really know where the truth lies in most of the narratives. Yet many of the unverified narratives are widely believed, recited and disseminated. I will refrain from the junk and tabloid narratives and as much as possible stick to respectable narrators.

There is probably no one else that represents the public face of opposition to the French neocolonial stranglehold of its ex-colonies in Africa as the Zimbabwean-born medical doctor, social activist and diplomat Dr Arikana Chihombori-Quao, who served as the Permanent Representative of the African Union Mission to the USA in December 2016, a position she held until controversially terminated in October 2019 by the AU Commission Chairman Moussa Faki Mahamat. Many believe that France was behind her termination because of her vocal critique of the French neocolonial exploits in Africa. I have limited my discussion in this section mainly to the views and discourses championed by Chihombori-Quao because in recent years her viewpoints have widely awakened and influenced popular discourses about the French–Africa Connection at the international stage.

Chihombori-Quao used her position as AU special envoy to the USA to among other things mobilize and incense the African diaspora to the devastating legacy of the nineteenth century's balkanization of Africa in the Berlin conference and the continuing exploitation of Africa by the Western neocolonial powers, especially France. The eloquent Ambassador has traversed America and Africa, giving public lectures, seminars and media interviews on the atrocities of France and most of her public speeches are available online.

Two striking revelations or claims have been made by Chihombori-Quao which many of her teeming followers have recited and spread beyond limits. The first is the so-called "Pact for continuation of colonization" which France made her former African colonies to sign as a condition for independence mostly between 1958 and 1961. The content of the Pact recited by the Ambassador in her various public speeches spelled out sequestrating conditions that utterly compromised the national security, economies, dignity and sovereignty of the ex-colonies in a manner that not only reverses their independence but also mortgages the future development and wellbeing of many generations of their citizens yet unborn.[7]

The second claim made by Chihombori-Quao is about the enormous wealth that France takes out of its ex-colonies through the mandatory deposit of their foreign reserves with the French treasury—funds she claims that France invests in stock markets to make super profits to the tune of $500 billion a year. As she asserts: "Today, France is taking out of Francophone Africa over US$500 billion. We, the Africans, the poor countries, are giving France US$500 billion year-in year-out." "France needs to be the Third World developing country, not Africa. No more shall we continue to be exploited. France can no longer take $500 billion out of Africa."[8] France is the biggest risk to peace and security and economic development in Africa, she submits.[9]

I do not have the evidence to comment on the amount of money the ex-AU envoy claims that France extorts or makes from its ex-African colonies yearly neither has the Ambassador provided the source(s) of her information in any of her speeches. On the other hand, the comments of Ambassador Chihombori-Quao about France signing Pacts with some of its colonies sequel to their independence are historical facts. The detail and scope of these secret agreements, the extent to which they have been enforced or are still in force, and their overall impact on national sovereignties and economies could be investigated and debated on a case by case basis. Writing in 2008, Richard Dowden had this to say about the French neocolonial Pacts:

> The French government also made bilateral military agreements with its former colonies and until recently kept about 9,000 troops in its African former colonies. Under the agreements the troops were stationed in French-controlled bases providing training and arms and sometimes intervening to keep their chosen rulers in power. Three decades after independence there were more French people in the Francophone territories than they had been in colonial times. French companies still got all the major contracts. Most ministries in Francophone Africa still contained a French official lurking in a back office to ensure that things did not go awry. That also meant Paris was kept fully informed of what was happening. In 2008 President Nicolas Sarkozy, embarrassed by France's outdated relationship with its former African colonies, offered to renegotiate the agreements. (Dowden 2008: 60)[10]

Dowden's revealing narrative essentially accords with Chihombori-Quao claims regarding French exploitation of its ex-colonies, albeit the latter is far more damning and supposedly embarrassing to France. But from their postcolonial antics in Africa, I doubt if the French government cares much about international embarrassments and its reputation in Africa. One might probably urge Ambassador Chihombori-Quao to write her memoir to further substantiate some of her claims with authoritative evidence. These claims and allegations are too serious to be consigned entirely to the platforms of public speeches and media interviews.

Beyond the controversial narratives about France, Chihombori-Quao deserves credit for her pan-African fervour, her mobilization of the African diaspora for multifaceted development activities and investments in Africa, including the Wakanda One Village Centre of Excellence[11] she initiated, for her promotion of intra-African trade and the African Continental Free Trade Area (AfCFTA) agreement, as well as for sensitizing African people and leaders to the need to unite against foreign interference, domination and exploitation. In her various pan-African engagements both before and after her stint as AU special envoy to the USA, Chihombori-Quao's commitment to Africa's total independence and transformation is arguably only second to that of the famous Ghanaian independence leader and Pan-Africanist Kwame Nkrumah.

The major shortcoming that I see in the perspectives espoused in most of the vociferous advocacy-oriented narratives about the French–Africa

Connection is the tendency to minimize the African agency and responsibility in the perpetuation of the ruins of Africa. Much of the blame for African failures is placed on the wrongs that the West did in history and continues to do in contemporary times. Little analytical weight is placed on the African agency in inflicting and aggravating painful setbacks on the continent. The real challenge in continuing to blame history and the outsider about African problems without duly acknowledging the incalculable damage that postcolonial African states have done to themselves is that it is an unhelpful approach in finding appropriate remedies. Accurate historical analysis is helpful in informing us about the sources, nature and scale of the African problem, but blaming history will not solve the problem. External actors and stakeholders will not solve Africa's problems either even though some of them could help a great deal if Africans can offer strategic leadership. African leaders and people need to rise to the occasion, be in the driving seat and take their national and collective destinies into their own hands.

Summary Points

1. To protect their strategic interests in Africa, the French have long championed a policy of active interference and engagement with their ex-colonies since the latter were granted political independence.
2. France aims to maintain postcolonial relationships with the African countries under its neocolonial orbit through a set of structural and relational arrangements loosely known as *Françafrique*.
3. There are different dimensions of *Françafrique*—the sociocultural, educational, geopolitical, military and economic dimensions.
4. Neocolonial capitalism which is dominant in postcolonial Africa has an added twist in the peculiar case of the 12 ex-French colonies in Sub-Saharan Africa—the refusal or denial of monetary sovereignty.
5. Refusal of monetary sovereignty means that one of the preconditions for the granting of political independence was that the French ex-colonies of Sub-Saharan Africa must maintain their ties with the French colonial currency union, the Franc of the French Community of Africa known as CFA Franc for short.
6. Post-independence CFA union has 14 countries split into two currency zones and operating under two monetary institutions

beholden to France—West African Economic and Monetary Union (WAEMU) and Central African Economic and Monetary Community (CEMAC). Guinea-Bissau, an ex-Portuguese colony and Equatorial Guinea, a former Spanish colony are the only two members of the Francophone currency union that were not colonized by France.

7. France guarantees the value of the CFA Franc, and in return, the countries that use it are required to keep 50% of their foreign exchange reserves with the French treasury (Al Jazeera 2019).
8. There have been extensive ripples about the French–Africa connection in recent years with many critics reproaching France for its continued undue exploitation and interference in the affairs of its ex-African colonies. France is also criticized for undermining African regional economic integration and the ECOWAS common currency project through its stranglehold and manipulation of its ex-colonies.

Discussion Questions

1. How would you define and characterize the term *Françafrique*?
2. What are some contemporary examples of the military dimension of *Françafrique*?
3. In what practical ways have the French government tried to maintain direct control and influence over its ex-colonies in Africa?
4. Why did the French government introduce the CFA Franc as a common currency in its colonies in 1945 and insisted on keeping the currency in postcolonial Africa?
5. Explain the attitude of France to the ECOWAS common currency project in West Africa and why?

Notes

1. Quote is taken from Riley Ricky (2016) "5 Quotes from French Leaders that Reveal How Much France Depends on Africa for Its Survival," *Atlantic Black Star*, 2 November 2016, https://atlantablackstar.com/2016/11/02/5-quotes-from-french-leaders-that-reveal-how-much-france-depends-on-africa-for-its-survival/.

2. "Françafrique is a term that describes the historical relationship between France and its former colonies in Sub-Saharan Africa. Like most colonial and postcolonial constructs, it was rarely challenged in France for decades, but today the idea of Françafrique is highly contested in both France and Africa"—Global Voices (5 February 2020) "Françafrique': A Term for a Contested Reality in Franco-African Relations", https://globalvoices.org/2020/02/05/francafrique-a-term-for-a-contested-reality-in-franco-african-relations/.
3. Al Jazeera (2019) "New African Currency: Will the 'ECO' Replace the CFA Franc?" 12 July 2020, https://www.aljazeera.com/ajimpact/african-currency-eco-replace-cfa-franc-190711162229142.html.
4. UNECA (n.d.) "ECOWAS - Macroeconomic Policy Convergence", United Nations Economic Commission for Africa (UNECA), https://www.uneca.org/oria/pages/ecowas-macroeconomic-policy-convergence.
5. UNECA (n.d.), ibid.
6. See Lamine Konkobo (2017) "African Protests over the CFA Colonial Currency", 30 August 2020, https://www.bbc.co.uk/news/world-africa-41094094.
7. I do not want to enumerate the embarrassing conditionalities of the so-called "Pact of Continuation of Colonisation" in this book. But they are available in many speeches and interviews granted by Ambassador Chihombori-Quao, as well as in several other sources that may or may not be attributed to her. Cf. Mawuna Koutonin (2014) "14 African Countries Who Still Pay Colonial Tax to France for the Benefit of Slavery and Colonization", Silicon Africa, 28 January 2014, https://siliconafrica.com/france-colonial-tax/; https://answersafrica.com/countries-subjected-pay-colonial-tax-benefits-salvery-france.html; Africa WebTV (2020) "Dr Arikana Chihombori | French Colonisation Of Africa Never Stopped | Speech That Got Her Sacked?", https://www.youtube.com/watch?v=v4DGqlq5BDQ; Roland Martin (2019) "EXCLUSIVE: Former AU Ambassador to The U.S. On Her Dismissal, France's Ongoing Influence in Africa", 6 November 2019, https://www.youtube.com/watch?v=HgMDuL9Ww7Y.
8. Cf. Mawuna Koutonin (2014), ibid., reference to note 7. Africa WebTV (2020), ibid., reference to note 7. Also cf. Tony Okeregbe (2020) "Arikana Chihombori-Quao: A Profile in Courage", *The Guardian* 1 January 2020, https://guardian.ng/news/arikana-chihombori-quao-a-profile-in-courage/.
9. Make Africa Great (7 July 2020) "Dr Arikana Chihombori without Fear, TOLD FRANCE and CHINA to Leave AFRICA"—video interview, https://www.youtube.com/watch?v=7hAKgF1RUOs.
10. I slightly rearranged the order of the sentences for logical coherence without changing a word.

11. *Wakanda One* is African Union's Diaspora Centre of Excellence which when completed will be fully equipped as model high-tech industrial and settlement hubs aimed to help fill the various capacity deficits in Africa – lack of capacity for development, healthcare, education, infrastructure, housing, power, science & technology, and pharmaceuticals. Five of such centres are envisaged for each of the African regions, and the first in the series will be located in a large expanse of land already allocated in the Zimbabwe-Zambia axis of Southern Africa. See Wakanda's official website for more details: https://ouraddi.org/wakanda-project/.

References

Al Jazeera. 2013. Al Jazeera Investigates 'The French - African Connection', August 6. https://www.modernghana.com/news/480169/al-jazeera-investigates-the-french-african-connect.html#:~:text=Al%20Jazeera%20Investigates%20The%20French-African%20Connection.%20On%20Thursdays,Al-Qaeda-affiliated%20groups%20from%20taking%20control%20of%20the%20country.

Al Jazeera. 2019. New African Currency: Will the 'ECO' Replace the CFA Franc? July 12, 2020. https://www.aljazeera.com/ajimpact/african-currency-eco-replace-cfa-franc-190711162229142.html.

Dewast, Louise. 2019. West Africa's Eco: What Difference Would a Single Currency Make? July 6, 2020. https://www.bbc.co.uk/news/world-africa-48882030.

Diop, B. Boubacar. 2018. Françafrique: A Brief History of a Scandalous Word. *New African Magazine*, March 23. https://newafricanmagazine.com/16585/.

Dowden, Richard. 2008. *Africa: Altered States, Ordinary Miracles*. London: Portobello Books.

Erforth, Benedikt. 2020. *Contemporary French Security Policy in Africa*. New York: Palgrave Macmillan.

Momoh, Mohammed. 2020. Buhari Expresses Concern over New Regional Currency. The East African, June 24. https://allafrica.com/stories/202006250081.html.

Nwachukwu, Onyinye. 2020. ECOWAS Urged to Focus on Convergence Criteria as They Meet on Eco Controversy. *Business Day*, January 16. https://businessday.ng/business-economy/article/ecowas-urged-to-focus-on-convergence-criteria-as-they-meet-on-eco-controversy/.

Sylla, Ndongo Samba. 2017. The CFA Franc: French Monetary Imperialism in Africa, July 12. https://blogs.lse.ac.uk/africaatlse/2017/07/12/the-cfa-franc-french-monetary-imperialism-in-africa/.

The Africa Report. 2020. Anglophone West Africa Kicks Back at Use of Eco to Replace CFA Franc, January 17. https://www.theafricareport.com/22312/anglophone-west-africa-kicks-back-at-use-of-eco-to-replace-cfa-franc/.

Tidey, Alice. 2021. France Rules Out Troops Withdrawal from Sahel to Cut off the Head of Terror Groups. *EuroNews*, February 16, 2021. https://www.euronews.com/2021/02/16/france-rules-out-troop-withdrawal-from-sahel-to-cut-off-the-head-of-terror-groups.

Tuğba, Korkmaz. 2019. La Françafrique: The Special Relationship Between France and Its Former Colonies in Africa, August 2. https://insamer.com/en/la-francafrique-the-special-relationship-between-france-and-its-former-colonies-in-africa_2307.html.

CHAPTER 4

Natural Resources and Rentier Capitalism

Enough is enough ... we need investors, but not this kind of exploitation. We are supposed to share profits.[1]—John Magufuli, President of Tanzania (2015–2021)

4.1 The Hope of Prosperity

The preceding chapters have shown how Africa's abundant natural resources became the core factors for the second scramble for Africa, and its consequent colonization. The anti-colonial struggles were largely framed around the expropriation of Africa's resources by the colonizers for the development of their Western homelands while Africans suffered and the continent stagnated. There was a great hope that should the African colonies regain their independence, the pillage and siphoning away of African resources would cease, and Africans will utilize their abundant resources for the transformation of the continent. The faith was palpable and expectations high. The regaining of independence came with discovery and/or commercial production and export of many more solid and liquid mineral resources in several countries, especially oil and gas, coltan, uranium, titanium and so forth. This second generation of resources comparatively generate more revenue in the global market than most of the resources comprised in the first generation of the colonial era—cash crops and solid minerals like copper, coal, aluminium ore,

K. Omeje, *The Failure and Feasibility of Capitalism in Africa*, International Political Economy Series,
https://doi.org/10.1007/978-3-030-75170-8_4

etc.). Cycles of commodity boom were experienced in the 1960s and 1970s, which reinforced the hope and expectations of African transformation. Indeed, in sections of the West, especially in America, early post-independence Africa was viewed with considerable optimism, albeit the Cold War politics and internal challenges of nation-building were beginning to produce cracks and instability in some of the resource-rich countries (Cooper, n.d.). By the late 1970s through the 1990s it had become evident that Africa's abundant natural resources were not producing the much-expected prosperity and growth but were becoming a major source of economic distress, instability and armed conflict, unravelling development and spreading or reinforcing mass poverty and underdevelopment (Karl 1997; Balthasar 2013). The failure of governance and development was almost uniform, especially across the richly endowed states. Africa's abundant natural resources became increasingly perceived as a curse rather than the expected blessing. Two related perspectives have dominated the explanations of the poor performances of most of the countries richly endowed with natural resources in post-colonial Africa that I wish to discuss in this chapter—the natural resource theory and the rentier state theory. Based on a stakeholder approach to natural resources, I have offered some explanations about how abundant natural resource rent sustains rentier capitalism, which is a recipe for squandermania, corruption and conflicts.

4.2 Resource Curse

The idea of natural resource curse implies the structural prevalence of a macroeconomic paradox in the operation of a natural resource-rich state whereby the vast majority of its citizens are consigned to extreme poverty essentially inflicted by the systematic expropriation of the resource wealth by an unscrupulous governing elite oftentimes working in collaboration with both visible and underground local and international business partners. The deliberate and vicious inability of the state managers to make the surplus resource wealth of a country impact positively on the lives of the vast majority of their citizens is the flip side of the resource curse. In contemporary dispensation, resource curse tends to be mainly fostered by a nexus of institutional and legal weaknesses in the resource-rich states which aid the unscrupulous political leaders, public officials and their business associates to loot the affected fragile and captive economies.

The phenomenon is not peculiar to Africa, even though the African continent is by far the worst affected.

> A survey of the institutional and legal environments in 58 resource-rich countries around the world found that only 11 manage their natural resource sectors effectively. These 58 countries represent 85% of the world's petroleum reserves and a significant share of global mineral wealth, including 90% of diamond reserves and 80% of copper reserves. Of the 58 countries included in the survey, 20 are in Africa – more than any other region in the world. None of these African countries was deemed to manage their natural resource wealth satisfactorily. (Mailey 2015: 5)

Some of the African countries often used as examples to highlight the tragedy of the natural resource curse include war-affected states like Liberia, Sierra Leone, Angola, the DRC, Cote d'Ivoire and Sudan; volatile conflict-prone countries like Nigeria, Cameroun and Chad, as well as hostage economies like Equatorial Guinea. Human development indices and infrastructural conditions in all of these countries are characteristically poor. As such, the vast majority of their citizens live in extreme poverty, well below $1.90 a day. Moreover, the economies of the seemingly resource-cursed states are lopsidedly structured around the production and export of one or a few natural resources (e.g., diamonds, oil and gas, timber, cobalt, etc.) as opposed to being diversified across several productive manufacturing sectors, which many international political economy experts regard as a necessary condition for sustainable growth and development.

Based on the analysis of empirical macroeconomic data from different oil-rich developing countries, scholars and policy analysts have proffered a number of arguments to explain the reasons for the prevalence of resource curse in many oil-rich developing economies, otherwise known as rentier states. These arguments can be summarised as follows. The first is that most natural resources are excessively subject to the vagaries (boom and bust cycle) of the international commodity market (Lehrer 2007; Frankel 2010). Secondly, many rentier states have volatile and narrow revenue bases, and volatile "rent" revenues are difficult to manage given the weak institutional, technical and regulatory capacities of the states (Collier 2008). Prebendal corruption by the hegemonic rentier elite becomes rife, which ultimately undermines investment in social development. To ensure regime survival and accumulation, the governing elite invests continuously in strengthening the security and repressive apparatuses of the state, a tendency which makes abundant natural resource wealth to systematically promote repression and authoritarian rule. This heightens the proneness of the state to armed insurgency and civil war. Armed rebellion in resource-rich states, as some experts argue, could be further instigated or aggravated and prolonged by factional greed for lootable natural resources and criminal obstructibility of the largely non-lootable resources (Collier and Hoefller 2000; Ross 2012). In fact, for certain companies that have mastered the art of doing business and profiting in disaster zones, armed conflict and volatile circumstances can provide a fillip for natural resource looting and accumulation. In her seminal book, *The Shock Doctrine* (2007), Naomi Klein calls this specific modality of accumulation the "Disaster Capitalism Complex."

Thirdly, access to plenteous rents such as often generated by oil revenue, for instance, tends to correlate negatively with democracy by minimizing government's reliance on taxation of its citizens or completely freeing the state from the need to levy taxes, and the corresponding obligation of representative democracy believed to be an inherent principle in citizens' taxation (Luciani 1997). Public taxation, theorists argue, leads to citizens' demand for democratic representation and accountability. Furthermore, in many petro-states with low-income per capita (e.g., Cameroun, Gabon, Equatorial Guinea and Congo-Brazzaville) attempts to introduce genuine multi-party democracy are invariably scuttled by an incumbent hegemonic party that persistently manipulates the electoral process to remain in power, thereby leaving the state with a form of dysfunctional rentier democracy tempered with sporadic outbursts of violence from below and militarized repression from above (Bratton 1998; Omeje 2008).

Fourthly, it is argued that preponderant reliance on natural resources could produce the deleterious effect of crowding out manufacturing and other productive sectors of the economy, especially sectors that offer dynamic benefits and spillovers conducive to growth—a tendency broadly known as the "Dutch Disease" (Moyo 2009; Frankel 2010). Paradoxically, in his study of the effects of oil wealth and changes in oil prices on political stability between 1960 and 1999, Smith (2004) posits that oil wealth is positively associated with greater regime durability, and significantly related to lower levels of anti-government protest and civil war in both democratic and authoritarian states. Smith argues from his findings that contrary to the thesis of a number of resource curse theorists, repression seems not to be the mechanism by which oil-rich rentier states of the Middle East and elsewhere maintain regime durability but by other positive investment factors that may relate to the dividends and blessings of oil wealth. Heilbrunn (2014: 9 & 16) amplifies the anti-resource curse discourse of Smith in a later study of the African oil economies in which he argues that "oil revenues are hardly a curse; rather, they are an opportunity for poor countries to grow economically and create institutional conditions that are conducive to democracy and development." In his critique of Smith's sceptical thesis on resource curse, Hlavac (2010: 3) remarks that "Smith's models assume that regime durability, civil war and political protest are all a function of economic growth and oil dependency." "Causality," argues Hlavac, could however, also run the other way: … "countries that suffer from conflict or instability may be less able to attract investment or develop industries in sectors other than natural resource extraction" (Hlavac 2010: 3).

The resource curse theory and the general debate on natural resource conflicts make interesting contributions to how the use of state power interfaces with the macroeconomic conditions and concomitants of growth, boom, development, bust, poverty and turmoil in postcolonial states. However, as Magrin, and van Vliet (2009) argue, "various studies that defend the resource curse thesis are based on a confusion between correlation and causation, thereby drawing unwarranted conclusions concerning links between resources and conflicts." The problem with most explanations from the resource curse and related perspectives is essentially twofold. The first is their preponderantly ahistorical narrativism, often mystified with quantitative regression analysis and econometric modelling, on the conditions for natural resource curse and the correlated conflicts. Both the quantitative and qualitative explanations of proponents are almost always of short postcolonial span and devoid of relevant historical depth. It suffices to say that the issue of how natural resource curse and conflicts are produced in transitional extractive economies is mainly a structural one which has a profound historical rhythm that logically connects present performance failures to past structural foundations. The globalization of production and trade in the late nineteenth century in the aftermath of the industrial revolution in Western Europe was the key factor in the emergence of dependent extractive economies in Africa and other regions of the global South. I have shown in the preceding chapters, as many a great deal of economic historians before me already demonstrated, how European colonial rule and imperial governance created outposts of dependencies in the global South for the primary purpose of exploiting economic resources (mostly minerals and agricultural produce) as a means to provide the crucial raw materials necessary to advance capitalist production and industrialization in the metropolitan West. To consign Africa and a greater part of the global South to dependencies for extraction of vital natural resources during colonial rule, Western imperial powers supplanted the sovereignty of the peoples they colonized and instituted a regime of impunity conducive to unaccountable exploitation and accumulation. Forced labour, compulsory cash crop production and delegation of sovereign power to transnational trading companies and individuals were all part of the regime of impunity widespread in the colonies (Mbembe 2001; Omeje 2015). The colonizers equipped and supported many TNCs with commercial and mining privileges and with sovereign rights allowing them to raise taxes and maintain an armed force (Mbembe 2001).

Colonialism was characterized by profuse obnoxious laws and gross abuse of law by colonial officials and agencies, including the big TNCs. From fiscal stewardship, legal justice and human rights perspectives, colonial agencies largely presided over a regime of impunity, hypocrisy and unaccountable rule. Mbembe aptly observes that the tendency to usurp the powers of the state for self-accumulation purposes under colonial rule was a rampart phenomenon that tended to occur in various guises and everywhere in the colonial service and economy, which ironically was a radical departure from the common law, individual rights and principles of legal justice that were already emerging in the metropole (Mbembe 2001).

It is the foregoing political economy of rentier capitalism, with its anomalies of unaccountable political superstructure, compromised political culture and a strategic corporate mining sector imbued with vestiges of state figure, personality and mentality that most postcolonial states inherited at independence. As a matter of fact, many of the lead TNCs, some of which have metamorphosed into global business conglomerates under different operational names, continued to preponderantly retain their colonial privileges well into the post-independence dispensation and even in the contemporary era. Under the prevailing circumstance, perpetuating the inherited culture of usurping state power for prebendal accumulation becomes a convenient political capital for the hegemonic postcolonial elites while taming and regulating the all-powerful TNCs becomes, for many states, a strategic dilemma in which diverse options are contemplated and explored. Confrontation and collaboration, nationalization and denationalization, co-investment and production-sharing partnership, displacement and replacement of firms, to mention a few, are some of the strategic options that have been explored with mixed results by different postcolonial states. The role of the strategic mining sector, which in most African states is dominated by TNCs, cannot be divorced from any serious analysis of how natural resource curse and the correlated conflicts are produced in Africa.

The second problem, the issue of state-centric explanations of natural resource curse and conflicts, is directly related to the preceding narrative. The dominant narrative in resource curse explanation is so much about the "harm" the state and its officials are doing and the "good" they are failing to do, which ultimately produces both the curse and armed conflict. The implicit assumption in this cyclical narrative is that if the state stops doing all the harm it is said to be doing, and starts doing all the good it is charged with failing to do, then the social maladies of resource curse and conflict would be automatically fixed. Whilst this explanation might be partially correct, it is fundamentally a half-truth over-simplification of the empirical reality. The key disconnect in all these theoretical assumptions is the phenomenon of stakes and the critical role of various stakeholders. The institutional state in weak developing countries of Africa is only one among many competing stakeholders, albeit in many instances, the most decisive stakeholder. But this is by no means to understate the instrumental significance of other stakeholders, as well as the specific historical, international and circumstantial environment in which they all operate.

One of the greatest tragedies of colonialism and colonial legacy in Africa is the fact that external metropolitan forces (states, TNCs, international NGOs and other foreign supra-national actors) have historically acquired strategic stakes and become important stakeholders in African domestic and regional affairs in a disproportionately disadvantageous way that their African counterparts cannot and would not have the slightest opportunity to replicate in their foreign home turfs. A simple example (not directly related to the politics of rent) will help to further illustrate this point. In February 2012 and May 2013, the UK government hosted a stakeholder conference in the famous Lancaster House in London on resolving the conflict in Somalia and turning around the Somali state. The 2013 conference which the UK government "co-hosted" with the Somali government was convened "to provide international support for the Government of Somalia as they rebuild their country after two decades of conflict" (UK Government FCO 2013). The stakeholders in attendance in the more crucial 2013 conference co-hosted with the government of Somalia were 54 friends and partners of Somalia, including the African Union Peacekeeping Force in Somalia (AMISOM) and all the troop-contributing countries, key regional organizations like AU and IGAD, European Union and leading EU governments, the World Bank, Organisation of Islamic Conference, Arab League and leading Arab Gulf states, UN, etc. Regarding the substantive issues discussed: the conference overly concentrated on issues of security, justice and public financial management—aspects that are conspicuously of concern to an international community that feels threatened by Somali [Islamist] extremism, worries about government corruption of donor funding, and prioritizes a human rights agenda; in fact, the conference communique is oriented to particular outcomes to be delivered by the Somali government, which includes "a commitment to form a fully federal government and deliver democratic elections in 2016" (Balthasar 2013; UK Government FCO 2013). Evaluating the "new deal" delivered by the London conference on Somali, Balthasar (2013: 1) remarks that:

> In view of the fact that the conference focused so narrowly on specific outcomes, the Somali government's policy space was significantly restricted. Among others, this shows in the communique´s insistence on the establishment of a 'fully federal government' – a process that has largely been objected by the Somali government thus far, due to fears that federalism could weaken its own standing and prospects of state-making. However, the Somali government is now pressed to comply with a greater devolution of power to regional states, which is likely to complicate matters, not least as this leaves Somalia's neighbours with continued influence to meddle in Somali politics.

A follow-up stakeholders' conference tagged a "New Deal for Somalia" was held in Brussels on 16th September 2013 with a similar broad range of Somali and international participation. In the London summit, some $130 million were pledged in aid to rebuild Somalia, while in the Brussels summit, international donors pledged $2.7 billion in aid for the same purpose (Al Jazeera 2013; VoA 2013). The Brussel's conference ended on a high hope and commitment that the pledged money will be spent according to a plan drawn up by the year-old Somali government, with international assistance (Gardner 2013). Another notable conference with the Somali federal government delegation in attendance was held in May 2017 in London that produced a new partnership framework agreement for fixing Somalia based on some calibrated areas of priority. Much of these deals are sham and their execution shambolic. I don't know how much of the pledged funds that were redeemed by donors, but anybody who has had the privilege of visiting Mogadishu for any "development" or service-related assignment as I have done knows something about whose priorities are driving the so-called reconstruction agenda in Somalia, who is controlling the funds, what they are spent on and who gets the chunk of the allocation to do all kinds of projects that are grotesque to the Somalis. The infrastructural development requested by the Somali government and desperately needed by the people are hardly part of the international development agenda. From the standpoint of reconstruction and development, Somalia has not been better off in the many years after the so-called "New Deal for Somalia" than the years before. Hypocrisy!

It seems quite normal in this postcolonial and post-Cold War era that a stakeholder conference to turnaround the war-affected state of Somali should be repeatedly held in Europe with both the agenda and outcomes of the summit profoundly shaped by Western stakeholders. It will be inconceivable that a stakeholder conference to turnaround the distressed economy of Greece or to resolve the conflicts in Bosnia and Ukraine should be held in Lilongwe, the capital city of the Southern African state of Malawi or in Pretoria, South Africa, let alone inviting any African agencies to such a summit as stakeholders. It does not take more than a sophomore-level course in international negotiation to know that where you host a problem-solving intervention summit, who sets the agenda; who attends the summit, their resource capability and what they bring to the table—can all have decisive influence on the outcome of the summit and possibly on the ultimate turn out of events on the ground. African states and agencies do not have the overall capacity to acquire important stakes in South/Eastern Europe and the Balkans, and therefore cannot be stakeholders in the Bosnian, Ukrainian and Greek troubles in a similar way that the UK, Italy, Germany, Turkey, USA and the EU can be considered important stakeholders in the conflict in Somalia. This is a well-structured case of asymmetrical stakeholding in international relations and the origin of the phenomenon transcends postcolonial history.

The capacity to project and foist decisive stakes on African states and institutions is no longer only peculiar to Western actors, even though they are credited with historically pioneering the phenomenon. Since the post-Cold War era, state-owned and private mining corporations from Russia and many Asian countries (notably China) and other emerging economies have rapidly acquired vast stakes and also become important stakeholders in African economies, states and societies in such a way that no African-owned agencies could operate in the home turf of these economies. In its most blatant forms, the predatory business corporations of China and other emerging non-Western economies have acquired harmful stakes in many African economies through a "marriage of convenience" with unaccountable African governing elites, a process akin to the ways by which Western imperialism has been sustained in the African postcolonial states. In his report titled *The Anatomy of the Resource Curse: Predatory Investment in Africa's Extractive Industries*, Mailey (2015) has examined the complex subversive linkages between predatory foreign businesses (mostly from the emerging Eastern economies) and the African ruling elites in relatively fragile resource-rich states. The author for instance provides a detailed anatomy of the dodgy business practices of one group of investors that has been particularly active on the continent since the early 2000s: a Hong Kong-based consortium known as the 88 Queensway Group. Cultivating relationships with high-level government officials in politically isolated resource-rich states through infusions of cash, promises of billions of dollars in infrastructural development (which they hardly deliver), and support for the security sector, Queensway has been able to gain access to major oil and mining concessions across Africa with massive operations in at least nine countries, including Angola, Guinea, Zimbabwe, Madagascar, Equatorial Guinea, Tanzania and Zimbabwe where they have signed deals worth billions of Dollars (Africa Confidential 2013; Mailey 2015: 1). The real names of these secretive companies are China International Fund and China Sonangol; they are nicknamed the "88 Queensway Group" for their network of opaque, affiliated firms based at that address in Hong Kong (Africa Confidential 2013).

Virtually all the important conflict and development intervention projects in Africa implemented by states and non-state actors have foreign donors and stakeholders. With some rare exceptions, peacekeeping and post-conflict peacebuilding in contemporary Africa have become almost inconceivable without some form of pivotal expatriate funding, technical assistance and overall stakeholding. Most successful regional policy think tanks and national NGOs in Africa are not only funded by foreign donors (mostly Western agencies) but also have the latter enlisted as key stakeholders. How many quangos in the West are funded by African donors or have the latter as part of their stakeholders?

There may be practically nothing wrong with foreign investors, states, donors and regional agencies acquiring diverse material and non-material stakes in foreign lands. But foreign stakeholding in a weak state almost always comes at a formidable price—deepening vulnerability in institutional, transactional, economic and managerial terms—especially if the weak state is not astute in domestic regulation, and economic and cultural diplomacy as is often the case. It is against this backdrop of deepening vulnerability that we can understand the lamentation in the Report of the Africa Progress Panel chaired for former UN Secretary General Kofi Annan that:

> tax evasion, secret mining deals and financial transfers through grossly inflated pricing are depriving Africa of the benefits of its resources boom; mining firms operating in many African countries use these mechanisms to shift profits to lower tax jurisdictions, costing Africa $38 billion a year.... Africa loses more money through these loopholes than it gets in aids and foreign direct investments. (BBC News 2013)

The Report gave the example of the Democratic Republic of Congo where between 2010 and 2012 five under-priced mining concessions were sold in "highly opaque and secretive deals," costing the country about $1.3 billion in revenues; and Zambia where between 2005 and 2009, 500,000 copper mine workers were paying a higher rate of tax than major multinational mining firms. Annan aptly recognized that Africa cannot fight these "illicit outflows" alone, stressing that "the tax evasion, avoidance, secret bank accounts are problems for the world and as such Africa needs to work together with the richer nations, particularly the G8 ... to ensure we have a multilateral solution to the crisis" (BBC News 2013). The findings of The Africa Progress Panel and Annan's reflection on the international complexity of the problem of tax avoidance and transfer pricing by mining companies operating in weak African states buttress the point about the deepening vulnerability of weak states inundated with foreign stakeholding in their economies even in times of extractive resource boom. Furthermore, it brings to the fore the need to break away from the state-centric supposition by some mainstream political economy analysts that resource curse only revolves around the dysfunctionality of the state and malpractices by its officials.

There are some well-meaning leaders in Africa who have seriously combatted the expatriate tax evaders and supplanters. Under the presidency of John Magufuli, the Tanzanian government launched an unprecedented anti-corruption drive in the mining sector, forcing many foreign mining companies to pay millions of Dollars in outstanding tax, and also instituting reform measures that have, among other things, helped to ensure more effective revenue collection and utilization. The mining sector reform includes a ban on the export of unprocessed ore in March 2017 and a drive for the construction of a local smelter.

The greatest culprit and catch in the Tanzanian anti-corruption drive is the Canadian TNC, Acacia Gold, the largest mining company in the country, indicted in 2017 for dodging tax and exporting more gold than they declared over many years and slammed with a $190 billion bill for unpaid taxes and penalties (Allison 2019). Two years later, "Canadian-based Barrick Gold, Acacia's parent company, announced an agreement with the Tanzanian government that will allow them to restart production. Barrick has agreed to pay a $300-million fine, as well as hand the government a 16% stake in each of its three Tanzanian mines and 50% of any royalties" (Allison 2019).

Even though a largely weak state phenomenon, the issue of tax avoidance and evasion by mining multinational companies on the continent is not just a problem that Africa can simply solve by states and state officials stopping the "harmful stuff" they do and doing the "good" they ought to do. To a lesser extent, tax avoidance by operating TNCs and wealthy tycoons who often exploit loopholes in tax laws to shift profits to offshore subsidiaries and bank accounts in tax havens (countries with low or lax taxation) is also a problem that affects and exercises the governments of some of the developed countries like the UK, USA, France and Germany. In a bid to combat tax evasion, the OECD in October 2019 published a new legal framework that would ensure that TNCs pay their fair share of taxes in countries where they have substantial sales or consumer activities (Minerva Analytics 2019). Hopefully, this will be a significant step to restore profits through taxation to countries where they are made.

Regarding the activities of TNCs and weaknesses in corporate governance in developing countries, proponents of "good [democratic] governance"—as important and well-meaning as the proposal could be—tend to be exaggerating their case. In its first anti-corruption report, the EU Commission remarked that "the extent of corruption in Europe is 'breath-taking' and it costs the EU economy at least 120 billion Euros annually" (BBC News 2014). This is Europe investigating and reporting itself to itself—"corruption in Europe, breath-taking," not corruption in Africa. An EU review of the UK in 2018 found serious weaknesses in the systems for holding top government officials—ministers, special advisors and senior civil servants—to account (Hawley 2019). "The UK's role in acting as a haven or a conduit for money stolen from rampant public corruption in other countries is well known and causes widespread anger there" (Hawley 2019). Way back in 2002, the then Nigerian President Olusegun Obasanjo remarked that corrupt African leaders have stolen at least $140 billion from their people in the decades since independence and accused European countries of "sitting" on much of the stolen money stashed in European banks (Basildon 2002). In recent years, there have been many leaks and revelations about the African leaders and politicians that have looted their countries, and the foreign banks and countries holding the looted funds in Europe and elsewhere. Some of these looters have already died, and the billions they stashed away in Western safe havens are probably gone forever. The Nigerian government deserves commendation for their efforts in recovering a significant part of the money that late maximum leader General Sanni Abacha stashed off in different banks and countries in the West, even if the government's accountability of the recovered funds remain suspect. But what about all other stolen wealth of the dead and the living plunderers of Africa held in Western banks? President Obasanjo sarcastically declared that "a man who provides a safe haven for stolen things is equally guilty as the one who stole the things" (Basildon 2002). If we go by the Transparency International Corruption Perception Index (CPI) for 2019, the levels of corruption in Russia and Ukraine surpass that of Zambia and Eswatini. And we know that what is happening in Zambia and Eswatini is not a child's play. Clearly, to a lesser extent, corruption and bad governance are also a problem in Europe. Of course, good governance, especially the quality of resource governance can make a difference in some countries as the examples of Botswana and Chile have demonstrated (Basedau and Lay 2009: 760). However, as Collier (2008: 65) has persuasively argued:

> Excellent governance and economic policies can help the growth process, but there is a ceiling to feasible growth rate at around 10%: economies just cannot grow much faster than this no matter what governments do. … Good governance and policies help a country to realise its opportunities, but they cannot generate opportunities where none exist, and they cannot

> defy gravity. Even the best governance and policies are not going to turn Malawi into a rich country – it just does not have the opportunities ***under the prevailing international trade and economic conditions*** (emphasis in italics mine). ... By contrast, terrible governance and policies can destroy an economy with alarming speed.

Despite its promise, the macroeconomic limitations of good governance cannot be overemphasized. Bad governance, on the other hand, is catastrophic.

4.3 Resource Rents and Rentier State

Abundant natural resources generally generate surplus rent. In his pioneering study on the Middle Eastern oil-rich states, Beblawi defines rents as "exports earned or income derived from a gift of nature" (Beblawi 1987: 85). Adopting a more classical economistic approach, Dunning (2008: 3) defines rents as a super-normal level of profit associated with economic return to natural resource extraction that exceeds production and transport costs and some "normal" return to capital. Deeper reflections on the present empirical dynamics on rent necessitate a more expanded definition. Rents are extraordinary profits and other related revenues derived from the development, extraction and sale of natural resources, under the direct control of the state and mining companies. The natural resource-rich states defined as rentier are usually those of developing countries whose economies are dominated by an export-oriented extractive resource sector, in most cases, oil and gas and solid minerals.

Most rentier theorists only associate rents with the state or government based on the etymological origin of the term which has to do with the money a tenant pays to a landlord for the contractual use or lease of his property. In the case of natural resources, the state in whose territorial jurisdiction a particular resource is extracted is the figurative landlord. In the case of most resource-rich African states, the state is an irresponsible and lazy landlord that hardly makes any significant investment in or add value to its natural property (the strategic resource). Similarly, the state seldom invests in developing its capacity to regulate resource exploitation by operating companies and other agencies. Most dismally, the state scarcely invests in expanding and strengthening its institutional and technical capacity to effectively manage and account for the revenues accruing to its coffers as natural resource rent. Resulting from the state's negligence in investing in its overall natural resource ownership capacity is that the state is easily outsmarted, short-changed and taken advantage of by the more experienced natural resource mining companies that are usually of expatriate origin. In addition to retaining a significantly high level of profit margin, mining companies frequently take advantage of the weak institutional and regulatory capacity of the weak resource-rich states to further leverage their financial buoyancy.

Furthermore, most expatriate mining companies operating in Africa make huge gains by relatively underpaying labour, and also by minimizing corporate environmental and social responsibilities. In fact, besides making extraordinary profits, some of the mining companies in Africa such as Shell Petroleum in Nigeria and Mopani Copper Mines (a subsidiary of the Swiss multinational Glencore) in Zambia are so politically powerful in relation to the state that they are no longer a typical tenant of the state but a de facto co-landlord with the state. In the day-to-day discourses, attitudes and orientation of members of the host communities where some of the mining companies operate, the perception that the powerful mining companies are a de facto co-landlord and apparently a "shadow-state" figure *à la* Reno (1998) is palpably strong. Informally, many government officials would readily admit and affirm this popular discourse in countries like Nigeria, Angola, Zambia and DRC (Omeje 2006, 2008; Mailey 2015). It is because of this practical anomaly regarding the institutionality of the big mining companies in Africa and the fabulous surplus wealth they control that I have expanded the meaning of rents to include the vast reservoir of rentier resources in the hands of the mining industry. Most significantly, the vast rentier surplus controlled by the extractive companies operating in the resource-rich developing countries, which are usually expatriate companies have far-reaching implications for armed conflict. Another consequence of the state's gross under-investment in its natural resource ownership and revenue management capacity is that too often a significant but usually unknown amount of rentier revenues are haemorrhaged from the state's fiscal coffers by the governing elites, sometimes in connivance with the mining industry and the highly patronage-driven private business sector. Large amounts of the state's rentier resources are frequently siphoned through well-known devices like under-reporting of revenue receipts, hyperinflation of government contracts, import-related money laundering and barefaced looting of slush funds (e.g., in countries like Nigeria, Equatorial Guinea and Angola) (Moyo 2009; Ross 2012).

Many experts argue that rentier states generally lack a productive outlook in the sense that their revenues do not depend on the growth of the domestic economy, coupled with the observation that the rent-yielding extractive sector is susceptible to the infamous Dutch disease (Dunning 2008; Magrin and van Vliet 2009). This type of inverse correlation hypothesized between natural resource-driven rentier revenues and manufacturing exports believed to be the trigger of the Dutch disease cannot be extended to developing economies without considerable caution. Clearly, the narrative seemed discernible in the Netherland's economy of the 1960s, a developed capitalist economy where the revenue influx from the discovery of natural gas made the Dutch Guilder rise in value, thereby producing a negative knock-on effect on manufactured commodity exports (Ismail 2010). Among the developing countries of Africa, the manifestation of the Dutch disease is comparatively different because most natural resource-rich states like Nigeria, Gabon, DRC and Angola do not have an export-based manufacturing sector, not least at the stage when their economies became manifestly rentierized. As such, a windfall in revenue receipts from primary commodity exports like oil and solid minerals does not necessarily destroy local manufacturing or its export competitiveness (which hardly exists). But it potentially destroys other sectors like agricultural and forestry production, which was for instance the case with the economies of Gabon, Congo and Sudan where the commercial production and export of oil practically destroyed all the robust agro-forestry exports on which their economies were previously based. Besides the rentier effect, African cash crop exporting economies were also badly affected by a convergence of the Dutch disease in the 1970s and the subsequent crash in the prices of primary agricultural commodities in the world market in the 1980s (Ademola 2012). In fact, a number of scholars have extended the concept of rent to analyse many African states whose economies are dependent on primary agricultural commodities (e.g., tea, coffee, cocoa, cotton, etc.) as a result of the boom and bust cycle of these commodities in the world market and the tendency of prebendal waste and aggrandizement among the state governing elites by courtesy of the commodity revenue windfall—a behavioural pattern associated with the typical rentier states.

Rentier states, especially those marked by weak low-income economies, are typically associated with a convoluted paradigm of behaviour and political culture linked to extreme levels of patronage, mediocrity, prebendal accumulation and institutional deformity that dialectically impede and even sometimes reverse development. Beblawi was the first proponent to use the term "rentier behaviour" or "rentier mentality" to describe the paradigm, which he argued was acquiring an inexorable transnational, pan-regional current in the Persian Gulf in the 1980s and infecting both oil and (to a lesser extent) non-oil states alike because of the tendency for guest workers from the poorer non-oil states to gravitate to the oil states for rentier income and to in turn remit their surplus savings back home for family support and investments (Beblawi 1987). Through this income transfer process, the guest workers make substantial contributions to economic growth in their home countries. Consequently, many state-led and voluntary sector projects in the non-oil Arab states depend on government grants and charity support from the oil-rich Arab states based on pan-Arab religious, political and cultural obligations. Beblawi described the entire process of structural dependency of the non-oil Arab states on their oil-rich counterparts as the "osmotic effects" of oil rents. At its worst, institutionalized rentier behaviour transverses the state, economy and society, largely contributing to a perverse national culture. Ostensibly, the most virulent expressions of encompassing rentier behaviour in Africa would be the cases of DRC, Nigeria and Angola where the dominant discursive language, political orientation and accumulation patterns and devices across the state, economy and society are extraordinarily rentier (Omeje 2006; Goldthau and Martin 2010; Global Witness 2012). Even the day-to-day media headlines, debates and popular stories in the encompassingly rentierized African states are awash with issues of accumulation by fronting, blackmail, deception and dispossession—interfacing structure of the state, economy and society. Further on its downside effects, rentierism (i.e., the condition or syndrome of rent dependency) can destroy cottage industries and perhaps can partly prevent largescale manufacturing from taking off subject to other crucial factors like availability of relevant cost-effective technology, a critical mass of technically skilled manpower and profitable local and export markets. From the foregoing discussion, it is evident that the nature of capitalism operated in rentier states is markedly twisted and driven by the imperatives of resource rent. This specific brand of twisted capitalism, more appropriately known as rentier capitalism, has many local and international stakeholders.

4.4 Rentier Stakes and Stakeholders: A New Conceptual Explanation

Natural resource rents dialectically generate stakes and stakeholders or put differently, stakes and stakeholders coalesce around resource rents, the core foundation of rentier capitalism. The concepts of stakes and stakeholders was first developed and popularised in the profit-oriented business management field from where they gradually made an inroad into the social sciences and public policy analysis. In the mainstream business management conception, stakes are regarded as "shares" and "interests" which individuals and groups hold in a business corporation (usually by way of capital investment, credits and loans, occupational engagement, customer service, etc.). By corollary, stakeholders are those who hold stakes in a business, a rather simplistic way of defining the concept. The original definition of stakeholder by Freeman who is popularly credited with pioneering stakeholder analysis in business studies conceives it as "any group or individual who can affect or is affected by the achievement of an organisation's objectives" (Freeman 1984: 46). Those that "affect" or are "affected" by the goals and actions of an organization are sometimes referred to as active and passive stakeholders in the natural resource stakeholder literature (Reed et al. 2009). The typical stakeholders in a business are those who have something to gain or lose as a result of the corporation's activities and include the employees, shareholders, management, creditors, consumers, suppliers, government, competitors, communities and trade unions (Fremond 2000; Buchholz and Rosenthal 2005). There is a wide range of other definitions of stakeholder which tend to build on Freeman's seminal study and also on the growing recognition of the interactive relationships between business corporations and the societies where they operate.

In the largely non-profit-oriented social and policy "science" where stakeholder analysis has been progressively popularised since the 1990s, the definition of stakeholder is not fundamentally different from the typical business school definition. Many social policy experts define the concept from the standpoint of normative theory as representing the diverse persons, groups, organizations and communities that must be taken into account (if possible consulted and involved) by leaders and managers in their day-to-day decision-making, and policy formulation and implementation (Bryson 2004; Buchholz and Rosenthal 2005). A

World Bank pilot study group defines a stakeholder from a more pragmatic rational actor theoretical perspective as "any entity with a declared or conceivable interest or stake in a policy concern" (World Bank, n.d.). In their various stakeholder analyses, both business and social policy experts have come up with various classifications of stakeholders, such as active and passive/dormant stakeholders, primary and secondary stakeholders, and key/major and minor stakeholders. Stakeholder analysis has become quite popular in the contemporary policy, development, security, conflict and governance studies. Virtually every social issue today (e.g., peacebuilding, terrorism, climate change, development provisioning, female genital mutilation and violence against vulnerable girls and women, etc.) is believed to have multiple stakeholders whose opinions and some form of participation are considered important for the viability of any policy or programme intervention. Conventional stakeholder analysis is a way of understanding a system through its stakeholders by looking at their interests, objectives, relative power/influence and relationships (ICRA 1997).

Extrapolating from the foregoing conceptions to explain the vicissitudes of events, phenomena and processes in the natural resource-rich African states, one can theorize about the nature of rentier stakes and stakeholders, as well as the social milieu in which rentier activities take place. Rentier stakes can be defined as the interests that different individuals, groups, classes, firms and other social agencies hold, claim and pursue within a rentier state. These interests are principally materialistic and pecuniary interests—financial resources, mining and mining resource-related positions and appointments; mining rights, concessions and contracts; compensation and redress against violations related to mining activities; rewards, perks and privileges associated with natural resource endowments and revenues, and so forth. The various interest-driven social agents spanning the entire spectrum of rentier resource chain can be labelled stakeholders and they represent diverse interests both within and outside a given state system. The stakeholders therefore include both domestic and external actors. From an economics perspective, the supply of all types of finite resources is relatively limited and scarce in relation to demand. Hence, rentier resources, as abundant as they are in the resource-rich states, are still relatively scarce in relation to demand. Competition among stakeholders therefore becomes inevitable, which makes the relative power and influence wielded by stakeholders at any given conjuncture important and sometimes decisive.

From a post-modernist perspective, power is ubiquitous, multifaceted and multidimensional; it is also relational and situational. Above all, power is essentially dialectical and political; politics itself being a correspondingly multifaceted activity in which diverse social agents strive to project and advance their interests, agendas and discursive representations at varied levels and spheres of human association and endeavour. Hence, every stakeholder is capable of wielding some measure of power, but it is certainly not all stakeholders that are capable of wielding the measure of power that can yield the outcomes they desire or expect in every circumstance. Similarly, it is not in all circumstances that the neorealist preferred instrument of hard power (coercive military force) confers decisive advantage to a conceivably more powerful stakeholder or determines rentier outcomes. Various stakeholders deploy a nexus of hard and soft power in different circumstances to maximize their competitive advantages and prospectively influence rentier outcomes. Occasionally, a threat of or resort to armed violence by stakeholder(s) occurs, and this is practically an extension of rentier politics. Of course, armed violence is a ubiquitous phenomenon in many rentier and non-rentier states and thus it is not every threat or use of armed violence that is tantamount to an extension of rentier politics.

4.5 Stakeholder Politics and Accumulation in Rentier Capitalism

Consequential stakes and stakeholders operate within a metaphorical space which can be regarded as the rentier space. The "rentier space" is a metaphoric platform that subsumes and upholds the diverse activities related to the acquisition and control of rentier resources in a state, including the disposition, appropriation and utilization of any accruable funds, perquisites, dividends and opportunities (Omeje 2008). Any rentier stakes and stakeholders operating outside the rentier space can at best be embryonic or putative. Aspirational stakes can be conceived by different actors both within and outside the rentier space, but consequential stakes can only be advanced within the rentier space where aspirational stakes have a chance of being converted into reckonable concrete stakes.

In the typical African rentier states as depicted in Fig. 4.1, the principal hubs where aspirational stakes could be converted into concrete stakes are those operated by the relevant state institutions (e.g., the ministry of petroleum resources) and the mining industry—the rentier landlord

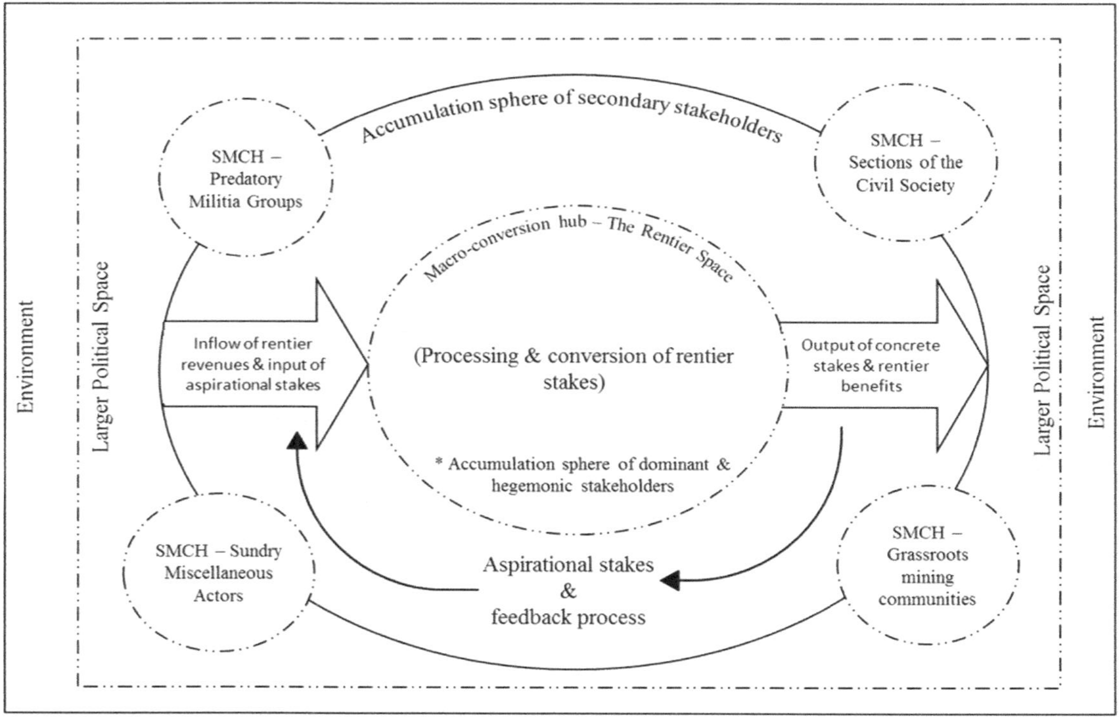

SMCH: Subservient Micro-Conversion Hub

Fig. 4.1 Patterns of accumulation in the typical African rentier state (*Source* Developed by the author)

and co-landlord as it were. These could be labelled the macro-conversion hubs. The mining industry is an amalgam of the state-owned mining corporations, TNCs (some of which operate diverse kinds of partnership ventures with the state) and the indigenous private sector (some of which have joint partnerships with the TNCs or are fronted by the latter). Consequently, the mining industry may represent diverse sub-sectoral stakes or interests. For instance, in a typical oil-rich rentier economy the sub-sectoral stakes might include oil exploration, production, shipping and export, refining and processing, marketing and distribution, servicing and maintenance, etc. (Solomon 2011). As such, the mining industry does not necessarily represent a monolithic interest and, similarly, the interests of the industry are not invariably consistent with the interests of the state and its top officials. However, because of the disproportionate and sometimes vulnerable reliance of the rentier state on rentier revenues, there exists a predictably high level of companionability and tolerance (call it a marriage of convenience) between the mining rent-dependent state and the mining industry. The state desperately needs a regular inflow of revenues from the mining rents to sustain the domestic politics of squanderation, patronage extravaganza and the consumerist economy at large while the mining sector requires the goodwill of the state to retain mining concessions and, to a lesser extent, guarantee security around the mining areas (Omeje 2006; Akpomera 2015). Similarly, the mining sector may require the goodwill of the state or, as is often the case, simply take advantage of its weak institutionality to maximize operational profits by local exploitation of labour, minimal corporate environmental and social responsibility and a host of other unwholesome contrivances (Deibert 2013).

Besides the macro-conversion hubs operated by the state and mining sector, there may similarly exist within the rentier space some micro-conversion hubs at the level of the (un)civil and grassroots society stakeholders; however these subservient micro-hubs rarely have an independent life of their own as they, by and large, derive their rentier current from their connection with or predation of the macro-hubs. An example of a micro-conversion hub operation is the occasional money some mining companies payout to local community chiefs as informal royalty and compensation for mining land expropriation and destruction of unharvested farm crops and economic trees (Omeje 2013). Such an occasional doling out of funds to local community chiefs or community leaders have almost invariably triggered a flurry of disbursement claims from many families and community members, allegations of fund embezzlement by the chiefs which too often results in varying levels of implosive conflict (Okonta and Douglas 2003; Deibert 2013).

The nature and configuration of the rentier space is context-specific and dynamic but given the decisiveness of rentier revenues in a rentier economy it is evident that the state and mining industry are the dominant stakeholders.

Box 4.1 Distinguishing Between the Territorial State and Institutional State in Rentier Politics

From a neo-Weberian perspective, an important distinction must be made between the territorial state and the institutional state. The territorial state is the state defined from the more legalistic Westphalian perspective in which a state is characterized by the existence of:

1. A defined territory and population.
2. A standing army or security forces.
3. A central government that has a monopoly of the legitimate use of coercive force within the territory.
4. Recognition of the state and its government by other states among the comity of states (juridical sovereignty).

Given the fact that many states in Africa and other developing regions vitiate from the Westphalian benchmark, a number of adjectival qualifiers have been adopted in defining and theorizing the African state, and the state in developing regions (e.g., weak state, fragile state, neopatrimonial state, rentier state and so forth). However, these adjectival qualifications are essentially academic because one cannot empirically sustain the argument that all the states in Europe (including struggling Albania, Bosnia and Herzegovina, Ukraine and Romania) are stronger than all the states in Africa in terms of institutional, security and economic viability.

Be that as it may, the institutional state can be loosely defined as the executive apparatus of government, and the gamut of formal and informal institutions and agencies that are linked to the dominance of hegemonic power at any given time. In most territorial rentier states, the institutional rentier state stands out either in isolation or in association with the mining industry (or sometimes with just a section of the industry such as the leading TNCs) as the "hegemonic stakeholder." This by no means implies that the institutional rentier state itself is a coherent force.

Too often, and depending on the historical and political struggles that have characterized the evolution of the state, the institutional rentier state can be a fragile coalition of social agencies purportedly representing salient (sub)ethnic, (sub)provincial, sectarian, cultural, business and other allied interests. Because the institutional state is usually structured into central and subnational administrative levels, stakeholders within the institutional state are correspondingly drawn from various levels that by no means wield equal measure of power and influence. Political power in general is fluid, likewise the significance of agencies that wield power in relation to others at different times, be they individual stakeholders or subnational states and institutions.

Beyond the dominant and hegemonic stakeholders, there is a myriad of subordinate or secondary stakeholders which operate from the civil society, grassroots communities and the larger political space. Some of them include specific opposition parties, NGOs, professional bodies, women's groups, cultural associations, community vigilantes, civil militia groups, regional and international organizations, etc. What distinguishes the secondary stakeholders from many other similar organizations and agencies is the issue of group perception that they (or in some cases the group they are acting on their behalf) have a stake in the "collective rentier resources" and more importantly, the articulation of some kind of strategies to press for the perceived claim or entitlement. In fact, the combination of perception and strategizing for rentier stakes is what ultimately gives rise to the politics of stakeholderization. Depending on their overall strategies and the intensity and impact of their activism, some secondary stakeholders can be reckoned as more active and consequential than others. A prolonged lack of consequential strategy and activism can render a stakeholder dormant or completely irrelevant. A stakeholder can also quietly give up its entitlement claim/pursuit or be forced by an overwhelming circumstance to do so, a tendency that can be described as destakeholderization. In practical terms, the relative fluidity of the rentier space which is partly explained by the preponderant self-serving tendency of rentier politics, entails a great measure of permeability between one category or segment of stakeholding and another. Hence, it is possible for an individual actor to start off as a civil society-based secondary stakeholder and over time advance to become a mining industry-based dominant stakeholder and ultimately an institutional state-based hegemonic stakeholder. A somewhat reverse trend can also be discerned in many African countries but perhaps to a lesser extent. The rentier state executive occasionally uses the direct appointment of vocal opposition figures to top government positions as a soft means to build elite consensus and silence opposition. This Machiavellian tactic was ingeniously perfected by ex-President Mobutu Sese Seko in former Zaire and ex-President Ibrahim Babangida in Nigeria during the heyday of pro-democracy campaigns in Africa in the 1980 and 1990s. Since assuming the reins of power in Cameroon in 1982, President Paul Biya has continued to rely on this method to "buy out" his political opponents some of whom were to be later dismissed and incarcerated by his government under allegations of corruption. Rentier stakes rise, mutate, become [partially] achieved and fall over time, and so do the stakeholders that champion them.

Box 4.2 Strategies for Transitioning from a Rentier State to a Transformative State

Natural resource rents generally produce and attract a multiplicity of competitive stakeholders, both domestic and external, in the resource-rich states, making a stakeholder analytical framework to the understanding of the patterns and dynamics of rentier accumulation imperative. The competition and jostling of stakeholders for access to, and appropriation of, rentier resources is too often an antagonistic process in many emerging economies that have consequences and implications for violent conflict. Content-specific nuances and variations in accumulation processes and the correlated conflicts abound, which can be accounted for using empirical case studies, but this does not however occlude the prevalence of some general patterns in the politics of stakeholder accumulation. The latter clearly calls for bolder explanatory paradigms and metanarratives.

It is pertinent to emphasize that stakeholder relations are not only adversarial and conflictual as seems to be the case in many rentier states but could also be relations of cooperation, co-governance and development—what one could call a transformative state model. A transformative state demands a [conflict] transformation, "good governance" and development-driven agenda. Furthermore, a transformative state model of stakeholder relations in natural resource governance is one that is based on the principles of:

1. Transparency
2. Public accountability
3. Devolution

4. Multi-stakeholder participation and sustainability throughout the natural resource value chain
5. An effective constitutional order.

The proposed framework involves the steps from the extraction of natural resources, to their processing and sale, all the way through to the ultimate use of the revenues, which if well managed, will help in ensuring that, as opposed to breeding conflicts, natural resource wealth transforms into citizens' wellbeing (cf. Collier 2008; Natural Resource Governance Institute, n.d.).

To be most effective, the state has to perform more of a regulatory, managerial, supervisory and service-delivery function as opposed to being an instrument for self-serving rentier accumulation. Changing the outlook and role of the state and empowering it to perform decisive regulatory and service-delivery functions is a major step towards deconstructing the obnoxious African rentier states and transforming them into more purposeful and functional development-driven states. Botswana probably represents one of the closest approximations of a transformative state model of natural resource governance in Africa, and one that calls for a focused empirical study with a view to exploring how the positive lessons could help to influence natural resource governance policies and practices in some of the most challenged economies (see Box 2.2). Clearly, the way out of the resource curse trap lies through a transformative state model of stakeholder politics in natural resource governance.

Summary Points

1. There was a uniform failure of governance and development across Africa after the first two decades of independence, especially across the countries richly endowed with valuable mineral resources. It was a failure that squandered the great hope held across many parts of Africa and beyond that independence was going to transform African countries and economies.
2. The catastrophic failure of development and governance was followed by political instability and armed conflicts in several natural resource-rich countries precipitating the theory and debate of "resource curse" in the international political economy literature.
3. The resource curse debate is associated with a heavy indictment of the African governing elites and their business collaborator—the

joint culprits behind the rentier character of the state and pervasive looting of the national treasury and sovereign resources of the people. Some of the typical examples of the natural resource-cursed states frequently cited in literature are DRC, Sierra Leone, Liberia, Nigeria, Sudan, South Sudan, Chad, Guinea and Angola.

4. Most expatriate mining companies operating in Africa make huge gains through transfer pricing in goods and services across national boundaries, tax evasion and avoidance, as well as by relatively underpaying labour, and minimizing corporate environmental and social responsibilities.
5. It is pertinent to mention that all the natural resource-rich states in Africa are not afflicted with the syndrome of resource curse. Botswana, a diamond-rich Southern African state has been well-governed since independence and has efficiently used its natural resource wealth to develop the country. Algeria and Tanzania are highly endowed with natural resources but have not typically had problems of resource curse.
6. Natural resource rents produce and attract a multiplicity of competitive stakeholders, both domestic and external, in the resource-rich states, whose activities and relations may sometimes lead to conflicts.
7. There are circumstances in which stakeholder relations in rentier states may not be adversarial but cooperative and transformative. The latter needs to be constructively cultivated to help counteract the self-serving accumulation tendencies that threaten political stability and development in most rentier states.

Discussion Questions

1. Why did the great expectation in the early postcolonial years that independence would lead to African development transformation prove abortive?
2. What do you understand by the term resource curse?
3. Is the concept of resource curse still analytically use? Explain in detail.
4. Describe the features of a rentier state?
5. What is the meaning of the term "rentier space"?

6. How do stakeholders' activities and politics generate conflict in a "rentier space?"

Acknowledgements An earlier version of this chapter was originally published in *Comparative & Commonwealth Politics* (CCP) with the following reference citation: Kenneth Omeje. 2016. Natural Resource Rent and Stakeholder Politics in Africa: Towards a New Conceptualisation. *Commonwealth & Comparative Politics* 54 (1): 92–114. I am grateful to the editors of CCP for granting me permission to revise and use the article in this book. The original article published in CCP can be accessed from the following website of the journal: https://www.tandfonline.com/.

Note

1. Reuters News (12 June 2020) "Acacia Mining Disputes Tanzania Audit as Shares Sink", https://www.reuters.com/article/acacia-mining-tanzania-idUSL8N1J91MB.

References

Ademola, Araoye. 2012. *Cote d'Ivoire: The Conundrum of the Still Wretched of the Earth*. Trenton, NJ: Africa World Press.

Africa Confidential. 2013. Spotlight on Queensway Group, 1July 2013. https://www.africa-confidential.com/article-preview/id/10942/Spotlight_on_Queensway_Group.

Akpomera, Eddy. 2015. International Crude Oil Theft: Elite Predatory Tendencies in Nigeria. *Review of African Political Economy* 42/143: 156–165.

Al Jazeera. 2013. Somalis Divided on London Conference, 8 May 2013. Al Jazeera. https://www.aljazeera.com/indepth/features/2013/05/20135813458147737.html.

Allison, Simon. 2019. Tanzania's Mining Dispute Ends – But at What Cost?" *Mail & Guardian*, October 23. https://mg.co.za/article/2019-10-23-00-tanzanias-mining-dispute-ends-but-at-what-cost/.

Auty, R.M. 1993. *Sustaining Development in Mineral Economies: The Resource Curse Thesis*. London: Routledge.

Balthasar, Dominik. 2013. The 2013 London Conference on Somalia: 'New Deal' But Old Principles? http://blogs.lse.ac.uk/africaatlse/2013/05/28/the-2013-london-conference-on-somalia-new-deal-but-old-principles-somalia2013/.

Basedau, Mathhias, and Jann Lay. 2009. Resource Curse or Rentier Peace? The Ambiguous Effects of Oil Wealth and Oil Dependence on Violent Conflict. *Journal of Peace Research* 46 (6): 757–776.

Basildon, Peta. 2002. Africa's Leaders Stole $140 Billion. *Independent*, June 14. https://www.independent.co.uk/news/world/africa/africas-leaders-stole-140bn-180078.html.

BBC News. 2013. Kofi Annan: Africa Plundered by Secret Mining Deals. BBC News, May 10. http://www.bbc.co.uk/news/world-africa-22478994.

BBC News. 2014. Corruption Across EU 'Breath-taking'—EU Commission. BBC News, February 3, 2014. http://www.bbc.co.uk/news/world-europe-26014387.

Beblawi, H. 1987. The Rentier State in the Arab World. In *The Rentier State*, ed. Hazem Beblawi and Giacomo Luciani, 85–98. New York: Croom Helm.

Berry, T. 1999. *The Great Work: Our Way into the Future*. New York: Bell Tower.

Bratton, Michael. 1998. Second Elections in Africa. *Journal of Democracy* 9 (3): 51–66.

Bryson, M. John. 2004. What to Do When Stakeholders Matter: Stakeholder Identification and Analysis Techniques. *Public Management Review* 6 (1): 21–53.

Buchholz, A. Rogene, and Sandra B. Rosenthal. 2005. Toward a Contemporary Conceptual Framework for Stakeholder Theory. *Journal of Business Ethics* 58: 137–148.

Collier, Paul. 2008. *The Bottom Billion: Why the Poor Countries Are Failing and What Can Be Done About It*. Oxford: Oxford University Press.

Collier, Paul, and A. Hoefller. 2000. *Greed and Grievance in Civil War*. World Bank. http://www.worldbank.org/research/conflict/papers/greedgrievance_23oct.pdf. Website accessed on 28 April 2012.

Cooper, Ryan. n.d. Why African Independence Was Such a Disaster. *This Week*. https://theweek.com/articles/574386/why-african-independence-such-disaster.

Deibert, Michael. 2013. *The Democratic Republic of Congo: Between Hope and Despair*. New York: Zed Books.

Dibua, I. Jeremiah. 2006. *Modernization and the Crisis of Development in Africa*. Aldershot: Ashgate.

Dunning, Thad. 2008. *Crude Democracy: Natural Resource Wealth and Political Regimes*. Cambridge: Cambridge University Press.

Frankel, Jeffery. 2010. *The Natural Resource Curse: A Survey*. Harpel Professor of Capital Formation and Growth: Harvard University.

Fremond, Olivier. 2000. The Role of Stakeholders. OECD Paper, October. http://www.oecd.org/daf/ca/corporategovernanceprinciples/1930657.pdf.

Freeman, R. Edward. 1984. *Strategic Management: A Stakeholder Approach*. Boston, MA: Pitman.

Gardner. 2013. EU Hails 'New Deal' for Somalia. European Voices, September 17. https://www.politico.eu/article/eu-hails-new-deal-for-somalia/.

Global Witness. 2012. *Rigged? The Scramble for Africa's Oil, Gas and Minerals.* A Special Report by Global Witness, January. http://gcs.dowjones.com/wp-content/uploads/2012/03/Global-Witness_RIGGED-The-Scramble-for-Africas-oil-gas-and-minerals-1.pdf. Website accessed on 10 March 2013.

Goldthau, Andreas, and Witte Jan Martin (eds.). 2010. *Global Governance: The New Rules of the Game.* Washington, DC: Brookings Institution Press.

Hawley, Susan. 2019. The UK Is Becoming More Corrupt and Our Democracy Is at Stake. Metro News, 1 February 2019. https://metro.co.uk/2019/02/01/the-uk-is-becoming-more-corrupt-and-our-democracy-is-at-stake-8418561/.

Heilbrunn, John. 2014. *Oil, Democracy and Development in Africa.* Cambridge: Cambridge University Press.

Hlavac, Marek. 2010. Comments on Benjamin Smith (2004): Oil Wealth and Regime Survival in the Developing World, 1960–1999. MPRA Paper No. 25797. http://mpra.ub.unimuenchen.de/25797/1/MPRA_paper_25797.pdf.

ICRA. 1997. Stakeholders – Key Concepts. ICRA. http://www.icra-edu.org/objects/anglolearn/Stakeholders-Key_Concepts.pdf.

Ismail, Kareem. 2010. The Structural Manifestations of the Dutch Disease: The Case of Exporting Countries. *IMF Working Paper*, WP/10/103. http://test.revenuewatch.org/rwiresources.071811/sites/default/files/Dutch%20Disease%20(IMF)%20Newest%20Version.pdf.

Joseph, Richard. 1987. *Democracy and Prebendal Politics in Nigeria: The Rise and Fall of the Second Republic.* Cambridge: Cambridge University Press.

Karl, Terry Lynn. 1997. *The Paradox of Plenty: Oil Boom and Petro-Politics.* Berkeley: University of California Press.

Klein, Naomi. 2007. *The Shock Doctrine: The Rise of Disaster Capitalism.* Toronto: Knopf Canada.

Lehrer, Jim. 2007. Analyzing the Natural Resource Curse. PBS News Hour. http://www.pbs.org/newshour/extra/teachers/lessonplans/world/conflict_diamonds_natural_resource_curse.pdf. website accessed on 2 February 2012.

Luciani, Giacomo. 1997. Allocation versus Production States: A Theoretical Framework. In *The Rentier State*, ed. Hazem Beblawi and Giacomo Luciani. New York: Croom Helm.

Magrin, Geraud, and Geert van Vliet. 2009. The Use of Oil Revenues in Africa. In *Governance of Natural Resources in Africa: Unfinished Business*, ed. Jacques Lesourne and William C. Ramsey, 103–164. Paris: IFRI.

Mailey, J.R. 2015. *The Anatomy of the Resource Curse: Predatory Investment in Africa's Extractive Industries* (ACSS Special Report No. 3). Washington, DC. African Center for Strategic Studies (ACSS).

Mbembe, Achille. 2001. *On the Postcolony*. Berkeley, CA: University of California Press.

Minerva Analytics. 2019. OECD Sets Out International Corporate Tax Proposal, October 12. https://www.manifest.co.uk/oecd-sets-out-international-corporate-tax-proposal/.

Moyo, Dambisa. 2009. *Dead Aid: Why Aid Is Not Working and How There Is Another Way for Africa*. New York: Penguin Books.

Ngoie, T. Germain, and Kenneth Omeje. 2008. Rentier Politics and Low Intensity Conflicts in the DRC: The Case of Kasai and Katanga Provinces. In *Extractive Economies and Conflicts in the Global South: Multi-Regional Perspectives on Rentier Politics*, ed. K. Omeje, 137–150. Aldershot, UK: Ashgate.

Okonta, Ike, and Oronto Douglas. 2003. *Where Vultures Feast: Shell, Human Rights and Oil in the Niger Delta*. London: Verso Publishers.

Omeje, Kenneth. 2006. *High Stakes and Stakeholders: Oil Conflict and Security in Nigeria Aldershot*. UK: Ashgate.

Omeje, Kenneth. 2008. Extractive Economies and Conflicts in the Global South: Re-Engaging Rentier Politics. In *Extractive Economies and Conflicts in the Global South: Multi-Regional Perspectives on Rentier Politics*, ed. K. Omeje, 1–26. Aldershot, UK: Ashgate.

Omeje, Kenneth. 2013. Avoiding the Natural Resource Curse: Lessons from Nigeria and Policy Implications. *Africa Insight* 42/4: 91–103.

Omeje, Kenneth. 2015. Debating Postcoloniality in Africa. In *The Crises of Postcoloniality in Africa*, ed. Kenneth Omeje, 1–27. Dakar: CODESRIA Books.

Reed, S. Mark. 2009. Who's in and Why? A Typology of Stakeholder Analysis Methods for Natural Resource Management. *Journal of Environmental Management* 90: 1933–1949.

Reno, William. 1998. *Warlord Politics and African States*. Lynne Rienner Publishers.

Ross, L. Michael. 2012. *The Oil Curse: How Petroleum Wealth Shapes the Development of Nations*. Princeton: Princeton University Press.

Smith, Benjamin. 2004. Oil Wealth and Regime Survival in the Developing World, 1960-1999. *American Journal of Political Science* 48 (2): 232–246.

Solomon, M.H. 2011. A Conceptual Approach to Evaluating the Political Economics of Mining in Africa and the Sector's Contribution to Economic Diversification. *The Journal of Southern African Institute of Mining and Metallurgy* 111 (July): 475–492.

UK Government FCO. 2013. Somalia Conference 7 May 2013: Key Outcomes. Foreign and Commonwealth Office (FCO). https://www.gov.uk/government/news/somalia-conference-7-may-2013-key-outcomes. Website accessed on 15 July 2013.

VoA. 2013. EU Pledges $860 Million for Somalia Reconstruction. Voice of America (VoA), September 17 https://www.hiiraan.org/news4/2013/Sept/41162/eu_pledges_860_million_for_somalia_reconstruction.aspx.

Wantchekon, Leonard, and Nathan Jensen. 2004. Resource Wealth and Political Regimes in Africa. *Comparative Political Studies* 37 (7): 816–841.

World Bank. n.d. What Is Stakeholder Analysis? http://www1.worldbank.org/publicsector/anticorrupt/PoliticalEconomy/PDFVersion.pdf.

CHAPTER 5

Dysfunctional Versions of Capitalism and the Political Economy of "Eating"

The greatest problem with dysfunctional capitalism is that it makes a total nonsense and mockery of the economics of policy planning, choice, reforms, resource allocation, growth and development.

5.1 The Institutional and Policy Framework

One of the widely held axioms of the rational choice theory in sections of mainstream behavioural economics, regardless of any mathematicized claims to scientific objectivity, is the assumption that political and economic actors in public life and corporate businesses are rational actors, and would invariably make the most rational calculations and choices in the midst of competing options that would ultimately be beneficial to the economy and society based on all the rational information at their command. That's strictly in an ideal world, certainly not in a dysfunctional capitalist economy. If governance is about public good, in the short or long term, then there are probably more irrational than rational actors wherever capitalism predominantly dysfunctions as in many of the African states. I am not by any means disputing the economics of choice, but the rationality of many government policy choices viewed from a basic governance, development and public good perspective is certainly questionable.

K. Omeje, *The Failure and Feasibility of Capitalism in Africa*, International Political Economy Series,
https://doi.org/10.1007/978-3-030-75170-8_5

I have argued in Sects. 1.4 and 2.1 that the African postcolonial elites who inherited power at independence progressively devised pragmatic ways of tinkering with the structures of the colonial frontier capitalism handed down to them in order to mainstream their own wealth accumulation interests in the neocolonial economy instead of genuinely transforming those structures to serve the interests of their people. This process was unleashed using the instrumentality of rule-making and the macroeconomic policy framework. In varied and diverse ways, the aggrandizing interests of the African governing elites, often tempered by those of their local business and expatriate partners, have majorly shaped the crafting and/or implementation of several economic development policies since the early postcolonial years. During the Cold War era, an avalanche of publications was churned out on this issue, especially by leftist political economists. A large part of the literature zeroed on dissection and analysis of the leading industrialization policies of most states which focused on import substitution and indigenization or nationalization of foreign enterprises, in most cases partial nationalization. Experts like Samir Amin (1976), Claude Ake (1981) and Bjorn Beckman (1982) repeatedly unmasked the hidden coalition of interests that informed these policies and how they promoted wealth accumulation by the dominant economic classes but ultimately represented bad economics and deformed development for the African states. The view that import-substitution industrialization was fundamentally anti-development was originally popularized by Latin American scholars of the dependency school of political economy such as Celso Furtado, Theotônio dos Santos and Andre Gunder Frank whose region had suffered corresponding development sham.

In her diagnostic critique of the structure of import-substitution industrialization in Africa and the interplay of interests that ruined it, Lynn Mytelka revealed that what was actually practiced in Africa was "import reproduction" and not substitution, arguing that genuine import substitution is salutary and makes both economic and development sense, from a developing country's perspective. In illustrating the difference between import substitution and import reproduction Mytelka wrote:

> Import reproduction strategies such as those implemented throughout Africa take "product" as their point of departure, rather than "purpose." They thus ignore the extent to which products incorporate concepts of

> functionality, cost, quality and aesthetics that corresponds to the producer's principal market of sale. An import substitution strategy reverses this process by first identifying the purposes embodied in imported products, then determining their relevance to the local environment, and lastly by designing a product that conforms most closely to domestically available inputs, material and non-material. (Mytelka 1989: 79)

Carefully designed as enunciated, Mytelka asserts, import substitution is able to produce needed products with maximum local inputs and that can functionally become a substitute for previous imports and the two do not necessarily have to be exactly identical. This functional model was neither the concept nor experience of the so-called "import-substitution industrialization" adopted and practiced in Africa in the first two to three decades of independence, which Mytelka argued should be more appropriately called import reproduction. The latter was a product-driven model unsuitable for the African market and which sought to induce capital, engineering, management and marketing skills to flow from the global North to South and to ensure a domestic market for the goods that these imported factors could produce (Mytelka 1989: 79). To that end, tariff, exchange rate, wage, price, tax and credit policies were combined to create an environment within which investments in manufacturing would be profitable for foreign capital (Mytelka 1989: 79). In this practical way, some of the import reproduction experiments (not all) were consumeristic, white elephant, wasteful and a drain on foreign exchange reserves of states. In terms of the ultimate beneficiaries, import reproduction as practiced in Africa served the interests of the expatriate investors, subsidiaries of foreign multinationals, as well as local middlemen, top government officials and compradors who participated in the investment and transaction networks. The much-expected technology transfer and local content development hardly happened because of the ill-conceived nature of the industrialization projects. Sustainable development took a heavy toll. However, marginal growth and infant industrialization were discernible in diverse circumstances. Some of the national and subnational governments constructed industrial areas in their major towns and cities in countries like Egypt, Ghana, Algeria, Nigeria, Kenya, Tanzania, Cote Ivoire, Senegal, etc., in the early decades of independence which combined with pro-industrialization policy incentives encouraged the expansion of local manufacturing and FDIs in various sectors. This fledgling manufacturing sector later took a heavy toll from the consolidated ascendancy of rentier economies (especially oil and solid minerals), the economic crisis of the 1980s and 1990s, and the World Bank/IMF Structural Adjustment Programmes.

Indigenization and partial nationalization of foreign enterprises were bold industrial development policies which provided an opportunity to encourage home-grown capital formation for entrepreneurial development but in several cases the policies were conceived and implemented to primarily enhance the wealth accumulation interest of the local governing and privileged elite. Nigeria probably provides the most revealing African example. The federal government promulgated the Nigerian Enterprises Promotion Decree otherwise known as the Indigenization Decree in two instalments (1972 and 1977), and the aim was among other things to expand local equity participation in the largely expatriate-controlled productive sectors of the economy (mining, oil, banking, manufacturing, etc.). The Land Use Decree of 1978 (subsequently renamed the Land Use Act, 1979) was promulgated alongside to free land from the shackles of traditional tenure systems for largescale industrial and agricultural development by bestowing ownership of all lands comprised in the federation and the power of expropriation of land for overriding public purposes on the state governors (i.e., within the jurisdiction of each subnational state). Two public sector development banks were established by the government to help provide long-term soft credits to local investors willing to take advantage of the government's entrepreneurial development policies in industry, commerce and agriculture. The two banks are the Nigerian Bank for Commerce and Industry (NBCI) and the Nigerian Agricultural Bank (NAB), both established in 1973. Later in 1978 NAB was renamed the Nigerian Agricultural and Cooperative Bank (NACB) with a tweaked mandate to support farmers' cooperatives. Many top civil servants, military officers and local businessmen took loans from the government development banks to finance substantial equity investments in the indigenized foreign enterprises, a few became local directors of the companies, and some others used the same credit facilities to set up or grow private enterprises across diverse sectors of the economy, but these loans were hardly recovered. A considerable number of the original big shots that benefitted from these government policies ultimately became national tycoons and top politicians in the various dispensations of civilian democracy.

In a more recent study on Nigeria, Matthew Page (2018), a nonresident scholar at the Carnegie Endowment for International Peace, has documented how the Nigerian federal government in the name of boosting local manufacturing grants import duty waivers to firms controlled by ruling party financiers, making the government incur a loss of $2.8 billion in revenues due to such import waivers over a five-year period (2011–2015), but with hardly any positive impact on the manufacturing sector which has declined steadily since the 1970s. Many African governments sometimes use import and export tariffs not necessarily in the most effective ways that can stimulate growth or foster productive capital formation, but to reward and favour influential patrons, financiers and cronies. Also, the application of fiscal measures like import and export tariffs is so erratic that governments can suddenly ban or unban the importation of certain products simply to privilege one or two influential financiers or to hurt the business of their perceived adversaries. This has happened time and again in Nigeria, and Page highlighted just a few of them in his research cited above.

Access to foreign currency in the face of the differential exchange rates between the official government rate and the parallel exchange or market rates is another highly manipulated policy measure that enables unproductive accumulation among the privileged and well-connected few at the expense of the real productive sectors of the economy and the overall macroeconomic performance. In several African countries, the foreign currency black market is substantially funded by influential politicians and public office holders who are given access to foreign currencies at the state-subsidized official rates, and then taking advantage of the "parallel premium"[1] sells to the black market. With little or no access to foreign currency at the official rate to pay for necessary imports and services, many genuine local investors and entrepreneurs are compelled to source foreign currencies from the more expensive parallel markets. This drives up production costs and even shuts down some otherwise thriving businesses. The parallel premium forex business is a big one in virtually all the African countries that have parallel exchange rates. It is a corruption-ladden device that defeats some of the key rationales for operating parallel currency markets—to insulate international reserves and domestic prices from shocks to the balance of payments and also privilege important financial transactions that can add value to the local economy (Kiguel and O'Connell 1995).

In most African short-term democracies, every change of government, and sometimes even a cabinet reshuffle, usually results in a new set of patronage-driven policy guidelines and measures that often reflect the dynamics of power struggles within the ruling party or coalition to enhance individual accumulation. In this way, the institutional and policy environment is ridden with parlous uncertainties and shenanigans which are disastrous for investments and business.

The African Power and Politics Programme (APPP) et al. found in an empirical study they published in 2012 that policy priorities and development outcomes in Africa, to a large extent, depend on the political incentives facing political leaders (APPP et al. 2012: 2;10). The political incentives range from winning elections and remaining in power to maintaining ruling coalitions, and creating necessary opportunities for close entrepreneurs in the economy which will ultimately benefit the public office holder in diverse ways. In theory, the issue of political leaders in Africa considering political incentives when faced with policy priorities may not be fundamentally different from the nature of democratic politics in different regions of the world. However, in practice, the African model is vitiated by a pathological level of patron-clientelism and rentier-type accumulation that is highly inimical to the business climate, investment and development.

The economic growth of recent years as argued in Chapter 2 has failed to substantially mitigate the high levels of extreme poverty and youth unemployment, especially against the backdrop of inadequate service delivery by the state (e.g., education, healthcare, water and electricity) and changing demographics—the youth bulge, and rural–urban migration, etc. Governments will need highly ingenious super-growth, wealth creation, job creation and income redistribution strategies to be able to make the necessary sustainable development impact. However, this is unlikely due to several local and international limitations. From a governance perspective, the greatest challenge that African states face in the context of the dominant neoliberal democratic framework is the enormous "rentier-type" resources required to service the patron–client system of politics in many countries which impairs the capacity and resources for development.

APPP et al. (2012: 10) observed in their study that in most African liberal democratic states, policies are often adopted that facilitate an uncoordinated and competitive "rent-seeking" by individuals or factions within the political and economic elite of the country. The authors use the concept of rent-seeking in a more generic sense that goes beyond the rentier state type I discussed in chapter four to imply "all those income flows which are additional to normal market-based profits and wages" including "revenues from natural and administratively created monopolies, subsidies, natural resources and, not least important, corruption and aid" (APPP et al. 2012: 10). Given the fact that the state and state power are largely perceived as mechanisms for personal enrichment and for meeting the demands of crucial groups and cronies, a huge patronage culture is fostered which is inimical to growth and development. Capital formation in the private sector in most African countries remains substantially small and mainly depends on patronage inflow, inflated contracts and looted funds from the state. In the context of weak institutional and law enforcement frameworks that can hardly rein in unruly non-state actors, let alone powerful political office holders and their cronies, impunity becomes an instrumentalized method of wealth accumulation which puts the economy on a dysfunctional trajectory.

The study of social and political institutions, and the conditions under which they can function or dysfunction is a long-researched subject in political science and sociology, among other social science disciplines. Most of the literature, which tend to focus on the state and its institutions, as well as on the society and its subsisting structures can be found within the scholastic ambit of theories of institutionalism, functionalism and structural functionalism (cf. Ake 1982; Barnard 2019). Some sociologists and economists have also extended the theories of institutionalism and structural functionalism to the study of large organizations, business corporations and the macroeconomy. In a large sense, these are theories concerned with how social order is constructed and maintained in society, states, social organizations and economic systems, as well as the place of individuals and social groups in the overall process. For order to be maintained, the integrity and interests of the whole must have primacy over those of its individual parts. Social institutions exist and operate within a sociocultural context with set values, norms and expectations for individual actors, groups and agencies, and as well as impose constraints on their actions, behaviours and relations. Social order is preserved when this arrangement operates or functions at its best, but may faulter when this socially constructed arrangement derails or dysfunctions. Dysfunctionality at its worst could spiral into violence and armed conflict. Proponents argue that social systems can function effectively or dysfunction at different levels—subnational, national, regional and international levels. Institutions, states, and economies can function effectively in whole or in parts but can also dysfunction. Dysfunctionality is a process and not a permanent state. As such, all aspects and incidents of dysfunctionality are subject to the variabilities constituted in space and time.

Without going into the specific assumptions, arguments, applications and limitations of each theory, it suffices to acknowledge that these theories of self-contained entities hardly take into considerations the destabilising impact of exogenous forces such as one vicious state invading a well-functioning stable state by an act of aggression. Clearly, there are many criticisms and limitations of these social system theories that apparently reached the peak of their discursive power in the 1980s, and since then have been on a slow decline.

Most studies on dysfunctionality are focused on the state. In the African context, Christopher Clapham edited an important book in 2006 titled *Big African States* in which, focusing on case studies of six big African states—Angola, DRC, Ethiopia, Nigeria, South Africa and Sudan—the chapter contributors revealed how their relative dysfunctionalities have not only hindered their capacities to deliver the highly needed political and economic development to their people, but also scuttled the expectation that they would ultimately stimulate regional transformation and development. “At the operational level, the dysfunctionality of African institutions can be explained by the dearth of responsible and ethical leadership on the continent, growing political alienation on the part of the African citizenry, inadequate state capacity to enforce rules, and limited economic opportunities, which encourages individuals and groups to subvert state institutions for rent seeking and the illegal accumulation of wealth” (SAIIA 2015).

5.2 The Dysfunctioning Process

Capitalism largely dysfunctions in contemporary Africa. The fundamentals essentially do not work. The reasons should be obvious by now following my analysis of the history, nature and political contexts of capitalism in the continent in Chapters 1–4. But to recap in simple terms, the driving motive behind dysfunctional capitalism is personal enrichment using state power, directly or indirectly. The logic behind it can be extrapolated *mutatis mutandi* from the 2009 epic rendition of the renowned British journalist and African correspondent Michela Wrong centred on Kenyan politics, *It's Our Turn to Eat*. The reasoning goes like this. We have been hungry and starved for so long. Now we have the power and we don't know for how long. Things can be unpredictably unstable over here and too many desperately want to get their hands on the pie. It is our turn to eat and we must make the most of it. Anybody that wants to help us eat—"a useful idiot"[2]—wherever they may come from, could get their own share. Let the masses eat the crumps and any leftovers!

Undeniably, the logic is backward-thinking economics—reverse economics, if you like, but that's in a nutshell the political economy of eating or squanderation! Even in corrupt dictatorships that have the benefit of longevity (e.g., the regimes of Obiang in Equatorial Guinea, Mswati in Eswatini and Denis Sassou Nguesso in the Republic of Congo) the logic is the same because most ruthless dictatorships end abruptly, especially when prebendal corruption and impoverishment of the people are added vices. There is more detail on the Kenyan corruption scandal investigated by Ms Wrong in Sect. 6.3. In some countries like Nigeria and Kenya, the predatory "eaters" too often overstep into the crumps and leftovers meant for the masses. Pension funds for retirees, benefits for the dead, food and funds for "internally displaced persons" (IDPs), agricultural subsidies for rural farmers, disaster and emergency relief supplies and funds, etc., are callously "eaten" by privileged overseers and managers of these government funds. Monthly wages of civil servants, schoolteachers and ordinary workers can be delayed for months while the elected executive office holders and their too many appointees that plunder state resources are officially over-paid for their services, and for some of them, "eating services." On coming to power in 2015, President Buhari of Nigeria approved a bailout package of about $2.1 billion or 413.7 billion Naira, shared between the federal government and 27 state governments, to help offset a backlog of salaries of hundreds of thousands of government workers (Winsor 2015). Some of the state governments were owing their workers up to ten months' salaries. Less than two years after the federal government bailout, 12 states were still in the same position of non-payment of their employees' salaries, some for periods of 6–15 months (Vanguard, 25 April 2017). The bloated wages and fringe benefits of political leaders and plunderers of public wealth are never part of the unpaid or delayed salaries.

To a large extent, dysfunctional capitalism is a product of the dysfunctionality of the state. The greatest problem with dysfunctional capitalism is that it makes a total nonsense and mockery of the economics of policy planning, choice, reforms, resource allocation, growth and developments. Furthermore, the political culture of squanderisation that pervades dysfunctional capitalism is bad for politics because it inhibits and compromises the development, consolidation and performance of public institutions, including the all-important institutions meant to regulate the conduct of public office holders and all other actors in the political space. As a political culture, it also affects the larger society because many who cannot competitively enter the political space to "eat" inadvertently turn their micro-organizations and agencies into platforms and devices for squanderisation—schools, universities, classrooms, hospitals, NGOs, banks and financial institutions, and so forth—they all become "eating" devices for those in charge with the rare exception of those constrained by their moral conscience. This societal dimension, external to politics, only happens to the extent that "eating" becomes a pervasively entrenched culture in politics. It is a cultural spill-over effect. The culture of "eating" fundamentally threatens the institutionality and formal sovereignty of the state, further corroding the capacity of the state to effectively re-engineer capitalism and regulate the economy for the good of all. Inadvertently, the dysfunctioning of capitalism spirals.

In dysfunctional capitalism, bad politics trumps everything, including economics, and bad politics is an aphrodisiac. For want of an appropriate terminology, I prefer to call this aphrodisiac that pervades dysfunctional capitalism in Africa the curse of impunity. The latter is driven by the pervading logic that "I need to get my own share because everybody else does it and gets away with it." In the pursuit of self-interest using state power, many African leaders and politicians are not prepared to heed any mantra about the transcendental soul of mankind despite their being overly religious. Their souls are desperately mortgaged to gaining all they can by all means, regardless of any existential and transcendental consequences. Impunity is the norm of the game. Aggrandisement is the end of it. Because most Africans are profoundly religious, the governing elites in Africa have predominantly perfected how to use religion to strengthen their support base and to cover the art of "eating" with impunity.

I have argued in Chapter 2 that Africa inherited a disadvantageous brand of capitalism at independence known as frontier capitalism which transitioned into neocolonial capitalism as the indigenous nationalist elites took over the reins of power. Frontier capitalism of the colonial order was impregnated with Western accumulation interests. This status quo was not completely acceptable to the postcolonial elites that had control of political power in independent Africa. Bereft of any significant material foundations, they needed to get their hands on the economic ladder.

The governing elites therefore took advantage of their control of state power to devise diverse mechanisms of mainstreaming their interests in the inherited colonial economies, in most cases without overriding the interests of the ex-colonizers and other Western stakeholders, most of whom were welcome into the neocolonial economies post-independence. I have argued that in the process of tinkering with the inherited frontier capitalism to mainstream their own accumulation interests, the governing African postcolonial elites have succeeded in proliferating diverse contraptions of capitalism that have largely impeded the development of genuine forms of capitalism capable of accelerating growth and development on the continent. One of the key logics that drives the devised dysfunctional contraptions is the political economy of "eating" or squanderation. The governing postcolonial elites have not been alone in the economy tinkering process; they have been joined and aided by many external players and racketeers—the useful idiots *à la* John Sweeney.

In the following section, I will discuss the various caricature and grotesque versions of capitalism that have developed in postcolonial Africa. It is important to observe that the various capitalist brands and devices are not mutually exclusive.

5.3 Versions of Dysfunctional Capitalism in Africa

5.3.1 Oligarchic Capitalism

An oligarchy is a political system in which governing power rests on a small and powerful elite. The leveraging of political power to substantially own and control the national economy by the few elites and their cronies therefore creates oligarchic capitalism. Convoluted moments of political and economic transition in modern history have occasionally created opportunities for oligarchs to gain control of a state's economy by implementing self-serving policies. The most well-known example of oligarchic capitalism in recent history is the Russian example in which the country's economy was usurped by oligarchs following the shady series of privatization implemented in the aftermath of the collapse of the Soviet Union in 1991. In fact, the emergence of oligarchic capitalism in Russia during the regime of Boris Yeltsin (1991–1999) was a culmination of the deep-rooted graft and corruption by public office holders that infested the last stage of communism in the Soviet Union, provoking widespread disillusionment with the system. The oligarchs were predominantly former communist bureaucrats who were in charge of big public companies during the Soviet era and therefore when privatization of these companies was implemented as part of the dismantling of communist structures, they simply bought the assets and transformed their control into ownership rights (Martirosyan 2016). Under Boris Yeltsin, the Russian oligarchs played very powerful roles in the economy and political governance, controlling public policies, the media and influencing the outcomes of elections. However, under Vladimir Putin's regime, the influence of the Russian oligarchs in national politics and the economy has significantly diminished but not disappeared. The oligarchs have been significantly reined in and subjected to presidential authority. Similarly, their economic operations have been effectively brought under the regulatory oversight and tax regime of the state to minimize subversion and enhance growth. However, in his critique of the changed pattern of oligarchy in Putin's Russia in the *Shadow State*, Luke Harding (2020: 270) asserts that "under Putin, Russia had become a virtual Mafia state in which the government, its spy agencies, and organized crime had merged into a single entity."

5.3.2 *Major Variants of Oligarchic Capitalism in Africa*

Postcolonial Africa has been widely associated with extreme variants of oligarchic capitalism, notably crony capitalism and hostage capitalism.

5.3.3 *Crony Capitalism*

Andrew Palmer (2016) defines crony capitalism as a systemic process where corporations have corrupt relationships with government officials and politicians in order to obtain an undue advantage over competitors, or to take over public assets for nominal or unfair prices. Crony capitalism is a pattern of oligarchic accumulation rampant in the large natural resource-rich countries (rentier economies) like Nigeria, Angola and Libya, but also widely prevalent in some comparatively less endowed large economies like Egypt and Kenya. In fact, most of the African rentier economies operate a virulent brand of crony capitalism largely associated with powerful companies (multinationals and local firms) and individuals that secure contracts, jobs and similar advantages through political connections, bribery and other forms of impropriety (Omeje 2015).

Box 5.1 Crony Capitalism, Despotism and the Arab Spring in North Africa

Crony capitalism, prebendal graft, nepotism and brutality by state security forces were the defining characteristics of the North African states prior to the youth-led Arab Spring that began in December 2010 in Tunisia, and rapidly spread to Egypt, Libya and the Middle East. The Arab Spring was sparked off by the horrifying self-immolation of a Tunisia street vendor and young graduate Mohamed Bouazizi after his vegetable cart was confiscated by a police officer for not having the necessary permit. Bouazizi's self-immolation generated sentiments of public anger that boiled over into mass street protests calling for the abdication of the entrenched corrupt oligarchies that had ruled each of the affected North African countries for decades. The protests brought down the regimes of Ben Ali in Tunisia and Hosni Mubarak in Egypt, the former more peaceful than the latter, and resulted in an armed insurgency that ended the 42 years dictatorship of Muammar Gaddafi in Libya, supported by NATO's aerial firepower.

Despite their relatively functional economies, economic growth in the three Arab countries was greatly impeded by the entrenched crony capitalism, rapacious "eating," nepotism and despotism in these countries which created high youth unemployment levels in Tunisia and Egypt, and popular discontent in Libya. All the ruling families in the three rebellion-affected countries and their local and foreign cronies that managed the opaque transaction-ridden economies reaped extensive plunders that hugely diverted resources from public infrastructures and development.

Ghaddafi reportedly amassed excessive wealth from oil-rich Libya with a net worth of about $70 billion, same as Mubarak in Egypt with a net worth of about $70 billion while Ben Ali in Tunisia amassed about $17 billion.[3] At the time of writing, Libya was still war-torn, albeit the warring sides signed a ceasefire agreement in Geneva on 23 October 2020. A couple of previous negotiated peace plans fell apart. The war in Libya has seen a constellation of regional and extra-regional powers taking sides with local war factions despite international arms embargo in a battle that has increasingly moved towards who controls the highly endowed oil fields in the larger Sirte basin (McKernan 2020). Given the complexity of the protracted war, the latest ceasefire agreement comes as a welcome relief, but its implementation will require diligent commitment to continuous negotiation and execution by all parties, and UN monitoring oversight, to ensure effective withdrawal of troops, including the complete disengagement and repatriation of foreign fighters.

Tunisia has managed to build stable democratic institutions but with a struggling economy, and in Egypt the political space remains as suffocating as in the Mubarak years. The Egyptian economy is dominated by security services and state-owned enterprises while cronyism, prebendal squanderation and nepotism are still entrenched in Tunisia and Egypt, to a larger extent, where the public sector and corporate business dealings and services are characterized by informal and hidden corrupt transactions (Holmes 2020; Sahajwani 2020).

The President Abdul *Fattah al-Sisi's* regime in Egypt has systematically reversed all hopes for political freedom and accountable governance by intensifying authoritarian rule and the military domination of the economy and political life. Inflation and poverty levels have deteriorated. Like most of Egypt's former rulers, Al-Sisi has a military background; he was a former Army General and Minister of Defense under the short-lived democratically elected government of President Mohamed Morsi which was ousted by the Egyptian military in July 2013. Al-Sisi's regime has been expanding the economy through debt-driven stimulus and massive infrastructural development projects in which government-owned enterprises and the military establishment are the principal beneficiaries through a contract system ridden with nepotism and corruption.[4] The dominance of state-owned enterprises and the military establishment in virtually all key sectors of the economy stifles competition and relegates the private capitalist sector to a second fiddle role as a sub-contract seeking appendage to the powerful state forces that dominate the economy.

Crony capitalism is also widespread in the West (e.g., USA, Italy, Greece and Spain), but with significantly different dynamics, outcomes and impact on the overall economy. The greatest disadvantage of crony capitalism in the African context where there are weak regulatory institutions is that it keeps inefficient businesses afloat at the expense of their more productive counterparts, compromises quality service delivery, short-circuits investments in the dynamic sectors of the economy and ultimately makes it more difficult for new companies to enter the economy, thereby restricting growth (Palmer 2016). Ostensibly, many of the African billionaires and rent-seeking tycoons are products of crony capitalism (*The Economist*, 15 March 2014; Mihalyi 2014). The staggering wealth accumulated by some members of the family of the former Angolan President José Eduardo dos Santos, who ruled the oil-rich African country for 38 years (1979–2017) is attributable to nepotism and crony capitalism.

In 2013, the young daughter of the Angolan President Isabel dos Santos emerged from relative obscurity to become *Forbes* magazine's Africa's first female billionaire with a net worth of over US$2 billion. At a later stage in her father's regime when she was already a billionaire businesswoman, Isabel was appointed the chief executive of the state oil company Sonangol, one of the most powerful positions in the oil-rich country. With her father no longer in power to shield her controversial wealth, Isabel has faced multiple charges of corruption under the successor regime of President João Lourenco who also sacked her from heading Sonangol. Isabel has been accused of misappropriation and embezzlement of funds during her tenure at Sonangol, an accusation she denies as a politically motivated witch-hunt. On 31st December 2019, an Angolan court ordered that all of Ms Isabel's assets be frozen, which include her stakes in Unitel, Angola's biggest mobile phone company, and Fomento de Angola, a bank, as well as myriad smaller enterprises such as a supermarket, a cinema and a mall (*The Economist* 2020). Isabel dos Santos, her late husband Sindika Dokolo and associate Mario Leite da Silva were subject to an asset freeze after accusations of steering more than $1 billion from Sonangol and official diamond trader Sodiam to firms where they held stakes (OAN 2020). In February 2020, Portugal ordered a freeze on all the bank accounts of Isabel dos Santos and subjected them to criminal investigations following a request by the Angolan authorities. Isabel's half-brother, José Filomeno, who was the head of Angola's Sovereign Wealth Fund under their father's regime (but later sacked by President Lourenco) was charged in court with stealing $500 million from the fund and transferring it to a bank account in Switzerland over which he was convicted in August 2020 and jailed for five years (BBC News, 14 August 2020). The Angolan authorities claim that assets worth more than $24 billion were looted during the previous regime of ex-President Dos Santos, an amount that according to the government significantly exceeds the country's debilitating debt of $20.1 billion owed to China.

One of the most bizarre features of crony capitalism in the rent-seeking economies of Africa is that it entrenches the tendency among the political elites and their local business associates to loot the resources of the state with impunity, and in turn use the looted funds to privately buy the loyalties of large sections of the impoverished grassroots populations through charitable help and support. This paradigm of legitimizing stolen public funds is a squanderation-driven version of "trickle-down economics," a clear case of primitive wealth redistribution. In many rentier cultures like Nigeria, Kenya and DRC the political elites and their local business cronies have perfected the art of distribution of largesse to the grassroots populations through donations to charitable causes, such as community fundraising to build places of religious worship, and to support the clergy and similar religious concerns; provision of scholarships to some indigent students covering different levels of education, sponsoring of lavish marriage and funeral ceremonies for some of their acquaintances, aides and constituents; funding popular sporting events and local football clubs, and perhaps most importantly bankrolling some of their trusted loyalists who run for public offices in national elections. In the peculiar case of Kenya, the time-honoured *Harambee* culture where relatives, friends and well-wishers come together in times of need to support a loved one with quiet contributions has increasingly been bastardized by grandstanding "big eaters" who literally hijack the events to make pompous political speeches and dole out money to the applause of the excited masses. Even funeral ceremonies are not spared. The "eaters" increasingly sponsor or bankroll funerals and turn them into mini-campaign rallies even when the next election may well be three to four years away. "Big eaters" sponsor all manner of social and political events for their self-serving advantages, but the most important event they sponsor is the election bids of loyalists.

The practice of sponsoring loyalists for elective offices is considered a vital clientelist investment by grand looters or "big eaters" because it not only helps to safeguard their stolen wealth from the long arm of the anti-corruption law enforcement agencies (where such is active), but it also guarantees future looting opportunities through diverse kinds of corrupt dealings, especially when the "patron-eaters"[5] are no longer in power. There are also many grand looters and "patron-eaters" outside the official realms of power. In Africa, crony capitalism is a major instrument for nurturing, cultivating and perpetuating patron–client networks of accumulation, primitive wealth redistribution, distorted democracy, as well as a regressive culture of dependency and corruption.

5.3.4 Hostage Capitalism

Hostage capitalism is another oligarchic brand discernible in Africa. I adopt the concept of hostage capitalism, often associated with "state capture," to describe a brand of oligarchy in which powerful families, dynasties and businesses collude with top state officials to hijack the policy machinery of the state to advance their mutual interests. Hostage capitalism thrives on a complex network of policy distortion, subversion of due process, patronage, kickbacks, tax avoidance and evasion, and money laundering—in fact, all vicious devices that promote the collaborative accumulation agendas of "eaters" and "useful idiots." Oftentimes, the dirty proceeds of hostage capitalism are significantly recycled into party politics and to influence election outcomes.

One of the most publicized examples of hostage capitalism in contemporary Africa is the prolific scandals that plagued the Jacob Zuma regime in South Africa (2009–2018) and ultimately brought it down, which prompted the setting up of the famous Commission of Inquiry into Allegations of State Capture. The inquiry involves allegations that President Zuma compromised his office in his relationships with the multimillionaire Guptas family whose chain of companies secured lucrative contracts from South African governments and also employed several members of the Zuma family in top positions. Revelations from the inquiry indicate that the Guptas (three brothers of Indian origin) enjoyed enormous influence in the South African state and allegedly "captured" the state to the extent that they masterminded the appointment, promotion and dismissal of some ministers and senior government officials; weakened the laws of the state and neutralized the powers of the government agencies that could potentially enforce those laws (Arun 2019). Among the public bodies allegedly "captured" by the Guptas to serve their business interests under Jacob Zuma's regime "include the ministries of finance, natural resources and public enterprise, as well as the government agencies responsible for tax collection and communications, the state broadcaster SABC, the national carrier - South African Airways, the state-owned rail-freight operator Transnet and the energy giant Eskom - one of the world's largest utility companies" (Arun 2019). At the time of writing, investigation into allegations of state capture and other related offences was still ongoing under the Judicial Commission of Inquiry into the Allegations of State Capture set up by the South African President and headed by the country's Deputy Chief Justice Raymond Bondo. In total, an estimated $33 billion was allegedly siphoned from state coffers during the nine-year tenure of Jacob Zuma, which ended in 2018 amidst public outrage over graft and bitter infighting within the governing party (Goldbaum 2021).

Without trying to diminish the enormity of the South African scandal, it is apparent that what the South Africans have extensively publicized as evidence of state capture pales in comparison with similar events in some of the African countries discussed in this chapter. The fact that the South African state seems to be efficiently probing diverse allegations of grand-scale graft that happened during Zuma's regime with the possibility of launching criminal prosecutions is an indication of hope in the functional capacity and resilience of the state institutions. The extent to which the incident of state capture and other related graft incidents in post-Apartheid South Africa have affected the fundamentals of the South African economy needs to be more thoroughly investigated and analyzed by policy researchers.

The incidents or allegations of state capture are not peculiar to Africa. In both past and contemporary history, powerful elites have from time to time captured the state even in some developed countries to advance their corporate and self-serving agendas. In his famous book titled *State Capture,* Alexander Hertel-Fernandez (2019) explains how, since the 1970s, conservative activists, wealthy donors and big businesses constructed a right-wing "troika" to advance conservative legislations, and in the process fostering epochal shifts in the American political economy: the decline of unions, party polarization and the skyrocketing concentration of wealth in the hands of the "troika."

Less dramatic incidents of state capture and hostage capitalism are widely discernible in Africa's past and contemporary history (e.g., Mobutu Sese Seko's Zaire [now DRC], Omar Bongo's Gabon and Yahya Jammeh's The Gambia). Ostensibly, the most horrendous examples of state capture and hostage capitalism in contemporary Africa are Equatorial Guinea and Eswatini (formerly known as Swaziland). President Teodoro Obiang Nguema Mbasogo of Equatorial Guinea who has ruled the small oil-rich island since he ousted his uncle in a military coup in 1979 makes no pretence that the state is literally owned by him and his family who have ruled it as a patrimonial fiefdom since independence in 1968. The country's oil economy is controlled by a predatory oligarchy comprising the President's family, in-laws, kinsmen, cronies and a network of foreign experts who mainly dissipate the oil wealth through a kleptocratic contract system. Writing in 2017, Sarah Saadoun, researcher with Human Rights Watch stated that Equatorial Guinea's total budget was around US$5 billion a year, and some 80% of it (about US$4 billion) had gone into funding of grand infrastructure projects (e.g., multi-lane highways, prestigious villas for visiting dignitaries, and presidential palaces, helipads, hotels, etc.) in which members of the hegemonic oligarchy are the contract beneficiaries (Saadoun 2017; see also Massoko 2019). Only a pittance of the country's national budget goes to health and education with the result that literacy level and life expectancy are below the African average which is ironic for an oil-rich country that has a large GDP per capita of $9,168 (the third largest in Africa in 2019) and a small population of 1.3 million (World Population Review 2019). The National Petroleum Company, GEPetrol, controlled by members of the president's family is ridden with corruption scandals and money laundering allegations (Massoko 2019).

In an astonishing book published in 2007 by John Ghazvinian, the author narrated how the ruling family in Equatorial Guinea dissipates the country's oil wealth, including how President Obiang lavished $2.6 million in acquiring a mansion in Potomac in Maryland, and his son (Teodoro Nguema Obiang Mangue) acquired a mansion of $30 million in Malibu, California where he runs his hip-hop label, TNO Records; a 2005 US Senate report disclosed that as much as $700 million of Equatorial Guinea's treasury deposits were held at the Riggs Bank in Washington DC with the president, his son and nephew as the three persons required to sign for the account (Sieff 2007; Cole 2019).

Equatorial Guinea is probably the only non-monarchical state in the world where the Vice President (Teodoro Nguema Obiang Mangue, nicknamed Teodorín) is the first son of the president. Teodorín has for several years been the subject of many Western governments' investigations for prolific corruption and money laundry scandals. In 2017 he was convicted in absentia by a French court for embezzling millions of Euros from his government and laundering the proceeds in France; the court handed him a three-year suspended jail sentence and a suspended Euro €30 million fine and seized over €100 million worth of his assets (Cole 2019).

The court demanded the confiscation of Teodorín's assets, including a €107 million mansion near the Champs-Élysées, which boasts a hammam, disco, gym, hair-dressing studio, gold-plated taps and hundreds of artworks (Chrisafis 2017). The French authorities had earlier in 2011 confiscated luxury cars, furniture, and artworks from Teodorín's $180 million Paris home in connection with money laundering, while in 2014, the US Department of Justice (DoJ) accused Teodorín of money laundering as well and seized 28 exotic cars, a Gulfstream Jet, and his $30 million mansion in Malibu, California, and a bunch of auctioned memorabilia of the late pop star Michael Jackson (Cole 2019). However, he later reached a settlement with the US DoJ to pay about $34 million from the funds held in his accounts to be allowed to keep some of his confiscated assets (Cole 2019). The DoJ's website reported that $20 million of the $34 million would go to a charitable foundation for the benefit of the people of Equatorial Guinea (Cole 2019).

In September 2018, more than US$16million in cash and luxury watches were seized at an airport in Brazil in the luggage of a delegation accompanying Vice President Teodorin to Brazil (*The Guardian* 2018; *The East African Standard* 2018). The confiscated cash was about $1.5 million. Teodorin was part of a delegation of 11 that arrived at Viracapos Airport near Sao Paulo on a private jet plane in contravention of Brazilian law which prohibits people from entering the country with more than R$10,000 Real in cash, (the equivalent of about $2,400) (*The East African Standard* 2018). Diplomatic source from Equatorial Guinea claimed that the confiscated fund was the money meant to pay for medical treatment that Teodorin was to undergo in São Paulo (*The Guardian* 2018). Over $16 million in cash and luxury watches are required for the treatment of a man who was neither packaged on a stretcher nor flown in on an air ambulance? I will not probe further. A year later in September 2019, Swiss authorities investigating money laundry charges of Vice President Teodorín seized and auctioned 25 luxury cars belonging to him which yielded £21.9 million—proceeds that would go to a charity to benefit the impoverished people of Equatorial Guinea (Cole 2019; Lamare 2019).

Outraged by the enormity of corruption in the country, the IMF in December 2019, handed down two conditionalities to Equatorial Guinea before the country could receive more financial support as a bailout for its worsening economic crisis. The first is a requirement that the country's leader Teodoro Obiang Nguema Mbasogo should declare his assets, and the second is that Equatorial Guinea should join the Extractive Industries Transparency Initiative (EITI), which promotes good governance in the oil and mining industries. End of story! The President will resist any effort requiring him to make an international asset declaration.

In a similar vein, King Mswati III of the tiny Southern Africa's Kingdom of Eswatini is Africa's last absolute Monarch, who has continued an unbroken tradition of extreme hedonistic lifestyle at the state's expense that only has its strongest parallels in medieval and early modern Europe, and perhaps in early postcolonial Africa. With a population of about 1.4 million people and almost completely eclipsed by South Africa, Eswatini is an illogical contraption of the British empire that since its independence in 1968 has maintained all the trappings of a hostage economy and captured state, or perhaps more appropriately a "bewitched state." In a bewitched state, the rulers and the ruled are bound together by a spell of Stockholm syndrome—a mystical rapport between a tiny elite that has taken the state hostage to serve their perverted interests and the "captive" population that cynically cheer the music of their collective dehumanization. In a poverty-stricken country (63% of the population live below the poverty line) known to have the world's highest HIV prevalence rate, King Mswati reportedly enjoys an official annual salary of US$50 million (based on 2014 known figure), in addition to controlling the key dominant companies in the local economy.[6] For instance, "he controls the Tibiyo Taka Ngwane, an investment holding company that holds stakes in sugar refining giants Ubombo Sugar and Royal Swaziland Sugar Corporation, dairy company Parmalat Swaziland, spirit manufacturing Swaziland Beverages, and hotel chain Swazi Spa Holdings. The company has asset worth US$140 million, but he holds it in trust for the people of Swaziland."[7] The King is known to have prolific top-of-range exotic cars and extravagant royal palaces for his 15 wives.

During his 50th birthday celebration in April 2018 which coincided with the golden jubilee independence anniversary of the country, King Mswati unilaterally changed the name of the country from Swaziland to Eswatini, received delivery of his second private jet—an A340-300 Airbus (valued at $30 million after VIP upgrades) (Reuters/Stringer, 5 May 2018). The royal birthday and national day extravaganza coincided with the time the country's Finance Minister Martin Dlamini had publicly admitted that the kingdom was broke, but the public admission notwithstanding, the government had also paradoxically earmarked the sum of US$125 million to build a conference centre and five-star hotel to host an African Union eight-day summit in 2020.[8] In the country's 2014 budget, King Mswati increased his annual household budget to more than 10% of the national budget (amounting to $61 million in the same year) (*The Guardian*, 14 May 2014). The IMF and US government have raised concerns that there is no oversight on how King Mswati and his vast royal family spend public money, often diverting money that should have been used on education and health to other purposes (*The Guardian*, 14 May 2014). In November 2019, King Mswati reportedly spent about £13 million to import 19 Rolls-Royces and 120 BMWs for his multiple "co-eaters," including wives and family members in a country where 12 of the

26 public ambulances available for the entire population are off the road in need of repair but there is no money to fix them[9] (*The Sun* 2019). Overall, the unconscionable spending spree of King Mswati and his vast royal family at the expense of the impoverished general public is ostensibly only matched in contemporary Africa by the extravagant lifestyle of the Western media acclaimed "playboy Vice President" of Equatorial Guinea and his ruling family.

Apparently, the main difference between the wealth accumulated by Isabel dos Santos and her family by courtesy of wielding state power in Angola and the wealth of the ruling families in both Equatorial Guinea and Eswatini lies in their use of the alleged looted funds. On her part, Isabel dos Santos, reputed to be an astute entrepreneur, has channelled significant portions of her wealth to productive investments in Angola, Portugal, and elsewhere and in the process has created thousands of jobs—benefitting humanity, generating more wealth and paying substantial taxes to the revenue coffers of the state. Isabel's business reputation could ultimately be diminished by the so-called Luanda Leaks scandal—a cache of 715,000 leaked papers presumably uncovering her business malpractices and that of many influential top state officials and rentier tycoons at the expense of the Angolan state during ex-President Dos Santos' regime. But without making any apologies for the embattled daughter of ex-President Dos Santos, it suffices to reiterate and elucidate the point made earlier that many African billionaires and business moguls are products of crony capitalism and high-level sabotage of the state's economy. Somehow, enrichment by subversive malpractices and acts of impunity is inherent in the nature of "unregulated" and dysfunctional capitalism. The phenomenon may exist in varied measures from one country to another depending on diverse empirical and sociological conditions (cf. *The Economist*, 15 March 2014; Omeje 2015). One of the key lessons of the global financial crisis and economic downturn of 2007–2008 is that lax regulation of the capitalist market encourages high-risk tendencies of predatory profiteering and subversive accumulation. On their own part, the ruling families in Equatorial Guinea and Eswatini who seem bereft of any serious sense of purpose, have a flair for prolific spending on vanities, indulgence in extravagant hedonism and accumulation of mammoth bank accounts.

Box 5.2 A Case Study of State Capture and the Officialization of kleptocracy in Burundi

There are varied degrees of state capture by powerful political leaders, state officials and business interests across Africa. Until the recent death of President Pierre Nkurunziza, the small Central African state of Burundi exhibited for several years all the characteristics of hostage capitalism. In January 2020, President Nkurunziza, who had ruled the poor and landlocked Central African country of Burundi for the past 15 years with an iron fist manoeuvred a new legislation through the national parliament that approved an incredible retirement package for him. On leaving office the president, who was a humble teacher and later a junior lecturer before entering politics, would get a luxury villa (to be built in a location of his choice) and a one-off payment of one billion Burundian francs (about $530,000). The retired president will also get the same benefits as a serving vice president for seven years after they step down and will for the rest of their life get an allowance equal to that of a legislator (Al Jazeera 2020). With a population of 11 million people, Burundi has a GDP of about $3.6 billion and per capita of $310.

In what could be best described as the officialization of kleptocracy, the rubber-stamp parliament of Burundi adopted the presidential retirement package proposal with an overwhelming majority of 98 votes and two contrary votes. Too many African parliaments are populated by handpicked clients of the executive who are there to legitimize the caprices and impunity of the latter. In Burundi, over 71.8% of the population lives in extreme poverty (World Bank Group 2020). The country had gone through a deadly 13-year civil war, the settlement of which saw Nkurunziza emerge as the first post-war elected president in 2005. In the violent election of 2015 in which the president was re-elected for an unconstitutional third term, more than 1,200 people were killed and over 200,000 refugees fled the country.

The European Union, which hitherto funded about half of Burundi's budget suspended all official aid and budgetary support and also imposed far-reaching sanctions on top government officials, but maintained full financial support to non-state organisations, especially those concerned with humanitarian assistance. Poverty and decline in basic services were exacerbated by donor sanctions. Unable to fund basic governance obligations, including the impending election in 2020, Nkurunziza introduced an annual election tax of 2,000 Burundian Francs ($1.09) per household and empowered the youth wing of the ruling party known as *Imbonerakure* to collect the tax (*The Irish Times* 2019). Not unexpectedly, the youth militias saw the assignment as an opportunity for extortion—a license for "petty eating" at their own pedestrian level. They collected the taxes both for the government and for themselves, forcing many people to pay the tax more than once a year. From the police corporal that extorts motorists on the highway to the charlatans that extort students for grades in some institutions of learning, and the civil servants that demand bribe to process basic documents for national passport or driving license—the "eating" culture, both petty and intermediate, is widespread and pathologically embedded in a number of African states. At the most pedestrian level the practice is poverty-driven. At sub-middle class and mid-ranging levels, "the intermediate eaters" are largely driven by the curse of impunity.

Less than five months after the adoption of the new presidential retirement legislation and two months to his official handover to a new President-elect Evariste Ndayishimiye, President Nkurunziza suddenly died of cardiac arrest; aged 55. Though the government announced that the President died of cardiac arrest, unconfirmed sources suggest that the President died of COVID-19, a pandemic disease that his government treated with levity.

Hostage capitalism and state capture did not originate in Africa. In particular, state capture was a term originally used colloquially by Russians to describe the corrupt oligarchs that assumed positions of political power and economic dominance in their country in the 1990s following the collapse of communism. In a special report published in 2000, the World Bank operationalized the concept and extended it to describe the new hegemonic classes and oligarchic regimes that emerged in the former Communist bloc in the process of their transition to liberal democracies. In its operationalization of the concept, the World Bank (2000: xvi) developed a State Capture Index which included variables like: "the 'sale' of parliamentary votes and presidential decrees to private interests; the sale of civil and criminal court decisions to private interests; corrupt mishandling of central bank funds; and illegal contributions by private actors to political parties." In a corresponding survey that applied the State Capture Index in the study of the former Communist bloc of Eastern Europe and Central Asia, the following five countries demonstrated the most deplorable evidence of state capture: Azerbaijan, Moldova, Ukraine, Russia and Latvia. In this present study, I have applied the concept of hostage capitalism to define the nature of capitalist economy and accumulation processes associated with state capture.

5.3.5 Predatory Capitalism

Another counter-productive brand of capitalism practiced in contemporary Africa is predatory capitalism. Extrapolating from Daniel Bash's theory of predatory neopatrimonialism, one could define predatory capitalism as a post-Darwinian trajectory of patron-clientelism and economic plunder characterized by extreme personalization of the state and looting of its resources by the governing oligarchy, with the result that there is a loss of any sense of public space or public policy (Bash 2011: 279). Writing on predatory capitalism in contemporary Brazil, Albuquerque and Faria (2019) identified two distinguishing pillars: the first is the persistence or deterioration of inequality as a result of the enormous hardship inflicted on the underprivileged masses; and the second, the allure of easy exploitation of natural resources regardless of the environmental damage. The pathological "eating" culture in predatory capitalism makes it profoundly anti-development, and a fundamental threat to the coherence and internal sovereignty of the state. I am inclined to argue that most of the African countries wobbling at the intersection of extreme fragility and corruption over the past five years following the global rankings published by the Fragile State Index and the Corruption Perception Index exhibit tendencies of predatory capitalism. Some of these countries include Somalia, South Sudan, Burundi, Sudan, DRC, Guinea, Guinea-Bissau and Chad.[10] With the complications created by protracted rebel insurgencies, warlordism and underground economies, large enclaves of countries like Somalia, Sudan and Central African Republic, as well as the embattled core of the Lake Chad Basin exhibit tendencies and features of "mafia capitalism" in which primitive patterns of accumulation and "eating" by dispossession[11] have acquired a normal current. Many African economies with a façade of all the formal state institutions and democratic structures are held hostage by an undercurrent and network of hegemonic predators who have strong vested interest in the perpetuation of prebendal corruption, countries like Kenya and Nigeria, among others.

Suffice it not to talk about Kenya and Nigeria in any detail because of the entrenched ubiquity of predation in both economies that practically makes it difficult to settle on specific case studies without the risk of writing two or three books in one. Michela Wrong and Kempe Ronald Hope (2014, 2019) have published well-researched works on the persistence of chronic and institutionalized culture of accumulation or "eating" by predation in Kenya. Former Nigerian Finance Minister and current Director General of the World Trade Organization Ngozi Okonjo-Iweala (2018) has written an outstanding professional memoir about predatory corruption and the dangers of fighting it in Nigeria, including how the phenomenon adversely diverts resources away from development. Okonjo-Iweala's book is replete with horrifying narratives of the mortal dangers she experienced for taking an uncompromising reformist stance against corruption during her tenure as Nigeria's Finance Minister, including the kidnapping of her 83-year-old mother and the kidnappers' demand that she should resign on a live television broadcast and leave the country as a condition for the release of her mum. The kidnappers were working at the suspected behest of fraudulent marketers importing processed oil products into the country based on the highly controversial federal government's oil subsidy contracts that drain well over a billion of petro-Dollars from state coffers annually. Nigeria has four oil refineries that operate significantly below their installed capacities, and all efforts to fix them have failed due to a multiplicity of factors, including the undermining exploits of the too many vested interests that profiteer from the ruins of the refineries. Between 1993 and 2016, the Nigerian government spent a whopping $6.065 billion in the rehabilitation or turnaround maintenance of the four refineries (Jeremiah 2019). President Obasanjo's government (1999–2007) sold two of the old and extremely dysfunctional oil refineries to a consortium of investors led by Nigerian billionaire Aliko Dangote at the sum of $750 million, which was apparently a good move to help rehabilitate the refineries since all government efforts to fix them had been persistently sabotaged. The succeeding regime of Umaru Yar'Adua, a candidate ironically handpicked and installed by Obasanjo, reversed the privatization of the refineries under pressure from the gangster profiteers and had the money paid by the Dangote-led consortium refunded (Vanguard, 30 July 2015). Nigeria loses more money than any other country in the world through high and low-level stealing of oil resources using diverse mechanisms ranging from pipeline perforation and siphoning of oil to offshore and nearshore piracy, among others. In a public statement released by Nigerian Extractive Industries Transparency Initiative (NEITI) in November 2019, Nigeria lost $41.9 billion to oil theft over the preceding ten years period, from 2009 to 2018—crude oil and refined petroleum products. The breakdown published by NEITI indicates that over the ten years period the country lost $38.5 billion on crude oil theft alone; $1.56 billion on domestic crude oil and another $1.8 billion on refined petroleum products—altogether averaging a theft of $11 million of oil products daily (Eboh 2019). Accumulation or "eating" by devious desperation! Way back in 1987, Richard Joseph propounded a new theory—the theory of prebendalism—to explain the convoluted entitlement and predatory dimensions of graft in Nigeria, a theory that seems far more relevant to the present-day Nigeria than when it was first propounded.

Evidently, Matthew Page (2018) has produced the most comprehensive empirical documentation and analysis of corruption in Nigeria, classifying it into 20 sectoral contexts of "eating" and showing the various tactics deployed in executing it, as well as the scope, scale and negative effects of the phenomenon. Corruption, writes Page, is the single greatest obstacle preventing Nigeria from achieving its enormous potential and it drains billions of dollars a year from the country's economy, stymies development and weakens the social contract between the government and its people (Page 2018). Lawlessness and insecurity are as big a problem in Nigeria as corruption. When the trio of extreme corruption, lawlessness and insecurity are added up, one may easily end up with serious contemplation on the validity of Richard Dowden's description of Nigeria as "a failed state that works."[12] In his famous book, *Nigeria: Dancing on the Brink* (2011), John Campbell, former US Ambassador to Nigeria raises similar issues about how state failure—endemic corruption, insecurity, the impunity and pernicious factionalism of the governing elites, and the likes—is driving Nigeria to the edge. About ten years after the publication of Campbell's insightful book, the condition of state failure in Nigeria is evidently worse. Renowned public intellectual and professor of political economy Pat Utomi published a highly indicting book titled *Why Not: Citizenship, State Capture, Creeping Fascism, and Criminal Hijack of Politics in Nigeria* in which he tried to explain why Nigeria has continued to dance on the brink after the hard-fought battle that rescued the country from many years of corrupt military dictatorship in 1999. Utomi (2019) argues that the Nigerian state has been captured by a bunch of criminals, ritualists, charlatans and conmen—the so-called political class—for their narcissist advantages, and as such is almost out of credibility and legitimacy in the eyes of both its citizens and the world. He further stressed that the Nigerian political class would use all the powers at their disposal to fight off and frustrate most well-meaning citizens who would venture to seek elective offices to offer visionary and service-oriented leadership.[13] The question of how long Nigeria could continue tottering at the precipice without decisive structural and governance reforms is a matter of endless intellectual speculation for experts given the fact that the liberal sciences have tenuous reliability in predicting the future.

From the Goldenberg scandal and the Anglo Leasing, to the Maize scandal, the Eurobond scandal, and the more recent hydropower dam scandal, Kenya has been rocked by a montage of staggering transactional sleaze spanning over two decades that makes the country look like "tales of state capture"—using the words of the Nairobi-based constitutional lawyer Wachira Maina (2019). In each of these scandals there are always local "eaters" in top government positions colluding with a network of local and international brokers, firms or middlemen to defraud the state and taxpayers of millions of funds. The intriguing dimension of Kenyan politics is that almost in all cases the kingpins are not invisible. Too often some are arrested, detained and investigated but not all. Somehow, virtually all of them go scot-free and many find their way back to public office and conspicuous limelight. The level of recycling is mindboggling. It can only be approximated and trumped by its similarities in Nigerian politics! Having said that, Presidents Buhari of Nigeria and Uhuru Kenyatta of Kenya deserve some commendations for their efforts in tackling high-level graft in government, but the wilderness is still full of too many "hyenas," reference to the "big eaters." Commenting about political hyenas, the Nigerian First Lady Aisha Buhari warned in July 2017 that the "hyenas and jackals" who were taking advantage of President Buhari's long medical leave in the United Kingdom to foster their inordinate shenanigans will soon be banished from the kingdom because of the imminent return of the President (BBC News, 11 July 2017). Mrs Buhari was responding to the Facebook solidarity remark from Senator Shehu Sani that "the absence of the lion king" has made the "hyenas and jackals fall over each other in their scheming to be in the front row of the palace temple," stressing further that "it is the prayers of the weaker animals that the lion king comes back to save the kingdom from the hyenas, the wolves and other predators" (BBC News, 11 July 2017). What an intriguing conversation using Hobbesian and Darwinian metaphors of untamed predators on the loose upsetting the body politic because of the temporary absence of the king of the jungle. More than three and half years after the return of the lion king, many Nigerians are yet to be convinced about the difference his return has made. Apparently, the lion king is constrained by the necessary institutions and structures of democratic governance.

5.4 A Postscript on Dysfunctional Capitalism

Many critics are not likely to take my arguments about the dysfunctioning of capitalism in Africa and its principal correlate, the political economy of "eating" or squanderation kindly. Without trying to preempt potential critics, I do not by any means intend to generalize that all capitalist economies in Africa essentially dysfunction or that the dysfunctionality of capitalism is an irredeemable state. Not at all! Africa comprises 54 sovereign states. This implies that there are 54 capitalist economies in Africa. All of them have not dysfunctioned. Likewise, the political economy of "eating" does not affect all African states, and those affected are not afflicted equally. There are some capitalist economies in post-colonial Africa that have never had any significant problem with the "eating" metaphor, the principal agency for dysfunctionality. In countries like Seychelles, Mauritius, Cape Verde, Botswana and Namibia, the political culture of "eating" has never been a serious problem since their independence. There are a few other capitalist economies that were previously for too long on the dysfunctioning trajectory but have managed to turn it around, the No 1 example being Rwanda. I imagine that many critics, especially from the West would not like to hear of Rwanda as a good example because of their apparent obsession with chaperoning and lecturing Africa about human rights. Strangely, the wealthy Middle Eastern Arab states are never lectured about human rights because there is enormous business to do in the Arab world. I don't in any way minimize the importance of human and people's rights. But Africa certainly doesn't need lectures on human rights, not least from the West. Other countries like Ghana and Tanzania started off relatively well under the governments of Kwame Nkrumah and Julius Nyerere, without the "eating" culture but thereafter things gradually derailed, especially in Ghana. Presently, they seem to be getting back on track away from the debilitating syndrome of "eating." Senegal and post-Arab Spring Morocco, to a lesser extent, are also gradually getting back on track with promising strategic approaches to development and governance, albeit the Covid-19 pandemic has had significant devastating impact on the Moroccan economy (Lloyds Bank 2021; World Bank 2021). Cote d'Ivoire has made significant progress in peacebuilding and economic growth since the end of its civil war in 2011.

However, the constitutional and political crisis surrounding the country's 2020 election and President Alassane Ouatarra's re-election for a controversial third term are a sign that key fundamentals of governance are still shaky in the country. These little strides and comeback are all happening despite the limitations that the short-term rituals and waste inherent in liberal democracy pose to growth and development in these small African economies. Liberal democracy, which postcolonial Africa has almost unanimously embraced as part of the settlement for the turbulence of the past few decades is a necessary albatross. I respect the take of Dambisa Moyo in her seminal book, *Edge of Chaos* (2018), on why liberal democracy is failing to deliver economic growth. Moyo's proposals on how to fix liberal democracy, if adapted to the context of the weak African states, are without doubt contestable but well-meaning.

In a large sense, most of the African economies that are either on track or tend to be coming back on track are all small economies. High levels of extreme poverty are still a big problem for many of them. At the pace at which they are growing, and with effective policy planning and resource allocation and management, most of them may not be able to effectively deal with the challenges of extreme poverty against population growth even in the predictable long term. I am of the view that Africa needs far more prosperity than what the small economies can deliver at their current pace of growth and development. Moreover, if a handful of small economies are getting on track while many of the relatively large economies and potential giants are failing to rise to their undeniable potentials, the latter could become a nuisance to the former through chaotic economic migration and influx of the desperately poor, especially as the continent-wide African economic community—the market integration project with its free movement protocol—gains momentum. Under such a scenario, a multiplicity of the kind of BREXIT backlash in Europe and xenophobic violence in South Africa are likely to occur in more parts of the continent. This explains the apparent reluctance among member states in ratifying the January 2018 Free Movement of Persons Protocol adopted by the AU Assembly of African Heads of State officially known as *Protocol to the Treaty Establishing the African Economic Community Relating to the Free Movement of Persons, Right of Residence and Right of Establishment*. African states have evidently shown more enthusiasm about the ideals of free trade (movement of goods and service) as opposed to free movement of people for fear of foreigners competing for or taking up the limited job and livelihood opportunities.

Finally, the concept of dysfunctionality has to be understood as a process. It is not a permanent state. I have essentially used dysfunctionality as an analytical construct to capture the obnoxious distortion and malfunctioning of the social economy largely due to the anti-systemic devices of powerful individuals and groups who deliberately take advantage of their control or access to state power to undermine the social economy in order to maximize their self-serving interests. Because dysfunctionality is a process and not a permanent state, one could for instance argue that the South African state and economy were probably more dysfunctional under ex-President Jacob Zuma than under his successor President Cyril Ramaphosa. States and economies differ in levels of dysfunctionality and likewise, for a specific state, dysfunctionality could vary from one political regime to another, especially because of the weak institutionality of the African postcolonial states which could sometimes make influential public office holders and non-state moguls more powerful than the formal institutional order. I am only being conceptual and analytic in a post-structuralist sense in my use of the concept of dysfunctionality. I will leave the empiric measurability of dysfunctionality to well-resourced institutions like the US-based Fund for Peace that computes and measures the global Fragile State Index (FSI) annually.

Summary Points

1. In varied and diverse ways, the aggrandizing interests of the African governing elites, often tempered by those of their local business and expatriate partners, have majorly shaped the crafting and implementation of several economic development policies since the early postcolonial years.
2. Capitalism, to a large extent, dysfunctions in contemporary Africa. The fundamentals essentially do not work because of "the political economy of eating" or squanderation.
3. Dysfunctional capitalism is mainly a product of the dysfunctionality of the state.
4. In dysfunctional capitalism, bad politics trumps everything, including economics, and bad politics is an aphrodisiac inexorably manifested in "the curse of impunity."
5. Diverse caricature and grotesque versions of capitalism have developed in postcolonial Africa, namely: oligarchic capitalism, crony

capitalism, hostage capitalism, predatory capitalism and mafia capitalism.

6. It is important to remark that Africa is a large and diverse continent comprising 54 sovereign states. All capitalist economies in Africa have not dysfunctioned and the dysfunctionality of capitalism is not an irredeemable state.
7. The concept of dysfunctionality must be understood as a process and not a permanent state.

Discussion Questions

1. Explain the term "import-substitution industrialisation"?
2. Is "import-substitution industrialisation" anti-development?
3. Why did the policies of indigenization and partial nationalisation of foreign enterprises implemented in many African countries during the early decades of independence fail to achieve the much-desired economic development outcomes?
4. What do you understand by the "eating" metaphor in African political economy?
5. What are the similarities and differences between the oligarchic capitalism practiced in Russia and the type discernible in Africa?
6. Using a specific empirical example, explain the phenomenon of "state capture" in African politics?
7. What is prebendalism?
8. Is the theory of prebendalism still useful in understanding African politics?

Notes

1. "The *parallel premium* is the percentage by which the parallel exchange rate exceeds the official exchange rate" (Kiguel and O'Connell 1995: 22).
2. Borrowed from the title of John Sweeney's book, *The Useful Idiot* (2020), but used in a different context to describe unscrupulous businesses, fronts and racketeers that connive with the African governing elites in the political economy of "eating" for the purpose of getting their own share. There

is no scarcity of useful idiots at home and abroad—contractors, business tycoons, middlemen, fronts, bankers, etc.

3. The reported scale of wealth amassed by the three ex-leaders Maummar Gaddafi, Hosni Mubarak and Ben Ali are unconfirmed but the fact that they all used state power to amass enormous fortunes cannot be disputed. See: Amy Austin Holmes (2020) "IMF Loans Will Further Entrench Corruption in Egypt", Foreign Policy 3 July 2020. https://foreignpolicy.com/2020/07/03/sisi-corruption-egypt-imf-loans/. Networth (2020) "Muammar Gaddafi Net Worth 2020 – Salary, House & Cars", https://networthbro.com/muammar-gaddafi-net-worth/#:~:text=Muammar%20Gaddafi%20was%20the%20longest%20serving%20ruler%20of,Gaddafi%20had%20a%20net%20worth%20of%20%2470%20billion. Manish Sahajwani (2020) "Seven of the Richest Dictators in History", 16 February 2020, https://www.investopedia.com/financial-edge/0912/8-of-the-richest-dictators-in-history.aspx#:~:text=Ben%20Ali%20is%20said%20to%20have%20a%20net,playground%2C%20killing%20most%20of%20his%20rivals%20and%20.
4. This observation is extrapolated from the views expressed by Timothy Kaldas in "Egypt's Revolution: Ten Years On", The Debate – A France 24 English Panel Interview Discussion, 25 January 2021, https://www.youtube.com/watch?v=tpWOmt7sssw.
5. Taken from the theory of patron-clientelism where favours and positions are distributed by powerful social agents known as patrons to loyalists they have propped up or who are beholden to them known as clients. The asymmetrical power between the patron and his clients is usually reproduced in the informal network of dependency of the latter on the former. The phenomenon exists in diverse forms and contexts in different parts of the world and its history has been traced to pre-modern social formations, such as the nature of relationships that existed between the patricians and plebians in the Roman empire or similar classes in feudalist Europe in general.
6. Cf. Mfonobong Nsehe (2014) "The 5 Richest Kings in Africa", June 3, https://www.forbes.com/sites/mfonobongnsehe/2014/06/03/the-5-richest-kings-in-africa/#7f200b4741d2; see also: MT (2018) "eSwatini: King Mswati III – Lifestyles of the Rich and Royal," *How Africa*, 8 June, https://howafrica.com/eswatini-king-mswati-iii-lifestyles-of-the-rich-and-royal/.
7. Cf. Mfonobong Nsehe (2014), ibid., reference to note 5; MT (2018), ibid., reference to note 5.
8. Information obtained from: AllAfrica.com (2018) "Swaziland Admits it is Broke", 15 June, https://allafrica.com/stories/201806150295.html.
9. Information partly obtained from: AllAfrica.com (2019) "Swaziland King Buys Himself Fleet of 15 Rolls-Royce Cars but There's No Money for

Public Ambulances", 25 November 2019, https://allafrica.com/stories/201911250170.html.

10. I came up with the listed countries by comparing countries recurrently ranked at the bottom 20 or quartile of both the most Fragile State Index and the Corruption Perception Index over the preceding 5 years. See the following sources: Fund for Peace (2019) Fragile State Index 2019. https://fundforpeace.org/wp-content/uploads/2019/04/9511904-fragilestatesindex.pdf; Transparency International (2018) Corruption Perception Index 2015 – 2018 Data Set, https://www.transparency.org/cpi2018; see also: World Population Review (2019) Most Corrupt Countries 2019, http://worldpopulationreview.com/countries/most-corrupt-countries/.
11. "Eating" by dispossession is coined from "accumulation by dispossession," a concept developed by David Harvey to refer to the fraudulent or forceful appropriation of natural or social commons by capitalists using neoliberal policies and their subsequent conversion into commodities. Cf. Richard Clayton Doughman (2016) "Might the Keys to Peace Open the Doors to Extractivism? Reflections on Colombia's Post-Conflict Extractive Economy", https://www.igi-global.com/chapter/might-the-keys-to-peace-open-the-doors-to-extractivism/142264; See also: David Harvey (2003) *The New Imperialism*. Oxford University Press. New York.
12. Quoted in: John Ryle (2008) "How to Write About Africa – Don't". Review of Richard Dowden's book *Africa: Altered States, Ordinary Miracles* in *The Guardian*, 31 October 2008, https://www.theguardian.com/books/2008/nov/01/africa.
13. See: Pat Utomi (2019) *Why Not: Citizenship, State Capture, Creeping Fascism, and Criminal Hijack of Politics in Nigeria*. Lagos: CVL Press.

References

Al Jazeera. 2020. Burundi to Give Outgoing Presidents Luxury Villa, over $500,000. *Aljazeera News*, 22 January. https://www.aljazeera.com/news/2020/1/22/burundi-to-give-outgoing-presidents-luxury-villa-over-500000.

Ake, Claude. 1981. *A Political Economy of Africa*. Lagos: Longman.

Ake, Claude. 1982. *Social Science Imperialism: The Theory of Political Development*. Ibadan: Ibadan University Press.

Albuquerque, Eduardo da Motta, and Cláudia Feres Faria. 2019. Uncontrolled Predatory Capitalism: The Core of Bolsonaro's Government. *International Socialism* (164), October 14. http://isj.org.uk/the-core-of-bolsonaros-government/.

Amin, Samir. 1976. *Unequal Development: An Essay on the Social Formations of Peripheral Capitalism*. New York: Monthly Review Press.

APPP, et al. 2012. The Political Economy of Development in Africa: A Joint Statement from Five Research Programmes. https://differenttakeonafrica.files.wordpress.com/2012/04/joint-statement.pdf.

Arun, Neil. 2019. State Capture: Zuma, the Guptas, and the Sale of South Africa, July 15. BBC. https://www.bbc.co.uk/news/world-africa-48980964.

Bach, C. Daniel. 2011. Patrimonialism and Neopatrimonialism: Comparative Trajectories and Readings. *Commonwealth & Comparative Politics* 49 (3) (July): 275–294.

Barnard, Alan. 2019. *Bushmen: Kalahari Hunter-Gatherers and their Descendants*. Cambridge: Cambridge University Press.

Beckman, Bjorn. 1982. Whose State? State and Capitalist Development in Nigeria. *Review of African Political Economy* 23: 37–51.

BBC News. 2017. Nigeria's First Lady Aisha Buhari warns of 'Hyenas' on Facebook, July 11. https://www.bbc.co.uk/news/world-africa-40569818.

BBC News. 2020. José Filomeno dos Santos: Son of Angola's Ex-Leader Jailed for Five Years. BBC News, August 14. https://www.bbc.co.uk/news/world-africa-53774288.

Campbell, John. 2011. *Nigeria: Dancing on the Brink*. Lanham, MD: Rowman and Littlefield.

Chrisafis, Angelique. 2017. Son of Equatorial Guinea's President Is Convicted of Corruption in France. *The Guardian*, October 27. https://www.theguardian.com/world/2017/oct/27/son-of-equatorial-guineas-president-convicted-of-corruption-in-france.

Clapham, Christopher (ed.). 2006. *Big African States*. Johannesburg: Wits University Press.

Cole, Williams. 2019. Luxury Cars Seized from Son of Equatorial Guinean President Sold in Switzerland, September 29. https://www.dailymail.co.uk/news/article-7517715/Luxury-cars-seized-son-Equatorial-Guineas-president-sold-Switzerland.html.

Eboh, Michael. 2019. Nigeria Lost $41.bn to Oil Theft in 10 years — NEITI. Vanguard, November 6. https://www.vanguardngr.com/2019/11/nigeria-lost-41-bn-to-oil-theft-in-10-years-neiti/.

Goldbaum, Christina. 2021. South Africa Court Set to Rule on Jacob Zuma, and an Era of Impunity. *The New York Times*, March 25, 2021. https://www.nytimes.com/2021/03/25/world/africa/jacob-zuma-south-africa-court.html.

Harding, Luke. 2020. *Shadow State: Murder, Mayhem and Russia's Remaking of the West*. London: Guardian Faber Publishing.

Hertel-Fernandez, Alexander. 2019. *State Capture: How Conservative Activists, Big Businesses, and Wealthy Donors Reshaped the American States and the Nation*. New York: Oxford University Press.

Hope, Kempe Ronald. 2014. Kenya's Corruption Problem: Causes and Consequences. *Commonwealth and Comparative Politics* 52 (4): 493–512.

Hope, Kempe Ronald. 2019. The Police Corruption 'Crime Problem' in Kenya. *Security Journal* 32 (2): 85–101.

Jeremiah, Kingsley. 2019. Refineries: Endless TAM as Money Guzzling Scheme. *The Guardian,* September 22.

Kiguel, Miguel, and Stephen A. O'Connell. 1995. Parallel Exchange Rates in Developing Countries. World Bank, February. http://documents1.worldbank.org/curated/en/690401468766186922/pdf/multi0page.pdf.

Lamare, Amy. 2019. The Insanely Blatant Kleptocracy of Teodorin Obiang – The Son of The President of Equatorial Guinea. *Celebrity Net Worth*, 28 October. https://www.celebritynetworth.com/articles/entertainment-articles/the-insanely-blatant-kleptocracy-of-teodorin-obiang-the-son-of-the-president-of-equatorial-guinea/.

Lloyds Bank. 2021. Senegal: Economic and Political Overview, April. https://www.lloydsbanktrade.com/en/market-potential/senegal/economical-context.

Maina, Wachira. 2019. Tales of State Capture: Goldenberg, Anglo Leasing, and Eurobond, September 5. https://www.theelephant.info/features/2019/09/05/tales-of-state-capture-goldenberg-anglo-leasing-and-eurobond/.

Martirosyan, Andre. 2016. The Changing Role of Oligarchs in Russia. *Market Mogul*, February 4. https://themarketmogul.com/the-changing-role-of-oligarchs-in-russia/.

Massoko, Delfin Mocache. 2019. Corruption: An Endemic Disease Plaguing Equatorial Guinea, January 9. IACC News. https://iaccseries.org/blog/corruption-an-endemic-disease-plaguing-equatorial-guinea/.

McKernan, Bethan. 2020. Gaddafi's Prophecy Comes True as Foreign Powers Battle for Libya's Oil. *The Guardian*, August 2. https://www.theguardian.com/world/2020/aug/02/gaddafis-prophecy-comes-true-as-foreign-powers-battle-for-libyas-oil.

Mihalyi, David. 2014. Crony 2014: Drilling Down into the Economist's Strike-It-Rich List, March 25. https://resourcegovernance.org/blog/crony-2014-drilling-down-economists-strike-it-rich-list.

Moyo, Dambisa. 2018. *Edge of Chaos: Why Democracy is Failing to Deliver Economic Growth and How to Fix It*. London: Little Brown.

Mytelka, Krieger Lynn. 1989. The Unfulfilled Promise of African Industrialization. *African Studies Review* 33 (3): 77–138.

OAN. 2020. Angola's Dos Santos Moots Presidency Run Despite Charges. *One American News*, January 16. https://www.oann.com/angolas-dos-santos-moots-presidency-run-despite-charges/.

Okonjo-Iweala, Ngozi. 2018. *Fighting Corruption Is Dangerous: The Story Behind the Headlines*. Cambridge, MA: The MIT Press.

Omeje, Kenneth. 2015. Natural Resource Rent and Stakeholder Politics in Africa: Towards a New Conceptualization. *Commonwealth and Comparative Politics*, 92–114.

Page, T. Matthew. 2018. A New Taxonomy for Corruption in Nigeria. Carnegie Endowment for International Peace. https://carnegieendowment.org/2018/07/17/new-taxonomy-for-corruption-in-nigeria-pub-76811.

Palmer, Andrew. 2016. Crony Capitalism. The World in Crises: Threats and Challenges, October 19. https://www.theworldincrisis.com/crony-capitalism/.

Reuters/Stringer. 2018. Swazi Royals Lavish Lifestyle under Scrutiny, May 5. https://www.enca.com/africa/swazi-royals-lavish-lifestyle-under-scrutiny-as-country-faces-grinding-poverty.

Saadoun, Sarah. 2017. How Equatorial Guinea Turned Corruption into an Art Form, June 15. https://www.hrw.org/news/2017/06/15/how-equatorial-guinea-turned-corruption-art-form.

SAIIA. 2015. Moving Beyond Africa's Crisis of Institutions. South African Institute of International Affairs (SAIIA) Occasional Paper, October 12. https://saiia.org.za/research/moving-beyond-africas-crisis-of-institutions/.

Sieff, Michelle. 2007. The Dutch Disease in Africa. *The New York Sun*, June 6. https://www.nysun.com/arts/dutch-disease-in-africa/55946/.

Sweeney, John. 2020. *The Useful Idiot*. Kidderminster: Silvertail Books.

The Economist. 2014. Our Crony-Capitalism Index: Planet Plutocrat, March 15.

The Economist. 2020. A Sticky Patch for Isabel dos Santos, Angola's Princess, January 11. https://www.economist.com/middle-east-and-africa/2020/01/11/a-sticky-patch-for-isabel-dos-santos-angolas-princess.

The East African Standard. 2018. Obiang Son's $16 m Seized at Brazil Airport, September 16. https://www.theeastafrican.co.ke/news/africa/Obiang-son-tripped-up-in-Brazil-customs/4552902-4762718-10g1k0a/index.html.

The Guardian. 2014. King of Impoverished Swaziland Increases Household Budget to $61 m, May 14. https://www.theguardian.com/world/2014/may/14/king-mswati-iii-swaziland-increases-household-budget.

The Guardian. 2018. Brazil Police Seize $16 m from Equatorial Guinea's VP Delegation. *The Guardian*, September 16. https://www.theguardian.com/world/2018/sep/16/brazil-police-seize-16m-from-equatorial-guineas-vp-delegation.

The Irish Times. 2019. Burundi's Hard-Pressed Citizens Being Forced to Pay for 2020 Election, 6 December. https://www.irishtimes.com/news/world/africa/burundi-s-hard-pressed-citizens-being-forced-to-pay-for-2020-election-1.4107266.

The Sun. 2019. King of Swaziland 'Shows Middle Finger' to Impoverished Workers by Blowing £13 m on 19 Rolls-Royces and BMWs for 14 Wives. *The Sun*, November 12. https://www.thesun.co.uk/news/10333552/king-of-swaziland-rolls-royces-wives/.

Vanguard. 2015. How Yar'Adua Was Pressurised to Revert Refineries Sold to Dangote, July 30. https://www.vanguardngr.com/2015/07/how-yaradua-was-pressurised-to-revert-refineries-sold-to-dangote-obasanjo/.

Vanguard. 2017. 12 States Owe Salaries Despite Bailout, April 25. https://www.vanguardngr.com/2017/04/12-states-owe-salaries-despite-bailout/.

Winsor, Morgan. 2015. Nigerian President Buhari Approves $2 Billion Bailout for Unpaid Workers. *International Business Times*, August 7. https://www.ibtimes.com/nigerian-president-buhari-approves-2-billion-bailout-unpaid-workers-1999222.

World Bank. 2000. Anti-corruption in Transition: A Contribution to the Policy Debate. The World Bank, Washington DC, November. https://books.google.co.uk/books?id=gpBvS3O17S4C&pg=PA3&redir_esc=y#v=onepage&q&f=false.

World Bank. 2021. The World Bank in Morocco. *The World Bank*, March 25, 2021. https://www.worldbank.org/en/country/morocco/overview.

World Bank Group. 2020. Poverty and Equity Brief: Sub-Sahara Africa – Burundi, April. https://databank.worldbank.org/data/download/poverty/33EF03BB-9722-4AE2-ABC7-AA2972D68AFE/Global_POVEQ_BDI.pdf.

World Population Review. 2019. GDP Ranked by Country 2019. World Population Review. http://worldpopulationreview.com/countries/countries-by-gdp/.

Wrong, Michela. 2009. *It's Our Turn to Eat: The Story of a Kenyan Whistle-Blower*. London: Harper.

CHAPTER 6

Key Governance Dimensions of Dysfunctionality

By far, politics remains the biggest business in Africa, and political entrepreneurs far outplay and overshadow the genuine business entrepreneurs in the local economy, which is an aberration for any capitalist economy.

6.1 The Seriousness and Decisiveness of Governance

Over the past two decades or more, there has been a groundswell of awareness, advocacy and agitation among the African public for an improvement in political and economic governance in their various countries for development, job creation and poverty reduction to be meaningfully achieved. The Arab Spring of the early 2010s that swept through North Africa like hurricane was the most popular and vivid rebuke of the entrenched culture of nepotism, kleptocracy and impunity that have been the bane of governance in many African states. Further popular revolts similar to the Arab Spring were to later pull down the corrupt and autocratic governments of Blaise Compaoré in Burkina Faso in 2014, Yahya Jammeh in The Gambia in 2017 and Omar Bashir in Sudan in 2019. There are a few more that need to fall. But the painful reality is that the lessons are hardly learnt, not even in most of the countries where popular revolts have brought down inept dictatorships.

K. Omeje, *The Failure and Feasibility of Capitalism in Africa*, International Political Economy Series,
https://doi.org/10.1007/978-3-030-75170-8_6

The *Ibrahim Index of African Governance* launched in 2007 by the Mo Ibrahim Foundation defines governance as "the provision of the political, social and economic public goods and services that every citizen has the right to expect from their state, and that a state has the responsibility to deliver to its citizens."[1] This definition is overly idealistic because the presumed "citizen's governance expectation right" and "the state's governance delivery responsibility" to a lesser extent scarcely exist in Africa. But the definition makes sense for advocacy and conscientization purposes and the Mo Ibrahim Foundation deserves commendation for their great strides in trying to raise the governance bar in Africa. According to the World Bank, governance is "the manner in which power is exercised in the management of a country's economic and social resources for development" (FHI360 2015: 1). Impliedly, misgovernance or bad governance occurs when power is exercised in the mismanagement of a country's economic and social resources to hinder development. In practice, misgovernance is arguably the greatest bane of Africa's development.

The advocacy, politics and literature on good governance and democratic governance have grown tremendously since the end of the Cold War. The growth and hype are due largely to the activist push of Western donors, states and institutions who have increasingly made "good governance" a major condition for their credit facilities and development aid. Contemporary politics of good governance is not without the concomitant ideological agendas of the West and as such proponents hardly make any distinction between the two variables—good governance and democratic governance—albeit some scholars have alluded to a hybridized third version, good democratic governance (Nyong'o 2021: 3). In the typical Western conception, governance is almost inconceivable without liberal democracy or liberal democratic governance with its major pillars of periodic and competitive multi-party elections, universal adult suffrage, market economy or marketization, civil society activism, as well as a constitutional and institutional framework logically akin to any of the established Western prototypes. But this is a misconception that cannot be empirically substantiated. Good governance is possible and has always had a place in history independent of liberal democracy, and conversely there is a plethora of bad governance within the liberal democratic spectrum, especially in the [semi-]developing regions of Eastern Europe, Latin America, Asia and Africa. The 2020 election in Belarus, a country in the heart of Europe, was massively rigged by Alexander Lukashenko, a despot who has ruled the country for more than 25 years, leading to mass protests in which many protesters were beaten and jailed (*The Economist*, 15 August 2020). But by courtesy of Russian firm support, Lukashenko got away with all the atrocities in utter defiance of the EU. Under Lukashenko's dictatorship, Belarus has been blighted by electoral fraud, manipulation of the constitutional framework, repression and incarceration of opposition party members, and occasional disappearances of vocal critics. Most apologists of liberal democracy would hasten to brand examples of bad governance from Eastern Europe and elsewhere in the developing world as symptoms of fledgling democracy, which under certain circumstances could be inevitable in the transition towards maturity. However, even in some of the developed Western countries—the so-called mature democracies—the content and quality of governance are questionable.

The Worldwide Governance Indicators project of the World Bank delineated six empirical indicators for measuring governance namely, citizens' voice and accountability, political stability and absence of violence/terrorism, government effectiveness, regulatory quality, rule of law and control of corruption (Kaufmann et al. 2010: 4). In discussing governance and good governance, some analysts have tended to revise and condense the World Bank's empirical benchmarks. Good governance, which ever way it is defined, is a process and not an absolute or permanent condition. Conceptually, the understanding of governance is focused on measurable empirical rubrics such as legitimacy of government, accountability of public office holders, competence of government to formulate people-centred policies and deliver services, as well as respect for rule of law and human rights (Fye 2015; Ahere 2021). Any of these processes could be achieved independent of the Western model of liberal democracy. The United Arab Emirates (UAE), China and Rwanda (to mention but a few countries) have significantly achieved good governance for their citizens without a "copy and paste" version of Western liberal democracy. African countries need to think outside the box to develop paradigms of governance most suited for their political, economic and sociocultural development.

The New Partnership for Africa's Development (NEPAD) was launched by the Organisation of African Unity (OAU later renamed African Union) in July 2001 to among other things "address the critical challenges of poverty, development and Africa's marginalization internationally."[2] The African Peer Review Mechanism (APRM) was established by the AU in 2003 as a "voluntary self-monitoring instrument to ensure that policies and practices of participating Member States conform to the agreed political, economic and corporate governance values, codes and standards contained in the African Union Declaration on Democracy, Political, Economic and Corporate Governance."[3] The African Union Agenda 2063 which was launched in May 2013 to mark the 50th anniversary of the OAU (later renamed AU) is a 50-year "strategic framework that aims to deliver on its goal for inclusive and sustainable development and is a concrete manifestation of the pan-African drive for unity, self-determination, freedom, progress and collective prosperity pursued under Pan-Africanism and African Renaissance" (MIF 2019: 01). Jakkie Cilliers (2020: 3) describes NEPAD and Agenda 2063 as part of "Africa's many plans and noble aims that rarely translate into reality." The APRM, NEPAD and Agenda 2063 were all launched to underscore the decisive importance of political and economic governance for Africa's present and future transformation but the cumulative impact of these regional initiatives on governance in the continent remains doubtful. As a matter of fact, political governance in many African countries has continued to operate on a dysfunctional trajectory with the result that capitalism—and by implication economic governance—as I have argued in the preceding two chapters have practically continued to dysfunction.

Governance is a serious matter, but not in many African states and dysfunctional economies. Self-interest politics is by far taken more seriously. Several African political leaders at both the national and subnational levels take governance with levity and unseriousness. They do not just stop at the unseriousness of what one could call the average "rational" politician who could oftentimes lie, cheat, dupe, steal and mislead, but pragmatically covering up their misdeeds, frequently with the help of a retinue of well-paid aide. Some of the best contemporary examples of sophisticated Machiavellian statecraft could be found in Luke Harding's thrillers, *Mafia State* (2012), *Collusion* (2017) and *Shadow State* (2020)—all chronicles of President Putin's mastery of the game of secret service politics and how he ingeniously perfects and deploys the art in the pursuit of personal agendas and "state interests" in post-Cold War's international politics with maximum returns. In this game of statecraft, morality and justice are the least considered values. Interests and results are what matter. Like it or loathe it, in reading Harding's trilogy, you may not but shudder in utter disbelief, if not respect, at the political engineering, adept calculations and breath-taking intelligence in President

Putin Kremlin's statecraft. This is not the case in the African dysfunctional states where for the most part politics is internally self-destroying. In most of these countries, the unseriousness with which governance is approached defies common sense. It is both dramatized and politicized. The unseriousness can sometimes be clownish and like in many stage performances of famous clowns, the theatricals almost always provoke widespread applause.

6.2 Fetish Celebration of Small Things and the Dramatization of Unseriousness

One of the most ridiculous features of democratic politics in many African countries is the fetish extravagance with which "small things" are celebrated by top government officials and the governed. It is in some places like a game of musical chairs. As a "political culture,"[4] the tradition has its origin in colonial history when African communities were frequently mobilized by their local chiefs (most of them warrant chiefs and stooges installed by the colonizers) to sing praises in appreciation of the colonizers for whatever development projects they received. Development projects like schools, pipe-borne water, paved roads, and health clinics had to be officially launched with pomp and pageantry. Colonial governments were neither democratically elected nor had any indigenous roots and therefore were unaccountable to the people. They owed all their allegiance to their metropolitan governments in Europe and therefore the Africans had to show undue appreciation for any governance benefits they delivered, including those that were primarily conceived to serve the purpose of colonialism. On their part, the warrant chiefs and local surrogates appointed or accredited to rule over the various local chiefdoms and communities owed their own allegiance to the colonial authorities. Mobilizing their local subjects for the celebration of small things was the chiefs' way of pleasing their commanding officers on the one hand, and claiming political mileage to strengthen their legitimacy among their subjects, on the other hand. Quite easily, the local subjects of the chiefs could see through the development projects delivered by the "native" administration of the colonizers (of which the chiefs were often a major part) to consider the entire colonial project as fit for purpose—impliedly, they are delivering development and therefore deserve commendation and supportive loyalty from the locals. Development projects were delivered not as a governance imperative, but as an act of charity and goodwill for which the "natives" owed a perpetual debt of celebratory thanksgiving.

The postcolonial state inherited this fetish tradition of celebrating small things which has become a major feature of politics and governance in many parts of Sub-Saharan Africa since independence. However, the practice has apparently been driven to reckless extremity during the current wave of democratization on the continent. These celebrations are always at a scandalous cost to taxpayers and ordinary citizens, many of whom the funds channelled into the frivolous fanfare and publicity could have helped to uplift from extreme poverty. In early June 2020, Governor Mutahi Kahiga of Nyeri County in Kenya mounted a giant billboard beside a public pit latrine at Kahara community of the County bearing his photo and that of Honourable Eric Mwangi Wamumbi, the Member of County Assembly (MCA) of Konyu Ward in the County. Many public projects cited by subnational governments in Kenya such as health centres, schools, asphalt feeder roads, local bridges, overhead water reservoirs, government buildings and job-creation investments are dotted with such billboards to give credit and honour to the elected politicians behind the projects. Elsewhere in Sub-Saharan Africa, including Kenya, the official launch or opening of some of these projects is usually marked by red carpet reception, pompous feasting, political speeches and outpouring of encomiums on the public office holders, performance by traditional dancing troops and an extravagant display of power. In fact, for many development projects, the celebration is often in two phases. The first phase is organized at the inception of the project when top government officials and elected politicians gather in a big public event to perform the ground-breaking ceremony to lay the foundation or mark the commencement of the project. The second phase of the celebration is when the project is completed (if it ever gets completed because some of these projects get abandoned midway especially when a new government comes to power). African villages and towns are always agog when elected politicians come to celebrate community projects they either wish to commission or have completed for the benefits of the people.

The billboard erected by the Nyeri County governor to publicize the small public latrine he constructed in a rural village provoked far-reaching outrage around Kenya as the pictures of the giant signage dwarfing the humble latrine went viral online. Many social media users and commentators speculated that the cost of the billboard far surpassed the cost of the latrine. The social media backlash prompted the County Deputy

Governor Caroline Karugu to quickly dissociate herself from the entire show of shame, describing the signage politics of her boss as "extremely unfortunate and ill-advised" "persistent cheap publicity stunts" (Mutura 2020). The same governor of Nyeri had been roundly reproached about a month earlier for reportedly spending public funds in repackaging into smaller units vast stocks of hand sanitizers donated by well-wishers to help contain the spread of Covid-19 in his County. The governor branded the hand sanitizers with stickers bearing his picture and the inscription of the County government which many thought was not only a cheap publicity stunt but one that was designed to deceptively take credit and claim political mileage from the generosity of some undisclosed privileged members of the public (Mutura 2020).

But for the social media age and the growing political awareness among the youths who increasingly demand responsible governance from their leaders, frivolous activities of this nature in African politics would ordinarily go unchallenged. A few days after the online frenzy over the Nyeri government's pit latrine billboard, some unknown persons pulled down the billboard supposedly at midnight.

The Nigerian political culture is evidently the most extravagant and bizarre in the celebration of small things and dramatization of unseriousness. While state governors and elected public office holders in Nigeria earned a reputation for celebration of small things in the second and third civilian republics, the present fourth republic that started in May 1999 has taken the phenomenon to a level of absurdity. In 2002, a Nigerian state governor constructed a 20 meters long road by-pass or tunnel in the state capital, which he claimed was the first of its kind in Africa and beamed the advert of its official commissioning repeatedly on CNN. Why would somebody go to CNN to repeatedly advertise a 20 meters road by-pass using public funds? The claim of being the first or best in Africa is a spurious claim that Nigerian politicians have frequently made about many of their so-called achievements to gain political mileage. Nigeria is the self-proclaimed "giant of Africa" and therefore every "big thing" they accomplish must either be the first or best in Africa. The official commissioning of the overly publicized tunnel was done by the then Nigerian president who praised the governor for his great achievement, describing the vision of the governor in constructing the road tunnel as "worthy of emulation" (Igata 2016). The by-pass is named after the political moniker of the governor. Too much hype and glory for just a 20-meters by-pass! That's what I call fetish celebration of small things, a widespread and institutionalized tradition in Nigeria. Using a "vain religion" metaphor, Moghalu (2014) calls it "worshipping at the altar of the god of small things." Media reports reveal that about twelve years down the line, the tunnel which was poorly designed with no drainage for the heavy seasonal rain and flooding in the area was under threat of caving in (Igata 2016). While this governor went on CNN to advertise his completed 20 meters tunnel, many other governors after him have even been more embarrassing. They have persistently bought exorbitant weekly airtime in leading Nigerian televisions with extensive international outreach to broadcast documentaries of their achievements which usually showcase all the development projects they have initiated, pursued or commissioned, including the grand ceremonies hosted to mark the commencement or commissioning of the projects. Some of these projects include rural electrification, community water boreholes, new and revamped roads, renovated school buildings, monuments of questionable leaders, monorails, local airports and so forth. Many of these projects are worthwhile even if some are shabbily designed and executed, but that is not the point. The undue publicity and hype given to mundane rural roads and water projects, not to talk of the advertorial waste, are a pointer to serious defects of political culture. A significant number of the projects are unsustainable or irrelevant white elephants with jaundiced feasibilities. Some of the white elephant projects, believed to be conduits for siphoning of public funds and money laundering, simply become abandoned when there is a change of government. More disastrously, most of the vanity-driven or unsustainable projects put the state governments in huge debt burden as many of them are funded with foreign loans. Matthew Page (2018) wrote the following about one of the several abandoned white elephant projects in Nigeria, in this case, a mile-long monorail project: "The previous governor of Rivers State spent $400 million on an inflated contract to build a mile-long monorail in Port Harcourt. Deeming it wasteful, the new governor abandoned the near-completed project." What a horrendous waste! $400 million is gone in a part of the world where extreme poverty, disease and non-motorable hard roads are widespread and cutting short the lives of many!

Nigerian elected leaders take undue credit for all variety of public projects they complete, most of which are characterized by inflated contracts and are shabbily executed. When they speak and brag about their accomplishments in office, you would think that they have used their personal fortunes to provide development for their people, when in fact a greater part of their personal fortunes have often been acquired by courtesy of the public offices they have held. The majority of state governors that have left office since the fourth republic have been investigated and charged to court by the federal government's anti-corruption agency for monumental corruption ranging from largescale stealing of public funds through exaggerated contracts to bribery and money laundering. Most of the corruption cases investigated by the government's anti-corruption agency, the Economic and Financial Crimes Commission (EFCC) are related to contracts and procurements (Yakubu 2019). Several high-level convictions involving ex-governors, ministers and heads of government parastatals, among others, have been secured by the anti-corruption agency with millions of looted funds recovered, including forfeiture of assets acquired with looted funds.

Uganda! Political governance in Ugandan is ridden with cronyism and malfeasance but what seems even more ludicrous is the unseriousness with which the government approaches the malaise. Uganda has all the relevant anti-corruption laws and agencies but there is hardly any serious enforcement action. The civil society has been fighting high-level graft in Uganda for a greater part of the long reign of President Yoweri Museveni which began in 1986. On 4 December 2019, President Museveni ironically led a highly publicized anti-corruption street protest in the national capital Kampala, joined by many of his top government officials. Attended by a large crowd, the rally blocked many streets going in and out of Kampala as top government officials marched against themselves to the enchantment of the participating members of the public. Speaking in an open-air rally at the Kololo Independence Grounds that marked the end of the long march, the deputy speaker of parliament Mr Jacob Oulanyah made a controversial remark that "everybody in Uganda is corrupt,"[5] by which I presume he meant "everybody in Ugandan government," but even that in itself will be an exaggeration. Oulanyah likened the ubiquity of the mess to the endemic nature of iniquity in Jesus' famous biblical pronouncement of clemency while acquitting the woman caught red-handed in the sin of adultery by the pretentious Pharisees when he declared to the latter—"If any one of you is without sin, let him be the first to throw a stone at her." Without mincing words, the deputy speaker had just admitted before the head of state and general public that "we are all eaters." The president who spoke after the deputy speaker cast a verbal stone on those who steal public funds calling all of them "parasites because they get wealth which they did not earn," but quickly exonerated himself with a claim that: "I have never stolen. But I am rich" (Eagle News, 4 December 2020). I am not sure there are many Ugandans who will believe their president's claim that he has never "eaten." Certainly, no one in Uganda would recommend that he swears to one of the potent African shrines in Ashantiland or Yorubaland, the type that ex-President Jerry Rawlings of Ghana has occasionally spoken about their instant retributive power. But jokes apart, it is overly unserious that the president who is elected to oversee the enforcement of laws against corruption is leading a public anti-corruption protest and rally. Despite all the controversies surrounding his longevity in power which I will not delve into, President Museveni has done many good works in Uganda. He has won international acclaims for engineering economic growth in Uganda, but his development efforts could have made greater impact had his government been less protective of well-connected cronies and more decisive in tackling nepotism and graft which is widespread in the higher and lower echelons of power. Under the watch of the president, there have been serious allegations of millions of bilateral donor funds stolen at high levels of government and Western governments (e.g. UK, Germany and US) cutting project funding to provoke thorough investigation and accountability. Between 2016 and 2018, Uganda was consistently ranked below Nigeria and Kenya in the bottom quartile of the Transparency International CPI. Uganda has a small economy ($31 billion GDP) relative to its population (42.7 million) which makes it indeed serious for the country to be consistently ranked below Nigeria and Kenya in terms of corruption for three years.

While small things are amplified and over-celebrated in many African countries, it is important to acknowledge that there are diverse big economic development projects happening in Africa without any undue hypes from the governments executing them. It will suffice to just mention a few of such mega-development projects. The Ethiopians are close to completing their controversial $4.8 billion Grand Renaissance Dam conceived to solve the country's electricity problem and also export power to some neighbouring African countries. The dam project, the largest in Africa, was started by late Prime Minister Meles Zenawi in 2011 and has been consistently executed by successive governments. If this mega-dam project were conceived somewhere in West Africa, the cost of the project could most probably have been inflated over five times and chances are high that a succeeding government would abandon it. Save for the controversy the dam project has generated with Egypt and

Sudan over the use of the River Nile waters, the project would hardly draw extensive media attention. Even at that, there has been measured celebratory bragging by Ethiopian politicians and leaders about this mega-hydroelectric power plant with an installed capacity to generate 6,450 megawatts of electricity. Most significantly, the first completed phase of Grand Ethiopian Renaissance Dam (GERD), involving about two-thirds of the project was largely executed with local expertise and labour. However, in February 2019, the Ethiopian government contracted the pre-commissioning activities of the dam, the last phase of the project, to the China Gezhouba Group Company Limited (CGGC). Negotiations are ongoing to help solve the dispute generated by GERD and one can only but hope that there will be a peaceful resolution of the dispute.

As part of its commitment to developmental capitalism, the Egyptian government of President Abdel Fattah al-Sisi in August 2015 completed its $8 billion mega project of expanding the Suez Canal [originally estimated to take three years] in just one year. The expansion added an additional lane of 21 miles (35 km) along part of the vital shipping channel to shorten waiting times for cargo vessels and dredged 22 miles (37 km) of existing water bodies to make way for larger ships (Malsin 2015).

Furthermore, in March 2015, President al-Sisi launched the construction of a new administrative capital project for Egypt, the 270-square-mile Galala city project, planned in three phases, at an estimated initial cost of US$45 billion (*Egypt Independent*, 27 September 2020). The different aspects of this mammoth engineering project are presently executed by at least 55 companies. Upon completion, the new smart city will help to decongest Cairo, attract diverse new profitable investments and create tens of thousands of new jobs for young people.

Elsewhere in Mozambique, the government is executing a major export-oriented $20 billion Liquified Natural Gas (LNG) project in partnership with leading international energy companies from France, US, Japan, India, among others. The French oil major Total is leading the LNG project reputed to be Africa's single largest foreign investment project. The mega-LNG project, which is just one among other natural gas projects involving major energy multinationals in Mozambique, is designed to extract, liquify and export natural gas from Mozambican offshore natural gas fields and the liquifying process will be facilitated by the construction of a two-train liquefaction plant with a capacity of 13.1 million tons per annum (Reuters, 17 July 2020).

6.3 Political Violence and Politics of the Unserious

In a brilliant research published in 2016 titled, "Types of Conflict in Africa: How Do the APRM Reports Address Conflicts?", Rebeka Gluhbegovic (2016), presented a fivefold empirical classification of armed conflicts in Africa based on the African Peer Review Mechanism (APRM) reports submitted by 17 member states.[6] The fivefold conflict classification includes political conflicts, identity conflicts, resource-based conflicts, civil unrest and terrorism. Of the five types of conflict, political conflicts are by far the most widely reported by member states which, based on their self-report, was primarily defined by the author as "conflicts over state power, often associated with liberal democracy—elections and democratic transition."[7] The findings of Gluhbegovic' study about liberal democracy being the greatest source of violent conflicts in contemporary Africa is instructive. It negates the neo-Kantian liberal peace assumption that liberal democracy and market capitalism will facilitate positive peace (Taylor 2017: 17). Furthermore, the recurrent violence associated with many African democratic processes tends to challenge the controversial assumption among many Western policymakers that democracy is the gateway to growth, development and stability among poor and heterogenous developing countries. In fact, as Acemoglu et al. (2018) summed up the discourse, democracy fosters "robust and sizeable economic growth" through its "positive effects on economic reforms, private investment, the size and capacity of government, and a reduction in social conflict." Instructive evidence from the history of many successful Asian economies and a few Latin American countries lucidly point to the fact that democracy is not a necessary condition for economic growth and social cohesion,[8] and indeed the emerging realities from the miscellany of African democracies do not present a convincing picture. Moyo (2009: 42–43) argues that, on the contrary, it is economic growth that is a prerequisite for democracy, and she further expounds the views of sceptics who contend that at the early stages of development, democracy is irrelevant, and may even be harmful, a perspective that Western policymakers have chosen to ignore. In a nutshell, violent conflicts do not only hurt positive peace in contemporary Africa, but it is a plain truth that investors, entrepreneurs and other anthropogenic drivers of capitalist markets recoil in an atmosphere of endemic and predictable violence.

Liberal democratic politics in Africa, both election-related activities and the process of governance, is characterized by unjustifiable levels of physical violence. The political violence is an indication or consequence of two things. The first is the enormous value placed on political power as an instrument for amassing personal fortunes, and "a means of production"—to borrow an expression commonly used to describe the politics of primitive accumulation characteristic of the African lumpen bourgeoisie in the heydays of leftist radicalism. This paradigm of politics and accumulation did not suddenly vanish with the end of the Cold War, even though one cannot diminish the measure of progress that has been made. By far, politics remains the biggest business in Africa, and political entrepreneurs far outplay and overshadow the genuine business entrepreneurs in the local economy, which is an aberration for any capitalist economy. The materialistic stakes in African politics are still exceedingly high and the stakeholders do not always fight jaw-jaw as honourable members of a hallowed parliament for instance would. Too often, politicians have thrown all caution to the winds, and fought with hard gloves. In this age of social media broadcast where everybody with a smart phone could effortlessly set up a worldwide television channel at zero cost, the news and footages quickly go viral. But the politicians seem to care less that they are brawling on camera because the stakes are just too high to act in honour of their hallowed position. For the reason of the enormous value placed on state power and the physical violence integral to the process, electable public offices and party positions in many African countries are largely attractive to those who can withstand the level of desperation required for both the right and wrong aspirations. Essentially, political parties in many African democracies are nothing more than machineries for capturing state power or retaining power. Political parties themselves are captured because to capture state power, you have to first capture the party structures or be well-connected to a king maker who has already captured the party and has the final say on who runs for office. Matthew Page (2018) calls it the "kleptocratic capture of political party structures" which is used to "unlock corruption opportunities across a range of other sectors" of the state. Depending on the specific nature of the alignment of political forces, parties may or may not be driven by primordial identities and demographics, but the struggle to capture and control the party machinery, especially if the party has substantial electoral clout, is as intense as the ultimate struggle to capture state power. The capturing of the party machinery can happen at different levels of the administrative structures of the state. An individual can capture the party machinery at the national level while other persons can capture it at any of the subnational levels—provincial level, municipal level and local council ward. Because the process of nominating or choosing candidates for elections within the party is hardly democratic but manipulated in many African countries, lack of control or effective access to the party machinery can effectively rule out a candidate from becoming a party's nominee, even if s/he is the most credible and popular candidate.

The incredible propensity among politicians to switch from one party to another and to form merged-coalition parties ahead of any elections is partly driven by the need to gain control or access to an officially certified machinery for capturing power. When a captured party is used to capture state power, then all other things could be literally achieved through unrestrained access to state resources. Money for funding political parties and elections campaigns are for the most looted through access to state power and government contracts with the result that incumbent parties in government at the national or subnational state levels have a head-start advantage in elections. Parties with no public coffers to loot will barely struggle through elections.

To become Nigerian president, General Buhari had to change political parties three times and among a large number of the opposition party stalwarts that supported and bankrolled him to victory in the April 2015 election were seven serving state governors and dozens of national assembly members of the then ruling PDP who decamped *en masse* to the mega-opposition alliance APC. Combined with other state governors from the parties that formed the mega-opposition alliance, the APC governors and elected politicians provided Buhari a solid resource base capable of matching the ruling PDP "money-for-money." It is estimated that the ruling PDP spent about $10 billion in the 2015 presidential elections which the party lost (Owen and Usman 2015: 462). Many veteran politicians in countries like Kenya and Uganda to a lesser extent have changed political parties or formed mega-party alliances for as many times as elections have been held in their country during their political career, literally running for office under a new party platform in each election. The end is what matters—to capture political power—not ideology or any cleverly crafted manifesto, which in several countries practically means nothing once power is captured. The proliferation of parties in countries like Lesotho, Liberia, Malawi, Mozambique and Guinea-Bissau, among others is not driven by competing ideologies and the need for effective representation but fundamentally by the permutation to capture power either at the national or subnational level. The tiny Southern African country of Lesotho with a population of about 2.1 million people has 25 political parties while Guinea-Bissau in West Africa with 1.8 million people has 24 parties.

For those motivated to join political parties by the right aspiration, for the most part highly accomplished citizens who are almost always in the minority, they are in politics because they are "desperate" or passionate to use political power to engineer and pursue the desired change against all odds. Many of them get frustrated midway by the monumental odds they always have to face and some ultimately become converted by the perverse majority. The cost of fighting the warped status quo is simply too hard to bear while the benefits of joining the bandwagon become too attractive to resist. So, if you can't beat them, join them! This is what occasionally happens to many well-meaning social critics with civil society, labour, academic and religious backgrounds when they join politics in Africa. Too often, they betray the high expectations the public place on them. There are indeed other well-meaning candidates, mostly accomplished technocrats and professionals who may have the reputation and mettle to do a good job if given the chance, but of course, are aware that they don't stand a chance in the corrupt mainstream parties and therefore opt to run for office under obscure parties that lack the necessary resources and political structures for making an impact in elections. These well-meaning candidates invariably excite the electorate with fascinating ideas and policy proposals for genuine change if elected. They are spectacularly cheered for their oratory, reputation and brilliance but hardly voted for. Even if we discount the undue advantage that ballot rigging confers on the dominant mainstream parties, such credible candidates usually don't stand a winning chance. That's the tragedy of practising liberal democracy in societies with largely uninformed and fragmented electorates who may have impaired judgement about how democracy can best serve their collective interests and about who their true heroes are. The likes of PLO Lumumba in Kenya and Pat Utomi in Nigeria—both potentially credible candidates for the required transformative change—can write bestselling memoirs on this subject. Commenting on how the African electorates too often elect their worst enemies and kleptocrats into positions of power, PLO Lumumba, the eloquent Kenyan anti-corruption activist rhetorically remarked that, "we are co-authors of our own misfortune ... we elect hyenas to take care of goats, and when the goats are consumed we wonder why" (Berman 2017). In the developed countries where bread and butter issues are largely taken for granted and where the outcomes of elections cannot fundamentally impoverish the people, the electorate can afford the luxury of impaired judgement and gambling with who they elect, including by electing leaders who can cause plenty of troubles around the world provided they are safe at home.

The masses in poor developing countries have incoherent fragmentation often cemented along primordial identity lines and politicized by the privileged elites to win and retain power. It will require a great deal of sensitization and political education to break the incoherent fragmentation of the masses and make them a force for purposeful democratic change. There are hardly any well-resourced detribalized non-state agencies in most countries that could undertake such a vital project of conscientizing and re-educating the masses to become a force for well-meaning democratic change. To some extent, the civil society and National Peace Council in Ghana have the grassroots operative structures, legitimacy and integrity to make such a desirable impact but are cash-strapped. Despite their lack of funds, the Ghanaian Peace Council and civil society have over the years done a great deal of sensitization and mediation work to foster non-violent elections, peaceful transfer of power and democratic consolidation in the country. Without delving extensively into the real and potential role of the civil society in interest articulation and governance, it suffices to say that there is the need for alternative and complementary sources of funding for the civil society in Africa. A civil society that is preponderantly dependent on donor funding is not in Africa's best interest because by so doing the civil society is inadvertently recruited and instrumentalized to promote donor [Western] interests, values and ideological agendas. The result is that the country becomes more irreconcilably fragmented and antagonistic. African states, regional institutions and the private sector need to prioritize the funding of local civil society organizations based on goals and agendas that are consistent with African interests and priorities, e.g. non-violent and transparent elections, peaceful transfer of power, accountability of public office holders, gender equity, informal and adult literacy, youths' skills training and employability, entrepreneurship development, ethnic and cultural integration, deconstruction and neutralization of violent extremism, etc. The relationship between the state and civil society is far less antagonistic in the West than in Africa and one of the reasons for this difference is that the agendas, priorities and funding of Western civil society organizations are, to a large extent, not externally driven. In the UK for instances, there are hundreds of Quasi-Autonomous Non-Governmental Organizations (QUANGO) that are funded by government using taxpayers money to pursue and execute specific programmes consistent with government's policies on inland security, diversity and social development. Other sections of the British civil society derive their funding from diverse internal or Western sources (e.g. private donors, the British state, Western governments, and until the recent BREXIT, the European Union). Consequently, they are all regulated by the state or Western institutions and agencies that do not fundamentally undermine the state. In fact, BREXIT was largely articulated and championed by political leaders, parties, as well as interests and business groups that were ideologically driven by what they saw as the need to rescue the sovereignty of the state from undue external (EU) interference and strengthen it to promote British interests.

Unlike the masses, the African political elites have the advantage of coherent fragmentation. They could be divided along party and ethnic or religious lines, but these divisions are secondary to their self-serving interest of aggrandizement of power, position and resources. It is this unity around self-serving prebendal interests that often lies behind the elites' political permutations involving frequent change of parties, reconciliation with former adversaries to form new parties and mega-alliances to capture or retain power, as well as power-sharing arrangements in the aftermath of political conflicts. The political elites could easily negotiate their disputes and interests to work together in a coalition government after an acrimonious and violent election in which many ordinary folks have lost their lives, but the incoherent fragmentation and acrimony of the masses would continue for a long time.

For politicians motivated by the wrong aspirations to seek political power who are always in the majority (albeit, their real motives are invariably disguised), they are unapologetic products and masters of the terrain and they easily get what they want. In the end, the surviving critical mass genuinely committed to positive change becomes hugely outnumbered, combatted, and most dismally, they may not find themselves in strategic positions of power where they can possibly make a difference. The neoliberal political space in Africa is often suffocating for activists and partisans of genuine change.

One of the greatest challenges of party politics in neoliberal democracies in general is the lack of rigorous mechanisms for integrity-vetting and capacity-grooming capable of preventing mediocres, charlatans and other contenders of questionable character from using ill-gotten wealth and sheer bravado to ascend to high positions of power. This is something that has repeatedly hurt the West in the past—and arguably in the present—but is profusely devastating Africa. The Chinese Communist Party, for instance has rigorous inbuilt integrity-vetting and disciplinary mechanisms to mitigate the possibility of people with questionable character climbing to high echelons of power. Western politicians and policy makers are unlikely to see this illustrious side of party politics in China. They only see one thing in the Chinese Communist Party—dictatorship!

The second indication of the physical violence frequently associated with neoliberal politics in Africa is that it dramatizes the politics of the unserious—a bunch of high-stake actors in the political space who are unserious with the issues of governance. In fact, a vast majority of these political actors are not prepared for governance neither are they in politics for this serious purpose. Many of them are career politicians who ventured into politics because of unemployment and under-employment which are critically high among school leavers in most African countries. With no [serious] career experience in life and nothing to lose if they fail, many of them venture into politics because they have the most vital requirement for seeking political power in the contemporary neoliberal dispensation—the physical and mental capacity to withstand the high level of desperation required for survival in the political space. Having been baked in the tough socio-economic and political milieu of Africa where they have survived unbearable struggles and hardship to secure things that are ordinarily considered basic in life in many parts of the world (livelihood, water, clothing and schooling), these political actors are mentally prepared to not only withstand but prevail in the rough edges of neoliberal politics in many African countries—the politics of thuggery, vote rigging, Machiavellian subterfuge and violence. Militias and thugs are recruited, sponsored or hired for the purpose of intimidation of opponents during political campaigns and elections using brute force and occasionally gun violence. This is an embedded political practice in countries like Nigeria, Kenya, Zimbabwe, Guinea, Togo, Burundi and Sudan—to mention a few countries. In countries like Uganda, Cameroun, Zimbabwe, Burkina Faso, Burundi, Gabon, among others, the state security forces are frequently used by the governments in power during election season to intimidate the opposition and facilitate vote rigging in the same manner that party militias and thugs do. Elections have not only been rampantly rigged but completely stolen with the defeated candidates cruising to victory and forming a government. It is a fate that veteran opposition candidates like Raila Odinga in Kenya, the late Morgan Tsvangirai in Zimbabwe, Ni John Fru Ndi in Cameroun, among others, have suffered. "The post-election violence in Kenya, following the stolen Nigeria election," argues Richard Dowden (2008: 531), "and the flawed polls in Uganda, Ethiopia, Cameroun, and Malawi, the post-election fallout in Congo and Zimbabwe's stolen election in 2008, all raise the question of whether winner-take-all, first-past-the-post multi-party democracy is ever going to work in Africa."

In Cameroun for instance, President Paul Biya, who has been in power since 1982, rarely campaigns in any election but always secures a landslide victory. President Biya, mockingly described by many Camerounians as "the absentee President" because of his frequent long trips to Europe, has perfected the art of winning elections but not governance. Even the BBC News described Paul Biya as Cameroun's "absentee President" in October 2018, reporting that he allegedly spent a third of the year abroad in 2006 and 2009, the Intercontinental Hotel in Geneva being reportedly his favourite destination (BBC, 5 October 2018). In the 2018 presidential election as in many others before it, there were many video footages of the president's campaigners handing out food items like loaves of bread, butter, sardine and even beer to the electorates, and many were captured on camera fighting over assorted T-Shirts, cloths and condoms bearing the presidents images.[9] These are campaign gifts that invariably help the president to get re-elected in addition to allegedly hiring fake election observers, while the entire state machinery, including the electoral commission is of course answerable to him and his ruling cabal. As is the case in the political economy of squanderation or "eating" the masses can "eat" the crumbs and leftovers, especially during the election cycle when they are most needed, even if their votes are sometimes inconsequential due to the effects of ballot rigging.

There have been too many flawed elections with questionable and manipulated outcomes at various levels, subnational and national, in Africa. Presidents like Paul Biya and a few others in Africa are contemporary reminders of the French monarch Louis XIV in early modern Europe who in his power-drunkenness was reported to have made the famous declaration: *L'etat c'est moi*, "I am the state." Biya is not as despotic as the kings in early modern Europe and the vicious potentates in early postcolonial Africa like Idi Amin of Uganda. In Biya's Cameroun, private citizens can publish the most satirical cartoons against Monsieur le Président or insult him in the pages of the newspaper without his security operatives coming after them. Nonetheless, President Biya personifies the state by his sheer longevity in power and mastery of the politics of using silence, fear and surprise to extract loyalty and mass compliance. The persistent absence of President Biya and his politics of silence even when present has created a fulltime job for several Cameroonian conspiracy theorists in print, electronic and social media. Under the political economy of squanderation, there are a few of the African states that are personified by their corrupt rulers and dictators. They are part of what I have earlier called the "bewitched states," and I don't mean any offence to the suffering citizens of these countries because they don't deserve the collective humiliation they are subjected to regardless of any support roles occasionally played by sections of the hoodwinked masses. From the standpoint of the "politically edgy" and agitational strand of critical theory, transformative scholarship is one that does not take side with hegemonic power, not least under circumstances of undeniable evidence of oppression and impoverishment of the masses (Leonardo 2004: 11). I do not wish to give out data about how much wealth the long-serving corrupt African dictators have amassed in office. One could find it in the American business magazine *Forbes*.

Away from the spoils of power, neoliberal democratic elections have facilitated the emergency of stable democratic governments in countries such as Ghana, Senegal and Benin Republic. Other countries like Tanzania, Malawi and Botswana have been stable since attaining political independence, with or without liberal democracy. Botswana and Malawi have been stable on the liberal democratic path. Post-apartheid South Africa has consistently held free and fair elections since 1994, even though the country's political space is becoming increasingly toxic with the unpredictable outbursts of xenophobic violence, especially as the economy struggles or stagnates, and opportunities available to the excluded and marginalized locals shrink. Under the prevailing circumstances of economic and livelihood insecurity for the masses, incendiary comments from local politicians and populist politics over immigration from many broken African countries fuel displaced aggression among the hopelessly marginalized local youth, which intermittently breaks out in xenophobic attacks on foreigners in the congested South African townships. The South African police and government in general do not always respond to these Afrophobic attacks with the required seriousness apparently because of their institutionalized belief that immigrants from some of the African countries contribute to South Africa's high crime rate, notably crimes like trafficking and retailing of drugs and human trafficking (Human Rights Watch 2019; JethroNews 2019). By and large, neoliberal democracy is associated with excessive violence in many African countries.

In an interview with a Nigerian national newspaper in May 2020, the Nigerian Transport Minister Rotimi Amaechi, gave the most brilliant portrayal of neoliberal politics in contemporary Africa, albeit his narrative may not be typical of all African neoliberal democracies in terms of degree. Responding to a question on why he joined politics the Minister declared as follows:

> My father was a politician. He ran for councillorship during his time. However, I didn't join politics because I wanted to be a leader or because I wanted to solve Nigeria's problems. I joined because of unemployment. I also believe there is a part that grace played in it. (Punch, 17 May 2020)

The truth be told. Many join politics in contemporary Africa not because they want to solve the problems of their country as the Minister confessed but as a desperate means of escaping unemployment. So, politics becomes their first job in life, and they don't ever want to leave the terrain because that is their only job and a job that in the context of most of the extremely dysfunctional states does not offer many transferable skills. Most people in Nigeria who go into politics for lack of jobs, including top elected officials at different levels of government are not better than uncultivated touts or *agboro* in Nigerian Pidgin English, but not the Transport Minister. He is a man of honour and integrity.

Since joining politics in the Nigerian third republic, Amaechi has held several positions, climbing through the ladder and weathering the storms. Among the positions he has held include Secretary of the defunct National Republican Convention (NRC) in Ikwerre Local Government Area of Rivers State, Special Assistant to the Deputy Governor of Rivers State (1992–1994), Secretary of the Democratic Party of Nigeria (DPN) Caretaker Committee in Rivers State (1996), Speaker of the River State House of Assembly (1999–2007), Governor of Rivers State (2007–2015), and Federal Minister of Transportation (since 2015).[10] At my time of research and writing, he was still in office as Minister. In his home base of Rivers State, the Honorable Minister has risen to become a political colossus and benevolent "god-father" or benefactor to many as is the trend in Nigerian politics. Most political god-fathers in Nigeria are devious and extractive "big eaters."

Despite the privilege of a great career in politics and enormous fortunes, Amaechi remarked in the media interview that he was concerned that his first son was showing strong interest in taking after him to go into politics. The Minister does not want the political career that both he and his father had enjoyed being passed on to his son for some intriguing reasons. Ameachi discourages his son from going into politics, remarking that:

> Nigerian politics is not something one would want one's child to go into because there are no rules. One can be easily destroyed. One must have the grace to survive. I don't know if he has that grace (and I'm not talking about tact or sagacity) to survive because it is a man-eat-man world. ... If God wasn't by my side, I may not have been standing till now. There is a lot of betrayal and I don't know if he can survive that because he literally grew up in Europe. One has to be a hard man to survive the betrayals in Nigerian politics. (Punch, 17 May 2020)

The Minister made three interesting disclosures in the preceding narrative which I simply wish to quickly highlight. Firstly, in neoliberal politics, arguably in the Nigerian variant, "there are no rules." This speaks about lawlessness and impunity. Secondly, "one can be easily destroyed" because "it is a man-eat-man world." I have postulated that in the political economy of "eating," men essentially "eat" money, and consequently, I have tried to analyse the structural conditions that enable the "eating," but here the Minister has introduced a puzzling dimension, metaphorically telling us that men also "eat" men. This speaks about political Darwinism in the "eating jungle," about the survivalist violence and chicanery that characterize the entire political space. And as he aptly added, "tact or sagacity" is not important for survival but "one has to be a hard man to survive ...," which points to a rugged mentality. Thirdly, the Minister said that his son may not survive the rough political terrain "because he literally grew up in Europe." Without specifically impugning the integrity of the Honorable Minister, this speaks about where and how the money that many African politicians and their local business collaborators make on the continent are preponderantly spent. Their children hardly grow up in Africa but in the West where they are also educated. Likewise, they and their families hardly shop in Africa, holiday in Africa, bank in Africa, and when they need medical attention—rarely in Africa—all mostly in the West. Africa's wealth is systematically transferred to the rich West without their asking for it. It's part of the tragicomedies of postcoloniality.

One might choose to lampoon the Transport Minister Mr Amaechi as some have done in the social media, but as an analyst, I am more interested in the unhidden truth he has courageously spoken. Again, without calling to question the integrity of the Minister, I do not begrudge anybody that lampoons the too many opportunistic politicians in Africa because they deserve the strongest indictment and opprobrium. Having said that, the point the Minister has made, wittingly or unwittingly, is that many things are fundamentally not working out well in neoliberal politics in Nigeria and Africa. When desperate young school leavers—products of the depreciated educational systems in many African countries—with no previous career experience "plunge" into politics as their first job in a sociocultural milieu with strong "acquisitive values" and expectations for the "successful," such as that you must own a car, get married in a lavish party, build and furnish your own house, support your poor siblings and relatives in every way that a government would do in functional political environments to uplift them from poverty, politics simply becomes a quick means to achieve all these value expectations. What I have called "acquisitive values" for lack of a more appropriate expression are values that have been largely shaped and reinforced by state failures and the abdication or incapacity of governments to fulfil the most basic obligations of governance. For most responsible hardworking citizens with a clear career path, fulfilling the value expectations of society in the context of their fragile national economies would progressively take a greater part of their career span, and for some almost a lifetime. For the desperate school leavers who can fight their way through the hullabaloo of illiberal politics, the desperation to fulfill these value expectations of the larger society is heightened by their understanding of the uncertainties and ephemerality of political power in the worst-case scenarios. As such, they are poised to make the most of every available opportunity, and the embedded culture of graft and impunity characteristic of liberal democracy in most African states becomes the final answer. Those sociocultural value expectations that would ordinarily take the average hardworking careerist a greater part of their employment life to progressively achieve could all be achieved in one year by the young graduate politician through access to state power. As already indicated in the preceding chapter, Michela Wrong (2009), captured this dominant culture of politics as a culture of using state power "to eat." *It is our turn to eat*, the title of Wrong's epic study is a typically Kenyan and African metaphor or euphemism for using political power to embezzle public funds whenever one is opportune to wield power. In her book, Wrong investigated the multi-faceted Anglo Leasing corruption scandals in Kenya. The Anglo Leasing scandal involved many top Kenyan officials and tycoons, the "big eaters", who connived with the proprietors of the British registered company Anglo Leasing to siphon millions of Dollars from the government treasury through multiple contract scams. The UK company had 18 contracts with the Kenyan government for the supply of everything from a forensic laboratory to a navy frigate and jeeps: 16% of the government's expenditure in 2003–2004 went to Anglo Leasing.[11] There is no scarcity of "useful idiots", expatriate and local, in the political economy of "eating." John Githongo, the respected Kenyan journalist and President Mwai Kibaki government's short-lived anti-corruption Tzar investigated and exposed the scandal at enormous personal cost. The pervading mentality and orientation to politics in most African states is one of cutting and eating the national cake as opposed to producing or baking it. The process of getting a handle on the cake for a cut can be brutal, highly brutal. The African metaphor of "eating" probably deserves elevation to a theory of political economy—if you like, the theory of squanderation.

The dysfunctional African capitalist economies and states are not in the political economy of squanderation alone. In the aftermath of the Rwanda genocide, more than 200 Western international development organizations flooded Rwanda, and literally displaced the government, but could not functionally replace it. While a few reputable charities like the International Red Cross and Médecins Sans Frontières did a phenomenal job, the vast majority of the organizations were free-riders and first-timers in Rwanda who had mediocre understanding of international development and no serious business with post-conflict intervention. They raised millions of dollars in aid money, posted huge expenses on humanitarian relief and development works in Rwanda but with little to show on the ground. Most of the international charities mushroomed around the national capital Kigali replicating similar activities. Many of them spent over 70% of the funds on fat staff salaries, international conferences and travels, workshops, official dinners and banquets, and the likes. When the

Rwandan government stepped in with sensible regulatory measures to arrest the gigantic fraud, some of the Western charities left the country labelling the government authoritarian. I make no apologies for the Rwandan presidency—just giving a tip of the iceberg on the prebendal "eating" culture of international development in Africa. One may need to read works like James Carafano's *Private Sector, Public Wars* (2008), Derek Paulhus' "Waste, Greed, and Fraud" (2016) and "The Economic Impact of Peacekeeping" (2009) by William Durch to fully appreciate the "supply-side" of prebendal "eating" in international development and how Western capitalism essentially drives their peacekeeping and international development engagements in developing countries.

Box 6.1 The Resonance of Gender Inequality in Neoliberal Politics in Africa

In terms of gender, the brutal and survivalist nature of politics in many African states practically disadvantages most young female school leavers who based on the prevailing sociocultural value systems are largely trained and cultivated for marriage and are expected to be good wives and mothers. This point was eloquently stressed by the celebrated African novelist and feminist Chimamanda Adichie in her indictment of the constraints that patriarchal power places on women and the girl child in Sub-Saharan Africa in her short riveting book, *We Should All Be Feminists* (2014). In explaining why both progressive-thinking men and women should all be feminists in Africa to fix the structurally institutionalized gender inequity, Adichie argued that girls are culturally prepared, socialized, educated and skilled essentially for the purpose of marrying a good husband, but men don't face similar expectations; they are not taught in their upbringing to view marriage the same way. Imported into the political space, the females' gender role preparation for marriage and the corresponding expectations of domesticity and docility place a clear disadvantage on their political participation potential beyond the ritual of voting and the tokenism of affirmative action in political recruitment and representation. The young female school leavers who could muster the equivalent of the rugged mentality required for entering the masculinity-driven political space are largely those the society would perceive as deviant clients and mistresses of politicians. Without intending any gender harm there is unfortunately no short supply of mistresses, female clients and pimps seeking political favours in the male-dominated corridors of power in Africa where sex is cheaply exploited for sundry favours. Pimping is done by both males and females. Without doubt, the playing field privileges masculinity, not just every kind of masculinity but what R. W. Connell calls "hegemonic masculinity."[12]

Lawmaking in many African neoliberal parliaments is not without the dramatization of unseriousness. As Africans and the rest of the world grappled with the lockdown occasioned by Covid-19 in June 2020, lawmakers in the Kaduna State House of Assembly were brawling and punching one another in the hallowed chamber, all wearing the protective face mask but completely breaching the more important rule of social distancing. It was a free-for-all fight, many of them struggling over the mace, the symbol of authority of the presiding Speaker of the House and the Legislative Assembly. The fighting was triggered by the impeachment of the Deputy Speaker, Mr Mukhtar Hazo over some alleged infractions. Instead of contesting his impeachment through the established constitutional procedure, the faction of the House loyal to the Deputy Speaker preferred to contest and overturn the impeachment by physical violence. Brawling by lawmakers and making the mace an object of struggle to frustrate parliamentary deliberation has happened repeatedly in Nigeria's national assembly. In one of such incidents in April 2018, the Senate's plenary was invaded by thugs believed to be led by a suspended well-known lawmaker (*Premium Time*, 24 April 2018). Amidst the fracas they caused, the thugs went for the mace and disappeared, but the police recovered the mace the next day. Acts of impunity of this nature hardly attract any lawful penalty or sanction in dysfunctional states. In fact, sometimes, they can be the ultimate catalyst for the negotiation and dispensing of reward. Comparatively, open brawling among law makers have been more frequent in the lower chamber of the Nigerian national assembly, the House of Representatives.

In the DRC, there were two days of fighting in the parliament on the 6th and 7th of December 2020 between the supporters of President Felix Tshisekedi and those of his predecessor and arch-rival Joseph Kabila who were using their parliamentary majority to control and frustrate the coalition government which they are part of. The fighting was aimed to frustrate the move to impeach the Speaker of Parliament, Jeannine Mabunda, an ally of Kabila, and pave the way for the formation of a pro-Tshisekedi majority, an action that Kabila's side claimed was illegal (Al Jazeera, 8 December 2020). Security personnel were brought in principally to control the mayhem and restore order.

The use of physical violence as an extension of political discourse in the parliament is neither novel in Africa nor is the phenomenon limited to the continent. In recent years, fracas and brawling have broken out among lawmakers in legislative chambers in many parts of the world including Nepal, Georgia, Turkey, Ukraine, Taiwan, Serbia and Montenegro, Venezuela and Hong Kong. In the US subnational states of Alabama, California and Texas, fighting has occurred between elected lawmakers in parliament over the past 15 years. Way back in history (over twenty years ago), brawling and fist punching were occasionally associated with lawmaking in India, Japan, Russia, Bolivia, Britain, and USA—to mention a few.[13]

However, the frequency and impunity with which brawling in parliament occurs in contemporary Africa is both a rebuke and ridicule of neoliberal democratic politics on the continent. Repeatedly, lawmakers have resorted to fist punching and brawling in national and subnational parliaments in Kenya, Nigeria, Sierra Leone, DRC, Lesotho, Uganda, Zimbabwe and South Africa, among others. Contemporary Africa has widely imported and constitutionalized neoliberal democracy but the practice of it has been largely characterized by a near bankruptcy of the core values of democracy—constructive debate, negotiated consensus-building, tolerance of dissenting views, transparency in voting and counting of votes, voters' sovereignty in elections, etc. Law and order can hardly be maintained in a dysfunctional political system operated by too many lawless lawmakers and promoters and apologists of legislative rascality and executive impunity. The dysfunctionality of the polity inadvertently batters and infests the larger society.

Summary Points

1. Diverse regional institutional arrangements have been launched in Africa since 2000 aimed at improving political and economic governance, such as NEPAD, APRM and Agenda 2063. However, the cumulative impact of these initiatives on governance in the continent remains doubtful.

2. Essentially, the governance dimension of dysfunctionality across many African states is expressed in squanderism, and the process can sometimes be chaotic.
3. One of the most ridiculous features of democratic politics in many African countries is the fetish extravagance with which "small things" are celebrated by top government officials and the governed. The tradition has a colonial origin.
4. Even though there is a culture of amplifying and over-celebrating "small things" in many African countries, it is important to acknowledge that there are diverse big economic development projects happening in Africa without any undue hypes from the governments executing them.
5. Rebeka Gluhbegovic (2016) has carried out an important empirical study on how the APRM Reports submitted by various African countries address the issue of conflicts. Her research demonstrates that liberal democracy is the greatest source of violent conflicts in contemporary Africa.
6. Several activities in the African "liberal democracy value chain" are ridden with violent conflicts.
7. There have been too many flawed elections with questionable and manipulated outcomes at various levels, subnational and national, in Africa. Some of these flawed elections have precipitated widespread violence.

Discussion Questions

1. Why have Africa's various plans aimed to improve political and economic governance rarely translated into reality?
2. Provide specific examples of the "small things" amplified and over-celebrated by top government officials and the governed in several African countries?
3. Identify the fivefold classification of conflicts in Africa reported by Rebeka Gluhbegovic in her research on "how the APRM Reports submitted by various African countries" address the issue of conflicts?
4. Why is liberal democracy in many African countries characterized by unjustifiable levels of physical violence?

5. What are the factors that contribute to the prevalence of xenophobic violence in South Africa?
6. In what specific ways are women disadvantaged in the African neoliberal democratic space?

Notes

1. The definition is taken from the Mo Ibrahim Foundation's website on 17 September 2020. https://mo.ibrahim.foundation/iiag.
2. See NEPAD website for the regional body's objectives: https://www.un.org/en/africa/osaa/peace/nepad.shtml#:~:text=What.%20is%20the%20NEPAD%3F%20The%20New%20Partnership%20for,%28OAU%29%20held%20in%20Lusaka%2C%20Zambia%2C%20in%20July%20200.
3. See the APRM website for their mission and objectives: https://www.aprm-au.org/page-about/.
4. I use the concept of political culture in the classical structural functionalist tradition popularized by Gabriel Almond and Sydney Verba as "specifically political orientations—attitudes toward the political system and its various parts, and attitudes toward the role of the self in the system." Almond had earlier conceptualized it as "the *dominant* pattern of orientations toward political actions in which every political system is embedded" [the italicised in my emphasis]. See: Gabriel Almond and Sydney Verba (1963) *The Civic Culture: Political Attitudes and Democracy in Five Nations.* Newbury Park, CA: Sage, p. 11. Also: Gabriel A. Almond (1956) "Comparative Political Systems", *The Journal of Politics* 18, no. 3, pp. 391–409.
5. *The Observer* (6 December 2019) "I Know Who the Thieves in Government Are – Museveni", https://observer.ug/news/headlines/62858-i-know-who-the-thieves-in-gov-t-are-museveni.
6. This research was limited to 17 states that submitted their APRM reports in English.
7. See Gluhbegovic (2016).
8. Moyo (2009: 42) lists several examples of Asian and Latin American economies that have achieved significant economic success through political systems that were bereft of democracy, namely China, Indonesia, Korea, Malaysia, Singapore, Taiwan, Thailand, Chile and Peru. See also, Baum and Lake (2003) for more empirical examples of the nature of relationship between democracy and economic growth. The authors, among other things, argue that "democracy is intimately bound up with the economic sources of growth," being "an important determinant of patterns of investment" (Baum and Lake 2003: 335).

9. See: Adeola Fayehun online news episode on "Cameroon President Biya Distributes Condom for Votes, Hires Fake Election Observers", 17 October 2018, https://www.youtube.com/watch?v=YPhpTFRceME.
10. See: Chuka Udeze (2018) "Rotimi Amaechi Biography", *Buzz Nigeria*, https://buzznigeria.com/rotimi-amaechi-bio-children-private-jet/.
11. See: Raymond Bonner (2009) "The Stink of Corruption", *The Guardian* 21 April 2009, https://www.theguardian.com/books/2009/mar/14/politics. Read also: Michela Wrong (2009) *It's Our Turn to Eat: The Story of a Kenyan Whistle-Blower*. New York: Harper Perennial Publishers.
12. Connell (1987: 184) defines hegemonic masculinity as "a social ascendancy achieved in a play of social forces that extends beyond contests of brute power into the organization of private life and cultural processes." See: R.W. Connell (1987) *Gender and Power*. Blackwell: Polity Press. See also: R.W. Connell (2005) *Masculinities*. Second Edition. Berkeley, CA: University of California Press.
13. Some video documentaries exist on the incidents of fracas and brawling in parliaments. See: https://uk.video.search.yahoo.com/yhs/search;_ylt=AwrIQZxw7edeY9wAxAd3Bwx.;_ylu=X3oDMTByZmVxM3N0BGNvbG8DaXIyBHBvcwMxBHZ0aWQDBHNlYwNzYw--?p=Brawling+in+parliaments+around+the+world&fr=yhs-arh-001&hspart=arh&hsimp=yhs-001#id=6&vid=449eef50eacec3d6a78034b5ac826732&action=view. See also: https://uk.video.search.yahoo.com/yhs/search;_ylt=AwrIQZxw7edeY9wAxAd3Bwx.;_ylu=X3oDMTByZmVxM3N0BGNvbG8DaXIyBHBvcwMxBHZ0aWQDBHNlYwNzYw--?p=Brawling+in+parliaments+around+the+world&fr=yhs-arh-001&hspart=arh&hsimp=yhs-001#id=7&vid=beab4cd2f5b09bad21e04c73575bacb9&action=view. See also: https://en.wikipedia.org/wiki/Legislative_violence.

References

Acemoglu Daron, Naidu Suresh, Robinson James, and Restre Pascual. 2018. Democracy and Economic Growth: New Evidence. *Money in Politics*, February 6. https://promarket.org/2018/02/06/democracy-economic-growth-new-evidence/.

Adichie, Chimamanda. 2014. *We Should All Be Feminists*. London: Fourth Estate.

Ahere, R. John. 2021. New Actors and Democratic Governance in a Rising Africa, January 29, 2021. https://www.frontiersin.org/articles/10.3389/fpos.2020.630684/full.

Al Jazeera. 2020. Parliament Descends into Chaos for Second Day as Rival Political Groups Flung Chairs and Buckets Before Police Restore Order, December 8. https://www.aljazeera.com/news/2020/12/8/drc-mps-brawl-again-as-president-nears-power-struggle-win.

Baum, A. Matthew, and Lake A. David. 2003. The Political Economy of Growth: Democracy and Human Capital. *American Journal of Political Science* 47 (2) (April): 333–347.

BBC News. 2018. Paul Biya: Cameroon's 'Absentee President, 5 October. https://www.bbc.co.uk/news/world-africa-43469758.

Berman, Eli. 2017. Colonialism is Complicated, and the 'Independent Africa' Mixtapes Show You Why. *The Princeton LP*, September 15, 2017. https://lp.princeton.edu/colonialism-is-complicated-and-the-independent-africa-mixtapes-tell-you-why-4c9434817ea1.

Carafano, Jay James. 2008. *Private Sector, Public Wars: Contractors in Combat - Afghanistan, Iraq, and Future Conflicts*. Santa Barbara, CA: Greenwood Publishing Group.

Cilliers, Jakkie. 2020. *Africa First! Igniting a Growth Revolution*. Policy Brief 146, June. Institute for Security Studies (ISS), Pretoria, South Africa.

Dowden, Richard. 2008. *Africa: Altered States, Ordinary Miracles*. London: Portobello Books.

Durch, William. 2009. The Economic Impact of Peacekeeping – An Update. http://www.xn–bundesheer-sterreichebc.net/pdf_pool/publikationen/eco_impacts_04_eco_impact_an_update_durch.pdf.

Eagle News. 2020. I am not corrupt – Museveni blasts Deputy Speaker Jacob Oulanyah, December 4. https://eagle.co.ug/2019/12/04/i-am-not-corrupt-museveni-blasts-deputy-speaker-jacob-oulanyah.html.

Egypt Independent. 2020. New Administrative Capital Costs Le380 Billion Over Seven Years, Says Sisi, September 27, 2020. https://egyptindependent.com/new-administrative-capital-costs-le380-billion-over-7-years-says-sisi/.

FHI360. 2015. *Guide to the Good Governance Barometer*. FHI360, April, https://www.fhi360.org/sites/default/files/media/documents/resource-good-governance-barometer.pdf.

Fye, Abdoulie. 2015. Democratic Governance in Africa: Myth or Reality. *American Scientific Research Journal for Engineering, Technology and Sciences*. https://core.ac.uk/download/pdf/235049642.pdf.

Gluhbegovic, Rebeka. 2016. Types of Conflict in Africa: How Do the APRM Reports Address Conflicts? EISA—Electoral Institute for Sustainable Democracy in Africa, EISA Occasional Paper AP8, September 2016. https://www.eisa.org.za/pdf/aprm2015aps8.pdf.

Harding, Luke. 2012. *Mafia State: How One Reporter Became an Enemy of the Brutal New Russia*. London: Guardian Faber Publishing.

Harding, Luke. 2017. *Collusion: How Russia Helped Trump Win the White House*. London: Guardian Faber Publishing.

Harding, Luke. 2020. *Shadow State: Murder, Mayhem and Russia's Remaking of the West*. London: Guardian Faber Publishing.

Human Rights Watch. 2019. South Africa: Punish Xenophobic Violence, April 19. https://www.hrw.org/news/2019/09/13/south-africa-punish-xenophobic-violence.

Igata, Francis. 2016. Enugu Moves to Stop Ebeano Tunnel Road from Caving In. http://news.bestnaira.com/posts/view/enugu-moves-to-stop-ebeano-tunnel-road-from-caving-in.

JethroNews. 2019. South Africa Says Drug Dealers Cause of Xenophobic Attacks. https://jethronews.com/2019/09/06/south-africa-says-drug-dealers-cause-of-xenophobic-attacks/.

Kaufmann, Daniel, Aart Kraay, and Massimo Mastruzzi. 2010. The Worldwide Governance Indicators: Methodology and Analytical Issues. Policy Research Working Paper Series No. 5430, The World Bank.

Leonardo, Zeus. 2004. Critical Social Theory and Transformative Knowledge: The Functions of Criticism in Quality Education. *Educational Researcher* 33 (6): 11–18.

MIF. 2019. *The Africa Governance Report: Agenda 2063 and 2030 – Is Africa on Track*? Mo Ibrahim Foundation (MIF), London & Dakar.

Malsin, Jared. 2015. Egypt to Open Suez Canal Expansion Two Years Early. *The Guardian*, August 2, 2015. https://www.theguardian.com/world/2015/aug/02/egypt-to-open-suez-canal-expansion-finished-in-a-third-of-projected-time.

Moghalu, C. Kingsley. 2014. *Emerging Africa: How Global Economy's 'Last Frontier' Can Prosper and Matter*. London: Penguin Books.

Moyo, Dambisa. 2009. *Dead Aid: Why Aid Is Not Working and How There Is Another Way for Africa*. London: Penguin.

Mutura, Jacinta. 2020. Nyeri Deputy Governor Karugu Distances Herself from Viral Billboard. Standard, Kenyan Newspaper, June 4. https://www.standardmedia.co.ke/article/2001374056/nyeri-deputy-governor-distances-herself-from-viral-billboard-after-online-backlash#.

Nyong'o, Anyang' Peter. 2021. Rethinking African Politics: The New Age of Political Parties. *CODESRIA Bulletin Online*, No. 9, April. https://codesria.org/IMG/pdf/9-_anyang_nyong_o_codbul_online_21.pdf.

Owen, Olly, and Zainab Usman. 2015. Why Goodluck Jonathan Lost the Nigerian Presidential Election of 2015. *African Affairs* 114 (456): 455–471.

Page, T. Matthew. 2018. "A New Taxonomy for Corruption in Nigeria" Carnegie Endowment for International Peace. https://carnegieendowment.org/2018/07/17/new-taxonomy-for-corruption-in-nigeria-pub-76811.

Paulhus, Derek. 2016. Waste, Greed, and Fraud: The Business that Makes the World's Greatest Army. *Harvard Political Review*, February. https://harvardpolitics.com/united-states/waste-greed-fraud-business-makes-worlds-greatest-army/.

Premium Times. 2018. Mace Theft: National Assembly tightens security, April 24. https://www.premiumtimesng.com/news/top-news/266072-mace-theft-national-assembly-tightens-security.html.

Punch. 2020. Unemployment Drove Me into Politics— Rotimi Amaechi, May 17. https://punchng.com/unemployment-drove-me-into-politics-rotimi-amaechi/.

Reuters. 2020. Total Signs $14.9 Billion Debt Financing for Huge Mozambique LNG Project, July 17. https://uk.reuters.com/article/us-total-mozambique/total-signs-14-9-billion-debt-financing-for-huge-mozambique-lng-project-idUSKCN24I2FZ.

Taylor, Ian. 2017. The Liberal Peace Security Regimen: A Gramscian Critique of its Application in Africa. *Africa Development XLII* 3: 25–44.

The Economist. 2020. Belarus's Election Was a Sham, The West Response has been Feeble, August 15, 2020. https://www.economist.com/leaders/2020/08/13/belaruss-election-was-a-sham-the-wests-response-has-been-feeble.

Wrong, Michela. 2009. *It's Our Turn to Eat: The Story of a Kenyan Whistle-Blower*. New York: Harper Perennial Publishers.

Yakubu, Umar. 2019. White Elephant Projects, Retrogressive Economy, and Misplacement of Priorities, April 4. http://www.opinionnigeria.com/white-elephant-projects-retrogressive-economy-and-misplacement-of-priorities-by-umar-yakubu/.

CHAPTER 7

China–Africa Relations: Averting the Risk of Deepening Subaltern Capitalism

As subaltern capitalist economies, Africa will be terribly disadvantaged by giving in, and surrendering to external monopsonies and monopolies, especially if the African states continue to operate and act as separate entities.

7.1 The Subaltern Context

Since the 1980s, postcolonial theory popularized subaltern studies with the object of writing and re-writing history from the lived world of the underprivileged majority whose struggles, experiences and realities are scarcely captured in mainstream historiography. In this neo-Gramscian and poststructualist analysis, there is a strong recognition of the fact that the power relations in the material foundations of society are discursively reproduced in the way history is written and interpreted to the advantage of the dominant elites who further extend their power to dimensions of ideological and cultural constructions, as well as control of the subordinate classes otherwise known as the subalterns. The Indian school of historiography led by renowned scholars like Ranajit Guha, Shahid Amin, Partha Chatterjee, and Gyanendra Pandey has made some of the most outstanding contributions to subaltern theory in the humanities and social sciences.

K. Omeje, *The Failure and Feasibility of Capitalism in Africa*, International Political Economy Series,
https://doi.org/10.1007/978-3-030-75170-8_7

Extrapolating from subaltern theory, capitalism is imbued with an extraordinary power relation that too often legitimizes the domination of the subalterns by the hegemonic capitalists both within the domestic and international political economy spheres. The many centuries of Europe's relations with Africa have produced and perpetuated various versions of capitalism that are all subaltern in relation to the West. Western capitalism has never been an underdog or subaltern capitalism. It is top-dog industrial capitalism. China has turned its economy around to become capitalist while retaining a communist political ideology—an ambiguity of some sort, but one that has worked fabulously well to reposition China as a strong economic power on the world stage. Undeniably, Chinese capitalism and state are not subaltern regardless of their modest and persistent claim of being a developing Third World country. That's part of their well-crafted international diplomacy. The Chinese have shed their Third World garb many years ago. You only need to visit different parts of China, England, America, and Spain successively to appreciate that China is no longer a developing country regardless of any macroeconomic indicators they might produce to try to justify their "Third World" claim and diplomacy. I am aware that from a positivist epistemological standpoint, you cannot use a casual observation method based on touristic visits to assess differences in levels of physical development between states without being charged with crude empiricism. However, this is perhaps the bluntest way of putting China's stellar achievements in comparative perspective without minimizing the spectacular achievements of the West. I am not a Chinese apologist but as is often said in the business world, it is what it is.

With the world's largest foreign currency reserve that stood at $3.112 trillion in June 2020,[1] China has enormous power for international investment and trade which it has in recent years used creditably to its advantage in bringing many developing countries under its sprawling economic orbit, albeit not exactly in the chequered neocolonial tradition championed by the Western powers that disempowers Africa.

Having been subalterns in the international political economy for over the past 400 years, there is a sense in which subaltern capitalism has over the years generated, institutionalized and perpetuated a subservient mentality and culture of subalternism among African leaders in the international system. It is a lazy and beggarly mindset that unduly predisposes them to frequently dabble into international [economic] relations least prepared and endlessly expecting favours and aid from potential "benefactors" in the belief that the latter is destined to help them. That's why any government in the West or East can effortlessly assemble most of the African heads of state for an economic summit, and the African bloc gathers for development assistance with no pre-negotiated and commonly agreed agenda as an economic bloc. China, US, Japan, Russia, France, UK, even India, not to talk of Turkey, have all convened African leaders to economic summits in the unfolding scramble for Africa. As subalterns in the international political economy, how well have African governments prepared themselves in negotiating with these well-established and emerging powers? What's Africa's strategic agenda in all these negotiations? Does the African bloc have any agreed bottom lines and red lines in these international economic negotiations? Beyond the negotiated deals, what measures and sanctions have the African bloc put in place to ensure that none of their members ultimately subverts any agreed terms to their self-serving advantage? Even in the best of collective intentions, extreme poverty can make the poorest of the poor to sell out. This is not a forum to discuss African economic and trade negotiations but the point being made is that African states are vulnerable subalterns in the international political economy, and as Mohammed Ayoob (2002) explained in his theory of subaltern realism, as subalterns in the international system, Third World states are more concerned with short-term utilitarian benefits than long-term strategic goals. Hence, akin to a survival-inclined wretched fellow, they have little patience and discipline for strategic thinking and committed long-term planning. It is all about what they can eat today, good or bad. Too often, the more powerful external actors and investors freely take advantage of Africa's subaltern status and vulnerability in the international marketplace where good conscience is not a prime value but strategic interest. China–Africa's relations have the risk of reproducing and deepening the existing structures of subaltern capitalism in Africa not necessarily because the Chinese intend to hurt Africa—even though some of their businesses do—but more fundamentally because Africa is not prepared to be in the driving seat and steer the relations to their advantage. If Africa fails to take the initiative to develop and pursue a concerted China policy capable of yielding more balanced and dignified win-win outcomes, the continent will be worse off for it. A similar observation would go for other states that are all wooing African leaders as a potential suitor would run after a mid-Summer maiden.

China–Africa relations have grown in leaps and bounds since the 1990s with the result that over the past decade or so, China has been Africa's largest trading partner, displacing historical and traditional allies like the European Union and the USA. The reason is largely due to the rapid growth in Chinese export-oriented manufacturing-intensive economy which hugely requires Africa's natural resources and markets. This is the story behind the third scramble for Africa—a scramble in which China has overtaken the West. China has had a remarkable economic growth that has seen its GDP rise from a record low of US$47.21 billion in 1962 to an all-time high of US$13.61 trillion in December 2018 (*Trading Economics* 2019). China is today not only Africa's leading partner in trade but also in productive investments and development. Chinese direct investments in Africa have grown in remarkable dimensions over the past two decades and there has been dramatic progress in technical cooperation, notably in sectors such as solid minerals, oil and gas, textiles, manufacturing, pharmaceuticals, energy production, aviation, agriculture, education and infrastructural development. Some of Africa's fastest-growing economies today, such as Ethiopia, Ghana, Tanzania, Mozambique, Zambia and Uganda are countries that have fostered robust trade, investment and development cooperation with China. Notwithstanding the noticeable mutual advancements, it is pertinent to point out that the rapid growth in "China – Africa cooperation" has generated mixed sentiments from many academic observers and policymakers in Africa and around the world. The sentiments range from "positive applause" to "cautious optimism" and "outright cynicism." In this chapter, I wish to place the China–Africa relations in a historical perspective. I have argued that the current phase of China–Africa relations presents a significant opportunity for Africa's growth and development. However, Africa needs to be in driving seat with strong strategies to steer the continent away from the noticeable trends of subaltern capitalism that the relationships seem to be reproducing.

7.2 The International Context and Historical Phases of China's Engagement with Africa

The first phase of the Chinese expedition to Africa is the precolonial phase, although China was not a colonial power. As already detailed in Chapter 1, Africa was colonized by countries of Western Europe during the nineteenth and twentieth centuries, a history that was preceded by about 300 years of trans-Atlantic slave trade in which millions of Africans were carted away from the continent to the West (the Americas and Europe, to a lesser extent) as forced labour in agricultural plantations and diverse European investments and infrastructural projects. Africa was colonized by five Western imperial powers—Britain, France, Belgium, Portugal and Spain who pursued different colonial policies that contributed to Africa's underdevelopment. Germany and Italy were involved in the colonial project in Africa until they lost the World Wars against the bigger powers when their colonies were taken away by the League of Nations and its successor the UN and handed over to some of the winners of the wars as trusteeship territories.

It is significant to note that China's expedition to Africa pre-dated European colonial contact but was devoid of any colonial or imperialist ambition. The Chinese involvement in Africa goes back to the early fifteenth century (1414–1431) when Chinese voyages repeatedly arrived in East Africa with thousands of troops, explorers and traders beholden to the Chinese Ming dynasty.

Zheng He, also known as Cheng Ho, a legendary Chinese Ming dynasty admiral, was said to have led a vast fleet of Chinese ships across the Indian Ocean to the Kenyan seaside town of Lamu (among other destinations) in one of the most famous of such expeditions in 1418. Oral history from different Lamu villagers claims that a ship from Zheng He's fleet sank in a storm and the surviving crew married locals, implying that some people in the area arguably have subtle Chinese features (Greste 2010). A few archaeological discoveries and DNA test results from locals have been used by recent historians to reinforce this legend about an early Chinese expedition to East Africa almost a hundred years before the first set of Europeans reached the region (Greste 2010).

The Chinese expeditions were peaceful, and they honoured the local chiefs with gifts from their emperor which made their mission respectable and friendly. The interests of the Chinese explorers were on trade and exotic wildlife, especially for the honour of their emperor. In this regard, the Chinese expeditions to Africa bear an interesting contrast with the expeditions of the Europeans that came later, first for slaves and later for Christian missionary work, colonial conquest and trade. Throughout the colonial era (and over much of the preceding period of trans-Atlantic slave trade, to a lesser extent), Chinese engagement with Africa was literally arrested and superseded by the domineering economic and political influence of the European colonial powers.

The second phase of the Chinese involvement in Africa is the Cold War phase, notably from the 1960s when most of the African countries regained their political independence from the Western powers. This marked the beginning of modern China–Africa relations. Following the famous Asian–African Conference in Bandung, Indonesia in April 1955 attended by 29 developing countries and which laid the foundation for the Non-Aligned Movement, China declared its intent to support decolonization struggles throughout the developing world, and this became the hallmark of China's Africa policy from the 1950s to the end of the Cold War in 1990 (Kobo 2013). The Chinese supported the liberation struggles in Algeria, Guinea-Bissau and many Southern African countries during the Cold War by providing ammunitions and training to freedom fighters. This friendly support endeared the Chinese government to most African countries.

The end of colonialism provided an opportunity for the newly independent states of Africa to expand their international relations away from the West and seek mutually beneficial partnerships with the rest of the world, including China. The international context of the new rapprochement with China was the ideological rivalry between the West and the East, as well as China's diplomatic need to promote solidarity amongst the various countries of the global South. The objective of the Chinese government during this phase was essentially to foster long-term international solidarity and friendship with the fledgling postcolonial states of Africa. Chinese Premier Zhou Enlai undertook a famous tour covering ten independent African countries popularly known as Zhuo's African Safari between December 1963 and February 1964 (Abegunrin and Manyeruke 2020: 1).

For a great part of the Cold War period, the Chinese government invested significantly in building public infrastructures and supporting social services in Africa—roads, bridges, railways, presidential palaces, hospitals, sports centres like football stadiums, and so forth. The classic example of Chinese support during this period was the $400 million interest-free loan provided between 1970 and 1975 for the Tanzania-Zambia railways, a landmark infrastructural project of 1,800 kilometers.

With the support of China and ex-Soviet Union, many African governments embraced the Communist-style short- and medium-term development planning, focusing mainly on agrarian and industrial developments. China was forced to curtail its internationalist ambition during the post-Mao Zedong's era, later followed by a new dispensation of inward-looking reforms introduced by Deng Xiaoping from 1979.

The third phase of the Chinese engagement with Africa is the post-Cold War phase which dates from the 1990s onwards. Starting from the 1990s, China's economy began to boom following years of successful reforms, necessitating expanded raw material requirements and market opportunities. In search of raw materials and trade partners, China launched a new phase of engagement with the developing world, especially Africa. The Chinese government sometimes calls the present phase their second engagement with Africa, but available historical evidence suggests that it is indeed the third phase. Since the 1990s, the volume of Chinese trade with Africa has risen astronomically—from US$5.6 billion in 1996 to a peak of $215 billion in 2014 before declining to fluctuating levels of $148 billion in 2017 and over $150 billion in 2018 due to weak commodity prices (CARI 2019).

A new partnership summit known as the Forum on China–Africa Cooperation Conference (FOCAC) was founded by the Chinese government in October 2000 to strengthen development cooperation and trade between the two sides. African heads of state, high-ranking ministerial teams and representatives of China–African business communities have been repeatedly hosted in Beijing and elsewhere in Africa under FOCAC. In the spirit of the booming partnership, the Chinese government designated 2006, "the Year of Africa." At the 2009 FOCAC summit, China pledged $10 billion in concessional loans to, among other things, support Africa's efforts to attain the Millennium Development Goals. From 2000 to 2009, China forgave poor African countries almost $3 billion in debt (Kobo 2013). China built a new $200 million ultra-modern headquarters complex of the Africa Union (AU), which was officially opened in 2012, and China has maintained a permanent mission to the AU since 2015.

With the establishment of FOCAC, China has advanced progressively to become Africa's largest infrastructural development funder and trading partner. Between 2000 and 2014, Chinese banks, contractors, and the government loaned more than $86 billion to Africa, about 61% of which were used for infrastructure construction, 16% are for industrial development, and a small portion of the remaining allocations were channelled to health, general budget support and education (Zhang 2016; Albert 2017). Over the same period, it is estimated that China funded about 1,700 official assistance projects in 51 African countries (Zhang 2016; Albert 2017; *The Conversation* 2016). Similarly, over the same 14 years period, merchandise exports from Sub-Saharan Africa to China (mostly primary commodities) increased from $4.0 billion to $68.1 billion, before decreasing significantly because of the fall in commodity prices (Langdon et al. 2018: 543). By the end of 2018, Sub-Saharan Africa's (SSA) debt to China stood at about US$154 billion (Green 2019; World Bank 2019).

Box 7.1 Chinese Foreign Direct Investments (FDI) in Africa
Chinese FDI annual flows to Africa, also known as OFDI ("Overseas Foreign Direct Investment") in Chinese official reports, have been increasing steadily since the early 2000s, surging from $75 million in 2003 to a peak of $5.5 billion in 2008 before declining minimally to $5.4 billion in 2018 (CARI 2020). Beyond the annual flows since 2003, China's total FDI in Africa can hardly be determined. "While China has not revealed the extent of its loans to Africa, the China-Africa Research Initiative team at Johns Hopkins University has tracked some 1,000 loans amounting to $152 billion, extended to 49 African governments and State-Owned Enterprises (SoEs) between 2000 and 2018" (EuroMoney 2020). Chinese investments cut across all strategic sectors of Africa's economy—solid minerals (copper, platinum, cobalt, aluminium, etc.), oil and gas, textiles, manufacturing, pharmaceuticals, energy production, agriculture, education and so forth.

Investments are spearheaded by both Chinese state-owned companies and the private sector, including smallscale traders.There are over 10,000 Chinese companies operating in Africa, about 90% of them being privately owned—among the largest and most successful privately owned being: (i) the mobile phone brand Tecno, (ii) Twyford—an industrial manufacturing joint venture between two Chinese firms: Sunda Group and Keda Clean Energy Company, (iii) the global telecommunications giant Huawei, (iv) Sunshine Group—a multifaceted investor in mining, agriculture, manufacturing and transport, (v) the digital satellite television giant Star Times, (vi) the famous travel agency Bobu Africa, and (vii) the vehicle assembly plant FAW (Maritz 2017). A classification of the privately owned Chinese businesses in Africa by industrial sector in 2017 suggests that 31% are in manufacturing, 25% are in services, 22% are in trade, and 15% are in construction and real estate (Nikkei Asia Review 2017).

The large Chinese state-owned enterprises are small in number, but account for about 77% of China's foreign direct investment (FDI) in Africa and have in recent decades built major development infrastructures like airports, highways, railways and power stations across Africa in growing numbers (Maylie 2014; Nikkei Asia Review 2017). Some of the largest

Chinese state-owned enterprises with commanding investments and operations in Africa are the energy giants Sinopec Group and China National Petroleum Company (Petro China), the alternative energy supply company State Grid; financial sector giants such as Industrial & Commercial Bank of China, China Construction Bank, Agricultural Bank of China, Bank of China and China State Construction Engineering Company; and China Railway Engineering Company.

The bulk of Chinese investments in Africa are concentrated in Nigeria, Zambia, Algeria, Tanzania, Ethiopia, South Africa, Kenya, Angola and Cote d'Ivoire. According to the report produced by Mckinsey and Company (2017a, b: 11), about 89% of the employees in Chinese companies in Africa are Africans, which in practical terms translates to tens of thousands of multi-sectoral jobs; 64% of the Chinese companies provide vital skills training for Africans and 44% of managers in these companies are Africans.

When the Chinese government announced in 2013 its multi-billion Dollar global development strategy, the Belt and Road Initiative (BRI), outlining massive infrastructural developments and investments to mainly connect Asia, Eastern Europe and Africa, it came to many observers in Africa and elsewhere in the developing world as a welcome grand plan for something that was already happening—Chinese investments around the world (*The Guardian* 2018). Originally known as the "One Belt One Road" (OBOR) policy until it was renamed in 2016, BRI is a transcontinental long-term policy and investment programme, which aims at infrastructure development and acceleration of the economic integration of countries along the route of the "historic Silk Road," a network of trade routes which connected the East and West, and was central to the multi-faceted interactions between these regions from the second century BC to the eighteenth century (BRI, n.d.). The name "Silk Road" is derived from the lucrative trade in silk carried out along the land and maritime trade routes. Described in many quarters as "the Chinese Marshall Plan," BRI is a global initiative but because it builds on the historic Silk Road, the programme puts a major focus on countries in South Asia, Eastern Africa, Eastern Europe and the Middle East, a region mainly composed of emerging markets (BRI, n.d.; *The Guardian*, 2018). Some of the flagship projects credited to BRI in Africa include a network of industrial zones in Ethiopia and elsewhere in East

Africa that serve as manufacturing hubs for scores of Chinese companies, the over 750 kilometres' Addis Ababa–Djibouti Railway, the 485 kilometres' Mombasa–Nairobi Standard Gauge Railway, the Lagos–Kano Standard Gauge Railway, etc. A total of about 44 African countries and the African Union Commission have signed cooperation agreements with China on the Belt and Road Initiative (*Global Times*, 10 July 2020).

President Xi Jinping announced at the 2015 FOCAC summit in Johannesburg, South Africa, some major aid package to consolidate China's diplomacy in Africa, which included a total package of $60 billion in various loans, grants and special funds; various assistance in industrialization, agricultural modernization, infrastructure, financial services, trade and investment facilitation, poverty reduction and peace and security; an additional amount of $60 million was pledged as free assistance to the African Union (AU) to support the building and operation of the African Standby Force and an African Capacity for the Immediate Response to Crisis (Ngoma 2016: 1). Since 2006, China has reviewed its foreign policy towards Africa to make a constructive shift from non-interventionism to active engagement. As such, China has become one of the personnel contributors to UN peacekeeping in Africa (notably South Sudan and Mali), as well as a key financier of peace and security support operations on the continent.

In August 2017, China opened a major military base in the East African state of Djibouti built with about $590 million and operated by the Chinese People's Liberation Army Navy (PLAN). Chinese government sources announced that the military base was established with the benign objective to provide logistical support to Chinese troops in the Gulf of Aden, and also Chinese growing interest in peacekeeping and humanitarian operations in Africa (Singh 2017). Djibouti has for many years hosted the military bases of three major powers—USA, France and Japan. Many critics are of the view that given the longer presence of the American, French and Japanese military bases in Djibouti, the coming on board of the Chinese military base is designed to increase the projection of China's power in the strategic maritime corridors of the Horn of Africa and Indian Ocean. In 2018, Beijing announced a whopping $60 billion aid package to Africa (Shepard 2019).

As the world was battered by the Covid-19 pandemic, an extraordinary China–Africa Solidarity Anti-Epidemic Summit against Covid-19 was held by video link on 17 June 2020. The summit deliberated on how China could assist the various African countries in the fight against Covid-19, and was jointly convened by China, South Africa, the rotating chair of the African Union (AU), AU and Senegal, the co-chair of FOCAC. In attendance were the Chinese President Xi Jinping, African Heads of State, AU Commission Chairperson Moussa Faki Mahamat, UN Secretary General António Guterres and the WHO Director General Dr Tedros Adhanom Ghebreyesus. China pledged to strengthen strategic and cooperative partnerships to win the fight against Covid-19. Prior to the summit, China was already helping many African countries to combat the microscopic virus by providing technical expertise and medical supplies. Furthermore, as part of the G20, China had already accepted the G20's commitment to temporarily suspend debt payments to the world's poorest developing countries, effect from 1 May 2020. About 39 African countries are members of the International Development Association's (IDA) world's poorest developing countries eligible for the announced Covid-19 related debt-repayment moratorium by the G20. IDA is part of the World Bank Group.

Following the growing strategic partnerships, there has been a corresponding increase in immigration between China and Africa. Over 200,000 Africans presently live in China, mostly businessmen, traders and students. About 25 years ago China was hardly a destination of choice for Africans. It is estimated that over one million Chinese presently live in Africa, mostly employees of Chinese state-owned companies and private companies, as well as businessmen and traders. Evidently, China is reaping significant benefits from its relationship with Africa through access to raw materials, expanded markets for exports of manufactured goods, interest on loans, the establishment of investment relationships, which could generate significant profits over time and diplomatic influence (Schiere 2011: 1).

7.3 Evaluating the Contemporary China-Africa Relations

In his film, *The Coming War on China*, the award-winning Australian journalist and film-maker John Pilger warns that the world's greatest military power, the US, and the world's second economic power, China, may well be on the road to war (Al Jazeera, 6 December 2017). In a state visit to the USA in May 2020 to seek and negotiate a new trade deal for his country, Kenyan President Uhuru Kenyatta reportedly warned that the US–China rivalry puts Africa at risk because it was exacerbating the continent's divisions (Shaun and Stein 2020). According to President Kenyatta, Western countries, and their counterparts in Asia and the Middle East, have returned to competition over Africa, in some cases weaponizing divisions, pursuing proxy actions and behaving like Africa is for the taking (Shaun and Stein 2020). The Irish professor of economic geography, Pádraig Carmody, in his popular 2016 publication described this phenomenon, centred on the competitive quest for Africa's abundant natural resources, markets and territory, as *The New Scramble for Africa*, which is also the title of his book. Chronologically speaking, it is the third scramble for Africa.

Africans and African leaders should not be misled to understand China from the standpoint of Western media and state propaganda. Listening to the Western media's persistent characterization of China as a communist dictatorship, you will hardly understand contemporary China. And if you have not been privileged to visit China to see things for yourself and have a first-hand experience of China and the Chinese system as I have done, you might be misled to believe that the Chinese live under daily oppression which is far from the truth. I make bold to say, even at the risk of a hyperbole, that most Chinese greatly adore their state and social system—a system that has lifted over 800 million of them out of poverty in recent decades—and do not want to be like the West. Same as the Middle Eastern Arabs—I imagine that most Middle Eastern Arabs are happy with their societies, and do not wish to be like the West. It does not mean that their societies are perfect, neither are the Western societies—with all their hypocrisy, licentiousness and self-defeating agnosticism—more perfect societies.

"If you stood on the tallest building in Beijing and looked out on the Pacific Ocean," write James Bradley, author of *The China Mirage*, "you'd see American warships, you'd see Guam is about to sink because there are so many missiles pointed at China. You'd look up at Korea and see American armaments pointing at China, you'd see Japan which is basically a glove over the American fist" (Al Jazeera, 6 December 2017). John Ratcliffe, President Donald Trump's last Director of National Intelligence warned that China "poses the greatest threat to America today," and "should be America's primary national security focus going forward," further claiming that: "The intelligence is clear: Beijing intends to dominate the US and the rest of the planet economically, militarily and technologically. Many of China's major public initiatives and prominent companies offer only a layer of camouflage to the activities of the Chinese

Communist Party" (Gabbatt 2020). I will not digress to talk about national security issues, the ongoing trade war between America and China, and the heightened American brinkmanship in recent years. It is a discourse that lies outside the purview of this book. However, it suffices to say that some of the most powerful sections of the neoliberal West, in their arrogance, find it difficult to understand that every part of the world cannot be like the West—politically, economically and culturally speaking.

Shanker Singham, Chief executive of Competere and former trade advisor to UK Trade Secretary and USTR[2] made an interesting observation in a recent article published in a UK daily *Express* on 12 July 2020 advocating for the placing of "Magnitsky Act-Style"[3] sanctions on Nigerian government officials complicit in horrific persecution of Christians in the Middle Belt region of the country. In justifying his position, Singham argued:

> The UK should ensure that its international economic policy, its foreign policy, and its development policy are aligned around the national interest. That national interest does not just mean the country's commercial interest, although that is part of it, but it includes the country's moral values – and its foreign policy should project them. As Britain stands for liberal trade, competition and the protection of property rights, its foreign policies should deliver those around the world. The protection of individual liberty and the protection of the security of your person and your property is a critical value of the UK's liberal economic democracy, and has been so since Magna Carta. The protection of human rights abroad is crucial to reflecting modern British values. (Singham 2020)

I will not comment on the issue of sanctions against Nigerian government officials, but I am particularly inspired by the observation of Singham that the UK's "national interest does not just mean the country's commercial interest, although that is part of it, but it includes the country's moral values – and its foreign policy should project them." The UK has moral values which the country's foreign policies should project, and I completely agree with that, but so do other countries and peoples. This is an essential philosophy the West needs to understand and respect.

The entire world cannot be like the West and cannot also submit ad infinitum to the neo-imperial governance of the West as they have done for a greater part of the past 400 years of Pax-Britannica and Pax-Americana. World history has shown that civilizations rise, peak, slacken and decline. Some civilizations rise as global powers, others as regional powers, but more importantly, multiple civilizations and hegemonic powers have sometimes coexisted side by side in the international system without one necessarily having to give way to the other, at least not before they have peaked and started their decline. The histories of the Egyptian empire, the Babylonian empire, the Medo-Persian empire, the Roman empire and the Greco-Roman civilization, the Ottoman empire, the Austro-Hungarian empire, the Japanese empire, the colonial era and the Cold War dispensation are particularly instructive. Some of the world's most influential and powerful empires practically emerged from obscurity but were able to make giant strides and great achievements by courtesy of a visionary leadership and the interplay of circumstantial opportunities. Many decision makers and politicians in the neoliberal West can still not relate to the reality that China, a previous Third World country they had once beaten and trampled upon has suddenly emerged from relative obscurity to become the world's second-largest economy and third-strongest military power. All scholarly predictions point to the fact that with the pace the Chinese have grown over the past 40 years, they are literally heading to become the largest and most powerful economy in the world in the near future, unless they are stopped. The neorealist theory of international relations, the dominant theory that has arguably informed much of American foreign policy since the end of the Word War II, teaches us that having a strong economic power is crucial for advancing your military capability. All these considerations have heightened the fear that the unexpected rise of China has provoked in the West.

To understand and relate with China, African governments and people should never buy into the rivalry and envy-driven fear of China spread by the West. The reality is that despite the fear-mongering, propaganda and hostilities, the West needs China (and vice versa) as much as Africa and many other regions of the world do. Western insatiable consumerism is significantly sustained by the prolific manufacturing industries in China and the well-integrated production networks of the South Asian countries which, to a large extent, depend on China for various inputs. "The Chinese state and its subsidiaries have lent about $1.5 trillion in direct loans and trade credits to more than 150 countries around the globe. This has turned China into the world's largest official creditor — surpassing traditional, official lenders such as the World Bank, the IMF, or all OECD creditor governments combined" (Horn et al. 2020). The US debt to China in March 2020 stood at $1.08 trillion (Amadeo and Anderson 2020).

One of the most significant developments in China–Africa relations is the strong perception in many African quarters that China is Africa's trusted economic and political ally and the most consummate example of South–South cooperation. The perception is partly informed by the fact that China has historically presented itself to Africa and the developing world as a fellow "Southern" country that shares all the detestable experiences of the "Third World." In sharp contrast with the Western powers, most of whom have been historically associated with colonizing, exploiting and degrading Africa, China is largely perceived as seeking genuine partnership and friendship based on mutual respect. It is this perception that has made many African statesmen and scholars to over the years idealize the Chinese developmentalist model as an alternative pathway and model for political and economic reforms in Africa. Countries that have embraced the philosophy of the developmental state in Africa such as Ethiopia (especially under late Prime Minister Meles Zenawi), Rwanda and Uganda, to a lesser extent, have all shown some fascination with the Chinese model [see Sect. 8.2.2 for more detail]. Many other African leaders who have taken part in FOCAC summits have paid great tributes to the Chinese model and partnership.

However, the growing presence of China in Africa has been a source of concern to traditional international players in Africa, notably the EU countries and the US. The vast space that China has taken in African economies and trade since the past two decades has largely come at the expense of the traditional Western players—the neocolonial powers.

Critics of the Chinese growing presence in Africa have variously remarked that China has increasingly replaced the West in dominating and exploiting Africa. Consequently, some commentators have sounded the alarm bell that China has a colonialist mission or is simply colonizing the continent, notably by using multi-faceted financial aid and loans designed to make African regimes more allegiant to China in international economic and political relations (cf. Shinn and Eisenman 2012; Mead 2018).

The Chinese have also been criticized for: (i) Their "unconditional approach" to business in Africa, not being mindful about issues of human rights, transparency and good governance as is often the case with the Western powers. (ii) Flooding Africa with cheap sub-standard goods and labour, which is otherwise in abundance in Africa, thereby not helping to expand skills acquisition and create jobs on the continent. (iii) Mixing commercial interests with development assistance, in response to which

China established the China International Development Cooperation Agency (CIDCA) in March 2018 to strengthen the strategic planning and overall coordination of Chinese foreign aid. (iv) Adoption of the unorthodox means of negotiated use of natural resources and award of mining concessions in payment for credit facilities in countries like Angola and DRC. In his critique of the Chinese presence in Africa, Muammar Gaddafi (former Libyan leader) reportedly remarked in May 2008 that: "Nowadays, the Chinese communities are in every African country. The plan is to take some of its population and put them in Africa, while Africans just look on and African leaders hold fruitless meetings" (Le Mauricien 2014).

I do not intend to respond to all these criticisms. Except for Gaddafi's undue hysteria, much of the criticisms can be evidently substantiated. However, I wish to point out that the experiences of China–Africa relations seem to markedly vary from one African country to another, which may diminish the validity or applicability of any generalized criticism. The truth is that the emergence of China as a global economic power has provided a great window of opportunity for African economies in terms of trade, investments and credit facilities. Much of the significant economic growth that many African countries witnessed in this millennium is largely attributable to the new vista of opportunities opened by economic relations and trade with China. Until the emergence of China, postcolonial Africa was held to ransom by the Western states and their international financial institutions for decades with practically no viable alternative sources of investments and development financing. Western credit conditionalities, and import restrictions, as well as their tutelage over issues of human rights, gay rights, democratization and good governance—all based on neoliberal values—are to say the least, crippling from an economic standpoint, and disrespectful of African values, from a socio-cultural and political point of view. Western priorities and values cannot be the same for Africa. On issues of trade, investments, credits, and economic sanctions the West has often spoken with one voice and acted in unison against disparate African states whom they preferred dealing with on individual basis, knowing that subalterns are much weaker when you subject them to a one-on-one prisoner's dilemma.

Despite all their imperfections, the rise of China and their approach to trade, investments and development financing are more respectful of the sovereignty and dignity of African states when compared to the Western approach. Significantly, China came to Africa and recognized

Africa's most pressing priority—bridging the infrastructural development gaps. Africa's infrastructural development needs, especially road networks have long been regionally recognized. The United Nations Economic Commission for Africa (UNECA) adopted the first masterplan for a Trans-African highway network in 1971 to boost continental trade, which they later further developed in partnership with AfDB and the African Union (Clacherty 2017). Among the long tracks of transregional roads envisaged in the Pan-African highway network are the 9,610 km Tripoli–Windhoek road, the 8,860 km Cairo–Gaborone–Cape Town road, the 8,636 km Cairo–Dakar road, the 6,260 km Lagos–Mombasa road, the 4,504 km Algiers–Lagos road, the 4,220 km N'Djamena–Djibouti road, etc. (Abegunrin and Manyeruke 2020: 51). Africa did not have the huge resources required to execute these massive road networks. The Chinese recognized the infrastructural gaps and resource deficits and more importantly prioritized them in their development aid to Africa. The Chinese President Xi Jinping once described inadequate infrastructure as "the biggest bottleneck to Africa's development" (Shepard 2019). China has heavily cooperated with African governments in helping to deliver on the much-needed infrastructural development—providing aid and helping African states to construct highways, bridges, railways, modern trains and city trams, airports, hospitals, power generation, sports and recreation infrastructures, special industrial zones, and so forth. These are by far more important than the much exaggerated human rights and gay rights to Africans. China has helped to complete one of the Trans-African highway networks, the 4,500 km Dakar–N'Djamena road spanning seven countries (Abegunrin and Manyeruke 2020: 50).

With their sprawling imperial presence in Africa and as major stakeholders in UNECA, the West certainly knew about Africa's massive infrastructural development deficit, especially the masterplan for the Trans-African highway network but failed to prioritize it. A recent report by the Global Infrastructure Hub—an initiative of the G20 group of the world's richest nations—evaluated seven sectors of the infrastructure needs of 10 African countries and found that they must invest $2 trillion between 2018 and 2040 if they are to meet the demands of their growing economies and populations (*The Telegraph* 2018). The evaluated seven infrastructural sectors are roads, railways, airports, seaports, electricity, water (including sewerage) and telecommunications, while the 10 assessed countries include Benin, Côte d'Ivoire, Egypt, Ethiopia, Ghana, Guinea, Morocco, Rwanda, Senegal and Tunisia (*The Telegraph* 2018). The projection is that if the evaluated countries continue on current spending trajectories—thanks to the Chinese Belt and Road Initiative—they will invest $1.4 trillion, a 40% shortfall (*The Telegraph* 2018). Estimates by the African Development Bank suggest that the continent's infrastructure needs amount to $130–$170 billion a year, with a financing gap in the range $68–$108 billion (AfDB 2018). In less than 10 years of the coming of the Chinese, African countries like Ethiopia, Angola, Kenya and Rwanda evidently had more to show in the area of development infrastructures and international economic relations relative to the rest of their postcolonial decades of hobnobbing with the West.

Having said all that, I recognize that some of the African countries have on different occasions gotten bad deals with the Chinese, especially in connection with infrastructure and development project credit financing. Several Chinese investors and companies have made headlines news in different African countries because of their unethical business practices. Commenting on the wider issue of Africa's relations with the BRICS countries, Kufakurinani (2017) argues that the latter's systems of exploitation are more amplified because when the Chinese, Brazilians, Indians, Russians and South Africans work in Africa, they are more extreme and exploitative than the Western countries who have better systems of accountability and approach to corporate social responsibility, among others. The issue of who is more exploitative of Africans is a disputatious one that can never have a conclusive answer. What seems to be evident from diverse research works is that international business in general often takes advantage of broken and less-law governed states to perpetrate outrageous atrocities and acts of impunity to maximize profit, violations that they would not ordinarily attempt in a law-governed society for fear of penalties (Omeje 2006, 2016; Mailey 2015). Hence, African states have serious need to strengthen rule of law and their governance institutions.

I made an earlier observation that needs to be reiterated at this juncture about Africa's lack of preparedness and capacity in negotiating deals with foreign partners, as well as the deep-rooted subaltern mentality that pervades the machinery of governance in many states. The Chinese or indeed any other international business actors cannot prepare, capacitate and set overarching policy frameworks for their international engagements and business negotiating team, and at the same time come over to the continent to do the same for their African counterparts. That would be as ludicrous as a football team preparing itself for a major international tournament and at the same time deploys their coaching crew to train and prepare their opponents for the match. It is this self-abnegation on the part of African leaders and states that risks the tendency of reproducing and deepening the structures of subaltern capitalism in the continent. It is squarely Africa's responsibility to prepare themselves at individual state and regional levels for the tough politics of international economic relations and map out their overarching policy frameworks.

Furthermore, in relation to trade, "China's prominent role as a buyer of resources increasingly displays monopsonistic characteristics"[4] loosely akin to the trade and credit markets controlled by the West before the rise of China. In economics, a monopsony is essentially a skewed market in which only one buyer faces many sellers, which is the opposite of a monopoly where there is one seller dealing with many buyers (Moyo 2012: 125). As subaltern capitalist economies, Africa will be terribly disadvantaged by giving in, and surrendering to external monopsonies and monopolies, especially if the African states continue to operate and act as separate entities. By reason of its enormous purchasing power over a wide range of commodities, China increasingly plays a leading role in setting resource prices and influencing whether market prices rise up or down, thereby helping to determine the value of assets in commodity-producing countries (Moyo 2012: 4). China's growing power in the international commodity market, including in price-setting dovetails with the point I made at the beginning of this chapter that there is a specific modality of power relations intrinsic to capitalism, local or international. In the international capitalist market, this power relation works to the advantage of primary commodity buyers, especially under monopsonistic tendencies. More disastrously, the power relations in international capitalism are further reproduced in the logic of interactions between the supply-side and demand-side of aid, technologies, and development assistance. In Sino–Africa economic relations, China is on the more powerful supply-side of the power relations. The less powerful has little or no chance facing the more powerful alone in a similar way that a featherweight boxer hardly stands a chance facing a heavyweight boxing champion in the ring. But 54 featherweight boxers together could stand a chance in facing one heavy-weight champion if there is a ring large enough to host such a bout. I recognize that all African states are not featherweights in the international economic arena. However, with an over $13 trillion GDP—five times more than Africa's GDP, a population and skilled workforce significantly higher than Africa's, as well as a foreign reserve largesse unparalleled in the history of capitalism, contemporary China is a colossus that African states cannot afford the luxury of continuing to engage in their isolated units or unprepared collectivity. The need for well-coordinated regional trade, investment and economic development policies and frameworks in Africa has never been more urgent. Is the African Continental Free Trade Agreement (AfCFTA) the answer? Time will tell.

Summary Points

1. Capitalism is imbued with a distinctive power relation that too often legitimizes the domination of the subalterns by the hegemonic capitalists both within the domestic and international political economy spheres.
2. In relation to both the developed capitalist economies of the West and the high-performing Chinese mixed-socialist market economy, Africa's capitalism is subaltern capitalism.
3. Historically, the Chinese engagement with Africa can be divided into three phases: the precolonial phase (howbeit, China had no colonial ambition in Africa), the early independence phase and the contemporary post-Cold War phase.
4. China–Africa relations have grown remarkably since the 1990s with the result that over the past decade, China has been Africa's largest trading partner, displacing historical and traditional allies like the European Union and the USA.
5. China has enormous power for international investment and trade, which it has in recent years used creditably to its advantage in bringing many developing countries under its sprawling economic orbit.
6. To understand and relate with China, African governments and people should never buy into the rivalry and envy-driven fear of China spread by the West.
7. Despite all their imperfections, the rise of China and their approach to trade, investments and development financing are more respectful of the sovereignty and dignity of African states when compared to the Western approach.

8. Africa needs to be in the driving seat to strategically steer the continent away from the noticeable trends of subaltern capitalism that its relationships with China seem to be reproducing.

Discussion Questions

1. How can subaltern theory be applied to explain contemporary China–Africa's relations?
2. What are the defining features of the three distinct phases of China–Africa's relations?
3. When was the "Forum on China–Africa Cooperation Conference" (FOCAC) founded and why?
4. What are the driving aims of the Chinese government's "Belt and Road Initiative" (BRI)?
5. Why did China establish a major military base in the East African state of Djibouti in 2017?
6. In what ways is "the third scramble for Africa" different from the preceding two scrambles?

Notes

1. Reuters (7 July 2020) "China's June Forex Reserves Rise to $3.112 Trillion", https://uk.finance.yahoo.com/news/chinas-june-forex-reserves-rise-082103417.html.
2. USTR stands for United States Trade Representative.
3. "In September 2019, U.K. Foreign Secretary Dominic Raab announced the government's intention to introduce unilateral post-Brexit 'Magnitsky' style sanctions for individuals deemed responsible for serious human rights abuses. The so-called Magnitsky sanctions refer to the US regime introduced sanctions to target officials responsible for the death of Russian tax lawyer Sergei Magnitsky, who died from mistreatment in a Russian prison in 2009, after revealing large-scale tax fraud." See Akin Gump (10 July 2020) "U.K. Announces "Magnitsky Act-style" Global Human Rights Sanctions And 49 Designations", Mondaq, https://www.mondaq.com/uk/human-rights/963242/uk-announces-magnitsky-act-style-global-human-rights-sanctions-and-49-designations.

4. Dambisa Moyo (2012) *Winner Take All: China's Race for Resources and What It Means for Us*. London: Penguin, p. 126.

References

Abegunrin, Olayiwola, and Manyeruke Charity. 2020. *China's Power in Africa: A New Global Order*. New York: Palgrave Macmillan.

AfDB. 2018. Africa's Infrastructure: Great Potential but Little Impact on Inclusive Growth. https://www.afdb.org/fileadmin/uploads/afdb/Documents/Publications/2018AEO/African_Economic_Outlook_2018_-_EN_Chapter3.pdf.

Al Jazeera. 2017. The Coming War on China, December 6. https://www.aljazeera.com/programmes/specialseries/2017/11/coming-war-china-171128124059730.html.

Amadeo, Kimberly, and Somer G. Anderson. 2020. US Debt to China, How Much, Reasons Why, and What If China Sells: Why China Is America's Biggest Banker, June 18. https://www.thebalance.com/u-s-debt-to-china-how-much-does-it-own-3306355.

Ayoob, Mohammed. 2002. Inequality and Theorizing in International Relations: The Case for Subaltern Realism. *International Studies Review* 4 (3): 27–48.

Albert, Eleanor. 2017. "China in Africa" Council on Foreign Relations, July 12. https://www.cfr.org/backgrounder/china-africa.

AU. 2019. African Continental Free Trade Area. African Union Documentary, January 28. https://www.bing.com/videos/search?q=africa+continental+free+trade+areadocumentary&&view=detail&mid=7EE60C60564E73FF591B7EE60C60564E73FF591B&&FORM=VRDGAR.

BRI. n.d. Belt and Road Initiative. Chinese BRI Homepage. https://www.beltroad-initiative.com/belt-and-road/.

CARI. 2019. Data: China – Africa Trade, published by China – Africa Research Initiative (CARI), May. http://www.sais-cari.org/data-china-africa-trade.

CARI. 2020. Data: Chinese Investments in Africa, published by China – Africa Research Initiative (CARI), February. http://www.sais-cari.org/chinese-investment-in-africa.

Carmody, Pádraig. 2016. *The New Scramble for Africa*. Cambridge: Polity Press.

Clacherty, James. 2017. The Trans-Africa Highway Masterplan: Of Masters, Plans and Master Narratives. Department of Urban Studies, University of Basel, Switzerland. https://criticalurbanisms.philhist.unibas.ch/publications/the-trans-africa-highway-masterplan-of-masters-plans-and-master-narratives/The-Trans-Africa-Highway-Masterplan_Of-Masters-Plans-and-Master-Narratives.pdf.

EuroMoney. 2020. China's Belt and Road Initiative: Can Africa Escape a Debt Trap? June 4. https://www.euromoney.com/article/b1lwrkkwwpxs0x/china39s-belt-and-road-initiative-can-africa-escape-a-debt-trap.

Gabbatt, Adam. 2020. China Conducting Biological Tests to Create Super Soldiers, US Spy Chief Says. *The Guardian*, December 4. https://www.theguardian.com/world/2020/dec/04/china-super-soldiers-biologically-enhanced-john-ratcliffe.

Global Times. 2020. Discrediting China – Africa Cooperation will not Make America Great Again. *Global Times*, July 10. http://www.globaltimes.cn/content/1194158.shtml.

Green, Duncan. 2019. From Poverty to Power: How Active Citizens and Effective States Can Change the World. https://oxfamblogs.org/fp2p/africa-in-2019-7-trends-to-watch-by-apollos-nwafor/.

Greste, Peter. 2010. Could a Rusty Coin Re-write Chinese-African History? BBC News Report. https://www.bbc.com/news/world-africa-11531398.

Horn, Sebastian, Carmen M. Reinhart, and Christoph Trebesch. 2020. How Much Money Does the World Owe China? February 26. *Harvard Business Review*. https://hbr.org/2020/02/how-much-money-does-the-world-owe-china.

Kobo, M. Ousman. 2013. A New World Order? Africa and China. *Origins: Current Events in Historical Perspective* 6 (8) (May). http://origins.osu.edu/article/new-world-order-africa-and-china.

Kufakurinani, Ushehwedu. 2017. The Political Economy of Africa and Dependency Theory. https://developingeconomics.files.wordpress.com/2017/06/chapter-8-the-political-economy-of-africa-and-dependency-theory.pdf.

Langdon, Steven, Achibald R.M. Ritter, and Yiagadeesen Samy. 2018. *African Economic Development*. London: Routledge.

Le Mauricien. 2014. Chinese Business in Africa: The Benefits and Problems of Such a Rapidly Expanding Business Relationship, March 4. http://www.lemauricien.com/article/chinese-business-africa-benefits-and-problems-such-rapidly-expanding-business-relationship/.

Mailey, J.R. 2015. *The Anatomy of the Resource Curse: Predatory Investment in Africa's Extractive Industries*. ACSS Special Report No. 3. Washington, DC. African Center for Strategic Studies (ACSS).

Maritz, Jaco. 2017. Seven Chinese Companies That Have Made It in Africa, August 8. https://www.howwemadeitinafrica.com/seven-chinese-companies-made-africa/59407/.

Maylie, Davon. 2014. Chinese State-Owned Enterprises in Africa: Ambassadors or Freebooters? October 25. https://journalistsresource.org/studies/international/china/chinese-state-owned-enterprises-in-africa-ambassadors-or-freebooters/.

Mckinsey and Company. 2017a. The Closest Look yet at Chinese Economic Engagement in Africa. https://www.mckinsey.com/featured-insights/middle-east-and-africa/the-closest-look-yet-at-chinese-economic-engagement-in-africa.

Mckinsey and Company. 2017b. Dance of the Lions and Dragons: How Are Africa and China Engaging and How Will the Partnership Evolve? June. https://www.mckinsey.com/~/media/McKinsey/Featured%20Insights/Middle%20East%20and%20Africa/The%20closest%20look%20yet%20at%20Chinese%20economic%20engagement%20in%20Africa/Dance-of-the-lions-and-dragons.ashx.

Mead, Van Nick. 2018. China in Africa: Win – Win Development, or a New Colonialism? *The Guardian*, July 30. https://www.theguardian.com/cities/2018/jul/31/china-in-africa-win-win-development-or-a-new-colonialism.

Moyo, Dambisa. 2012. *Winner Take All: China's Race for Resources and What It Means for Us*. London: Penguin.

Ngoma, A. Leslie. 2016. Introduction China-Africa Relations: Political and Economic Engagement and Media Strategies. *African Studies Quarterly* 6 (3–4): 1–6.

Nikkei Asia Review. 2017. Some 10,000 Chinese Companies Now Operating in Africa, Report Says, July 10. https://asia.nikkei.com/Business/Trends/Some-10-000-Chinese-companies-now-operating-in-Africa-report-says.

Omeje, Kenneth. 2006. *High Stakes and Stakeholders: Oil Conflict and Security in Nigeria Aldershot*. Farnham, UK: Ashgate.

Omeje, Kenneth. 2016. Natural Resource Rent and Stakeholder Politics in Africa: Towards a New Conceptualisation. *Commonwealth and Comparative Politics* 54 (1): 92–114.

Schiere, Richard. 2011. *China and Africa: An Emerging Partnership for Development*. Tunis: Africa Development Bank (AfDB) Working Paper No. 125, May.

Shaun, Tandon, and Chris Stein. 2020. Kenya Leader Warns Against US, China Rivalry in Africa, February 5. https://news.yahoo.com/kenya-leader-warns-against-us-china-rivalry-africa-172204859.html.

Shepard, Wade. 2019. What China Is Really Up to in Africa. *Forbes*, March 10. https://www.forbes.com/sites/wadeshepard/2019/10/03/what-china-is-really-up-to-in-africa/#372be9975930.

Shinn, H. David, and Joshua Eisenman. 2012. *China and Africa: A Century of Engagement*. Philadelphia: University of Pennsylvania Press.

Singh. 2017. Chinese Military Base in Djibouti: Strategic Implications for India. War on the Rock Special Series, August 21. https://warontherocks.com/2017/08/chinas-military-base-in-djibouti-strategic-implications-for-india/.

Singham, Shanker. 2020. Sanctions Must be Placed on Nigeria After Horrific Christian Persecution, Lobby Group Says. *Express*, July 12. https://www.exp

ress.co.uk/news/uk/1308371/christian-persecution-nigeria-uk-Competere-foreign-aid-sanctions.
The Guardian. 2018. What Is China's Belt and Road Initiative? July 30. https://www.theguardian.com/cities/ng-interactive/2018/jul/30/what-china-belt-road-initiative-silk-road-explainer.
The Telegraph. 2018. African Countries must Spend their Way out of Poverty by Investing Trillions in Roads, Water and Power. *The Telegraph*, July 3. https://www.telegraph.co.uk/global-health/climate-and-people/african-countries-must-spend-way-poverty-investing-trillions/.
Trading Economics. 2019. China GDP. https://tradingeconomics.com/china/gdp.
The Conversation. 2016. How and Why China Became Africa's Biggest Aid Donor, April 26. http://theconversation.com/how-and-why-china-became-africas-biggest-aid-donor-57992.
World Bank. 2019. 2019 International Debt Statistics. The World Bank. http://datatopics.worldbank.org/debt/ids/region/SSA.
Zhang, Junyi. 2016. Chinese Foreign Assistance Explained, July 19. https://www.brookings.edu/blog/order-from-chaos/2016/07/19/chinese-foreign-assistance-explained/.

CHAPTER 8

Productive Forms of Capitalism: Trends and Prospects

As important as it is in today's global economy, entrepreneurial capitalism has its weakest regional expression in Africa, a region that on the contrary has perfected diverse forms of pseudo-capitalism.

8.1 The Philosophical Context

In his *Protestant Ethics and the Spirit of Capitalism* (1905), Max Weber, the famous German Sociologist and Philosopher makes an important intellectual contribution that is almost completely lost in contemporary discourses of capitalism, and that's the recognition that there is "a spirit of capitalism." With their avowed predilection for agnosticism, contemporary Western social sciences will dismiss any talk about "spirits" as intellectual mumbo jumbo. Right-wing America of course appreciates the supremacy and power of the spirit, best captured by the American official motto "In God We Trust." In "post-modern" Europe, to a large extent, they predominantly trust in themselves and perhaps in their imperial past. Modernist Europe of Max Weber's generation, like contemporary right-wing America believed in the omnipotence of the Spirit, hence Weber's recognition of a potent "spirit of capitalism."

The phrase "spirit of capitalism" can be understood in the context of the historicity of a people's civilization, as a nexus between spirituality

K. Omeje, *The Failure and Feasibility of Capitalism in Africa*, International Political Economy Series,
https://doi.org/10.1007/978-3-030-75170-8_8

and materiality. As a historical reality, the "spirit of capitalism" encompasses the underlying ethos of business and the dominant worldview that sets the place of capital, labour, technology, investments, production and profits in society.[1] Writing on the essence of the spirit of modern capitalism, Weber argues that: "Man is dominated by the making of money, by acquisition as the ultimate purpose of his life. Economic acquisition is no longer subordinated to man as the means for the satisfaction of his material needs" (Giddens 1992: xi).

In examining the relationship between religious worldview and capitalism, Weber demonstrated how, based on their teachings and professions, Protestantism, especially the Puritan sects such as Calvinists, Methodists and Baptists, played a key role in the rise of modern capitalism in Europe. Puritanism required a "this worldly ascetic" way of life that, in Weber's view, emphasized normative values such as frugality, the equation of time with money, entrepreneurial industriousness, profit rationality, the moral legitimacy of wealth and an obligation to earn it by hardwork and self-discipline.[2] Comparatively, the Puritan ethics emphasized the core values of capitalism in such a way that Catholicism and other world religions studied by Weber did not (e.g., Judaism, Confucianism, Buddhism and Hinduism).[3] Impliedly, countries with predominantly Protestant populations (the Puritan sects) embodied a spirit of capitalism different from the spirit that predominantly Catholic countries or indeed countries of other religions had.

Weber's work has been widely criticized for its crude empiricism, mischaracterization of Catholicism and Protestantism, and a flawed interpretation of the causal relation between Puritanism and modern capitalism (Giddens 1992: xxi–xxiv). Furthermore, there are other important dimensions to the growth of modern capitalism in Europe that Weber apparently overlooked which I have already discussed in Chapters 1–4 of this book, notably the role of trans-Atlantic slave trade and imperial conquest, colonization and exploitation of foreign lands—the Third World. There is a density of reputable literature on this subject going back to more than a hundred years. Weber was a social evolutionist of the positivist tradition and as was the trend with most social evolutionists of his generation, his studies created binaries and hierarchies of social structures between and across societies in such a teleological manner that many critics have charged his theories with the core criticism associated with the works of social evolutionists of Victorian England—ethnographic distance or insensitivity.

Having said that, what I consider most significant from Weber's positivist analysis is a logical deduction I am inclined to make—that different societies have different spirits of capitalism or social economy. Put in another way, there is no universal spirit or episteme of capitalism. This is contrary to the fallacy promoted by Western neoliberalism over the years—that there is a "one-size-fits-all" model of capitalism and its concomitants the whole world must conform to. The spirit behind the social economy—be it capitalism or any other system—is not static. It is eternally developing and dialectically reproduced as in Hegelian idealism or Marxian materialism.

In a post-mortem analysis of the 2007–2008 global financial crisis, Dominic Barton, Canadian Ambassador to China and former Managing Director of the renowned American consulting firm McKinsey & Company, makes an interesting comparison between the nature of Western capitalism and Asian capitalism—a comparison that may point to contrasting spirits. Barton calls the capitalism operational in the West "quarterly capitalism," a reference to the short-term profit maximization values and devices that drive businesses in the West which were also at the root of the financial crisis. In the words of Barton:

> As a Canadian who for 25 years has counselled business, public sector, and non-profit leaders across the globe (I've lived in Toronto, Sydney, Seoul, Shanghai, and now London), I've had a privileged glimpse into different societies' values and how leaders in various cultures think. In my view, the most striking difference between East and West is the time frame leaders consider when making major decisions. Asians typically think in terms of at least 10 to 15 years. ... In the US and Europe, near-sightedness is the norm. I believe that having a long-term perspective is the competitive advantage of many Asian economies and businesses today. Myopia plagues Western institutions in every sector. In business, the mania over quarterly earnings consumes extraordinary amounts of senior time and attention. Average CEO tenure has dropped from 10 to 6 years since 1995, even as the complexity and scale of firms have grown. In politics, democracies lurch from election to election, with candidates proffering dubious short-term panaceas while letting long-term woes in areas such as economic competitiveness, health, and education fester. Even philanthropy often exhibits a fetish for the short term and the new, with grantees expected to become self-sustaining in just a few years. (Barton 2011)

Without delving into the catalogue of policy errors and governance failures spanning over 50 years at the root of the 2007–2008 financial crisis which Barton and many academic experts have brilliantly analysed,[4] the point I wish to underscore is that values and norms cannot be divorced from the way that social economies—and in this context capitalism—operate in different societies and across generational dispensations. In the context of early modern Europe, Max Weber called the core Protestant ethics that encouraged capitalist ingenuity, entrepreneurship and professionalism the spirit of capitalism. The spirit of capitalism at its best generates stupendous prosperity as exemplified by the emergence and growth of capitalism in Europe which Weber demonstrated in his study, and indeed, further exemplified by the unparalleled wealth that capitalism has generated in world economic history which makes it an irreplaceable system—at least, foreseeably. But at its worst, and going beyond Weber's discourse, the spirit of capitalism can precipitate a catastrophic crisis of global proportion, such as the subprime mortgage crisis in the USA and the mega-financial meltdown and economic crash that followed it. Moreover, at its worst, the spirit of capitalism can generate fratricidal wars and aggravate armed conflicts in different parts of the world. The legendary Adam Smith recognized the devastating impact of the contrary spirit of capitalism at its worst when he wrote about the "monopolizing spirit" of greedy merchants and manufacturers, as well as "a nation looking with an invidious eye upon the prosperity of all other nations with which it trades" in the following discourse:

> Nations have been taught that their interest consisted in beggaring all their neighbours. Each nation has been made to look with an invidious eye upon the prosperity of all the nations with which it trades, and to consider their gain as its own loss. Commerce, which ought naturally to be, among nations as among individuals, a bond of union and friendship, has become the most fertile source of discord and animosity. The capricious ambition of kings and ministers has not, during the present and the preceding century, been more fatal to the repose of Europe, than the impertinent jealousy of merchants and manufacturers. The violence and injustice of the rulers of mankind is an ancient evil, for which, I am afraid, the nature of human affairs can scarce admit of a remedy. But the mean rapacity, the monopolizing spirit of merchants and manufacturers, who neither are, nor ought to be, the rulers of mankind, though it cannot perhaps be corrected, may very easily be prevented from disturbing the tranquillity of anybody but themselves. ... As it is the interest of the freemen of a corporation to hinder

> the rest of the inhabitants from employing any workmen but themselves, so it is the interest of the merchants and manufacturers of every country to secure to themselves the monopoly of the home market.[5]

To arrest the multifaceted failures that preceded and triggered the global financial crisis, Barton called for the reform of capitalism in the West, and many noted business experts and economists have equally made the same call. It is remarkable that most of the reform proposals of Barton are centred on values and normative frameworks of Western capitalism—"rewiring the fundamental ways we govern, manage, and lead corporations" and "changing how we view business' value and its role in society" (Barton 2011). His proposed reform framework requires a fundamental shift in business and corporate governance values in Western capitalism:

> There are three essential elements of the shift. First, business and finance must jettison their short-term orientation and revamp incentives and structures in order to focus their organizations on the long term. Second, executives must infuse their organizations with the perspective that serving the interests of all major stakeholders—employees, suppliers, customers, creditors, communities, the environment—is not at odds with the goal of maximizing corporate value; on the contrary, it's essential to achieving that goal. Third, public companies must cure the ills stemming from dispersed and disengaged ownership by bolstering boards' ability to govern like owners. (Barton 2011)

There are discernible nuances within Western capitalism, as well as in any other regional capitalist bloc. The distinctions can take varied philosophical and empirical dimensions depending on the intellectual persuasions of analysts and I don't wish to explore the intellectual debate in this book. Chinese intellectuals have a classic way of often comparing Western capitalism and their civilization heritage (contemporary state capitalism inclusive) in academic seminars and workshops. Their argument is that the driving unit of Western capitalism, especially the American model is individual wealth for his own good—the bottom line of the popular rhetoric called "the American dream." For the Chinese, the driving unit and motif of their capitalist economy are the good and strength of the community. The individual finds his fulfilment in community well-being and solidarity. I will approximate this Chinese analogy to loosely represent the driving spirits of capitalism between the West and most of the successful Asian market economies regardless of the huge state's social welfare investments in individuals and households in the European model (essentially the wealthy countries in Europe).

Notwithstanding the policy nuances that different national economies have pursued, Michael Schuman has identified the following striking differences in the nature of capitalism that the successful Asian economies and the West have pursued:

> (1) Asian policymakers don't trust that free markets always produce the best results, and they are more willing than their Western counterparts to intervene directly to alter their direction (through, for example, industrial policy, or the control of interest rates or exchange rates).
>
> (2) Asian governments have traditionally avoided the extensive welfare programmes popular in the West (though that is changing).
>
> (3) All Asian economies are obsessed with exports *while the West seems obsessed with financial capitalism,*[6] *as well as "easy wealth" from the service and entertainment industries.*
>
> (4) Asian policies tend to favour industry over services and investment over consumption to drive growth (Schuman 2012).

In a similar comparison of capitalism in the West and Asia in the aftermath of the 2007–2008 financial crisis, Lord Meghnad Desai, the renowned Emeritus Professor of Economics at the London School of Economics had this to say:

> Capitalism is alive and well, but not in the Western countries - it has migrated eastwards. Russian capitalism is somewhat old and in need of urgent repair, but the spirit of capitalism - risk-taking, saving, investing, hard work - all those virtues have now migrated and are happily ensconced in China, India, Indonesia, Korea and Japan - the countries which we never thought would ever get out of poverty. Western capitalism probably had half a century of over-indulgence - continued prosperity, full employment, almost guaranteed growth - and that in its turn meant that our costs went up and manufacturing industry migrated abroad, while finance has proved to be a fickle friend. (BBC, 23 September 2011)

Many things are certainly wrong with capitalism in the West but that is not the point I wish to pursue here. Remarkably, Lord Desai recognizes that there is a spirit of capitalism—all those virtues that characterize capitalism—pointing out that this spirit or those composite virtues of capitalism have now migrated from the West and are happily ensconced in the East.

In a large sense, the contemporary spirit of capitalism in Asia cannot be disconnected from their religious and philosophical foundations of Confucianism, Buddhism and in the case of India, Hinduism. In their brilliant empirical study titled *Confucianism, Discipline, and Competitiveness* (2019), Chris Baumann, Hume Winzar and Doris Viengkham have analysed the significant impact of the sociocultural values of discipline and competitiveness rooted in Confucianism in the transformation of the East Asian educational systems, productivity of the future workforce and ultimately their national economies. This viewpoint concurs with the cultural explanation for the Asian economic miracle, one of the five theoretical perspectives postulated by Richard Stubbs (2018: 3–14) discussed in Sect. 2.3.

Can one identify any constructive spirit or worldview behind capitalism in contemporary Africa? Africans are deeply religious people with a rich heritage and worldview founded on Christianity, Islam and various indigenous faith systems. The chequered colonial and postcolonial experiences of Africa have not destroyed the African ontology which is deeply influenced by their religious heritage but have thus far mostly prevented this ontological outlook from robbing off on the state system in a constructive way that can help to transform the African educational systems, productivity of the future workforce and ultimately the national economies—courtesy of the South East Asian model. This is where the struggle for the African renaissance greatly popularized by ex-president Thabo Mbeki of South Africa while in office needs to be waged.

8.2 The Marginalized Productive Forms of Capitalism in Africa

The dominant models of capitalism in contemporary Africa as I have argued in this study are the dysfunctional models, which ostensibly are not capable of generating a constructive spirit of capitalism to power accelerated and transformative growth and development in the continent. There are several considerably functional models of capitalism that are regularly taught in the African business schools and business economics in general, models developed from some of the "best practices" in different parts of the world, especially from the West. These models include:

a. *Fordism*—This is the quintessential model of mass production and consumption by large specialized companies, originally associated with Ford Motors in the USA, which helped to power post-war economic growth and boom. The history of Fordist capitalism goes back to the 1930s.
b. *Managerial capitalism*—This model is based on entrusting big firms to a professional managerial cadre headed by a CEO who runs the day-to-day affairs of the business on behalf of the owners and shareholders, as the case may be. It is a rational bureaucratic model that tends to make a distinction between ownership and management which was developed in the West in the late nineteenth century but popularized as a business management practice in the post-war era.
c. *Shareholder capitalism*—This is the capitalist model in which dominant enterprises are owned by shareholders and the primary responsibility of a company is to maximize the profit-making interest of shareholders. The post-war ascendancy of shareholder capitalism can be traced back to the 1970s' deregulation that unduly empowered the Wall Street and its unproductive risk model of short-term profit maximization in the highly speculative global financial market. It is the synergy between shareholder capitalism and managerial capitalism that gave rise to financial capitalism already mentioned above. Gerald Epstein has defined financial capitalism (also known as financialization) as "the increasing role of financial motives, financial markets, financial actors and financial institutions in the operation of the domestic and international economies" (cited in Engel 2015).
d. *Customer service capitalism*—This brand of capitalism implies that business exists to fundamentally serve the interest of customers because they pay the bills and guarantee profitability. The customer-centric model is strongly associated with the popular cliché that in business the customer is king.
e. *Social market capitalism*—This is an economic model that has grown in post-war Germany which aims at a blend of market efficiency, social protection and social justice for all (Sally 2015). German politicians and intellectuals often call it a third-way between mainstream capitalism and socialism, which makes it remotely coterminous with mixed economy, but with the state promoting advanced level of social welfare and social justice, especially for the underclass. The social market economy is often associated

with neo-corporatism,[7] which in the German context is characterized by a hierarchically structured system of interest articulation, bargaining and representation by diverse intermediate groups (e.g., trade union, professional associations, business lobbies, etc.) liaising between their social constituencies and the government, but cooperating among themselves to build broad consensus on issues of common interest. The intergroup negotiation and bargaining to build common consensus on policy matters help to strengthen the case of the organized and institutionalized unions before policy-makers. The German model of neo-corporatism is also found among the Scandinavian countries.

f. *Community capitalism*—This is basically a model of capitalism in which corporations prioritize the interest and overall well-being of the human and ecological communities where they operate in doing business. Community capitalism is the model mainly espoused by the Chinese. The whole idea of corporate social and environmental responsibility which is highly developed in many Western countries is integral to community capitalism. In proposing community capitalism, a special report prepared by a coalition of 65 business and community leaders and government officials brought together under the auspices of The American Assembly of Columbia University, encourages businesses to work with non-profit organizations, community groups, organized labour and government to harness the underdeveloped economic potential of urban neighbourhoods (Brookings 1997).

The list of the various models of capitalism taught in Business Economics cannot be exhausted, and the models are not mutually exclusive. In Africa, teaching and learning about these relatively functional models, their pros and cons, as well as practical relevance to the African business environment do make brilliant academic sense. In practice, the functional application of some of these models in many African countries may make sense in a microeconomic context, but in the wider macroeconomic spectrum, with the possible exception of financial capitalism, their applicability is highly constrained by the dominance of dysfunctional models of capitalism discussed in Chapter 5. Having said that, one can identify a few relatively marginalized but sublime models of capitalism in postcolonial Africa out of which the hope of reconstruction and transformation could be possibly built if the executive managers of the state systems can get their act together. Let me briefly examine them.

8.2.1 Mixed Economy Capitalism

In mixed economies, there is a blend of market forces and government intervention, markets play a dominant role, but are regulated to a greater extent by the government to correct market failures, such as to promote social welfare; defence and public safety (Jahan and Mamud 2015). It is a market economy characterized by a reasonably balanced coexistence of privately owned enterprises and state-owned enterprises, which is often tempered with a measure of state regulation of the private sector using a combination of some monetary and fiscal policies. In practical terms, the mixed economy model integrates ingredients of socialist control by an interventionist state and free-market capitalism. The state plays a significant role in investing in strategic sectors of the economy for diverse reasons which may include consumer protection, affordable service delivery and social welfare. In fact, the welfare capitalism that emerged in most countries of Western Europe in the early twentieth century and became significantly expanded in the post-World War II era is an offshoot of the mixed economy system. Many countries in the world today operate varied levels of welfare capitalism in which the state promotes the welfare of various vulnerable social groups through diverse policies of wealth redistribution, social security programmes and collective bargaining agreements.[8]

Most of the African postcolonial states started off with varied forms of the welfare state model of mixed economy capitalism, albeit not as developed as the versions in Western Europe. The economic crises of the 1980s and the subsequent World Bank/IMF Structural Adjustment Programmes literally wiped out the embryonic welfare state in most of the African countries leaving the populace exposed to the harsh economic realities of neoliberalism. Some of the countries with relatively good Human Development Index in Africa (e.g., Algeria, Tunisia, Botswana, Gabon and Morocco) are for the most part reasonably functional states in which large sections of the citizenry still enjoy significant measures of welfare support from the government and in some cases, from big private employers (UNDP 2019; The SDG Centre for Africa 2019). Key areas of welfare assistance are education, health, agriculture, household subsistence, housing and sanitation. The sparsely populated Atlantic and Indian Ocean islands of Seychelles, Mauritius and Cape Verde whose economies are largely underpinned by fishing, tourism and financial services have also significantly excelled in human capital investments. These island economies largely thrive on "safari capitalism" (tourism and its associated economies), which in the context of globalization requires a strong push and bolstering investment in Africa. Generally, the feasibility of mixed economy capitalism culminating in the form of advanced welfare state (welfare capitalism) achieved by Western Europe is doubtful in contemporary Africa because of the challenges of high population growth rate, low industrialization, low productivity and weak governance institutions.

8.2.2 Embryonic State Capitalism

State capitalism is an economic development model in which the state not only sets the parameters for investments and transactions but by reason of its massive investments and spending is also the dominant driver of growth in the economy. The commanding heights of the economy are owned by the state not only for the purpose of fostering efficient and quality service delivery but also for the purpose of ensuring that they are competitive and profitable in both local and international contexts. Private capital is supported and encouraged by the state, especially in manufacturing, trade and commercial service sectors, and most importantly the state supports the internationalization of private capital by its nationals. The space occupied by the private sector is regulated by and subordinated to the state in the business environment, and heavily resourced state-owned corporations are leading foreign investors and exporters of profitable capital. Technically speaking, state capitalism, which is best exemplified by the contemporary Chinese model is a "misnomer" that rewrites the doctrinal scripts of liberal capitalism which thrives on private ownership of the factors of production with the state mostly confined to regulatory functions (using fiscal and monetary measures), extractive duties, infrastructural development and strategic public service delivery. In the Chinese model, basic factors like land, banks, finance, energy, mining and large industries are mainly state-owned; village lands are de facto owned by smallscale cultivators but nominally administered by county/village authorities, while the export economy is dominated by a technically vibrant entrepreneurial or private capitalist sector (David

2017). The state itself is controlled by the Chinese Community Party in a functionally dynamic manner that creates a State–Party nexus. The driving philosophy of state capitalism in China is the well-being of the country as defined in the policy framework of the Communist Party and delivered by the state's use of encompassing regulations, allocation of its vast public funds, including the country's foreign reserves, as well as efficient control of the workforce and citizenry (Moyo 2012: 6–10).

The meteoric rise of China between the late 1970s and early 2000s from being a relatively poor developing country to the world's second largest economy in a space of less than 30 years and their ubiquitous presence as Africa's leading investment and trade partners have greatly inspired many African countries to idealize and partly imitate the Chinese model in the belief that it could help them achieve similar performance outcomes. The Chinese government has also been actively promoting its development model in Africa through diverse exchange programmes for top African government officials and policy intellectuals sponsored by the various Chinese state ministries, especially the Chinese Academy of Social Sciences, which is a central government think tank that officially enjoys the status of a fully fledged ministry. China also awards many scholarships to African students to study in China annually and funds a growing number of Confucius-related Centres in African Universities dedicated to the study of Chinese civilization.

In a 2016 survey conducted by Afrobarometer across 36 African countries, China emerged as the second most popular model for national development (cited by 24% of respondents) in Africa, trailing only the USA (30%) but rated far ahead of the model represented by their former colonial powers (13%). Specifically, the Chinese model matched the USA or took the lead among countries of Southern Africa, North Africa and Central Africa, and the most important factors contributing to a positive image of the Chinese model in Africa are its infrastructure/development and business investments and the relatively affordable cost of its products (Afrobarometer, 24 October 2016). Among the countries in Africa that have tried to copy the Chinese model are Ethiopia, Egypt, Rwanda, and to a much lesser extent, Uganda, Sudan and Eritrea. China's state-led economic reforms and prioritization of stability over a boisterous externally funded or driven civil society have been particularly appealing for countries like Ethiopia and Rwanda (Kuo 2016), what for want of appropriate terminology could be dubbed "embryonic state capitalism." Egypt under the post-Arab Spring leadership of President Abdul Fattah al-Sisi has greatly deepened its economic rapprochement with China and seemingly embraced a new dispensation of state-led capitalism that combines neoliberal reforms with the state's centralized control over the economy; envisions national mega-projects as the locomotive of development; and is further marked by the emergence of the defence establishment as an autonomous economic actor with assured access to public procurement contracts and a central role in managing government-funded initiatives (Calabrese 2020). The real question is whether the African countries copying the Chinese model of state capitalism have a significant chance of making a quantum leap like China, albeit the remarkable progress that some of these countries have already made cannot be minimized.

The success of the Chinese model has shown that state capitalism requires an omnipotent government with high levels of strategic decision-making and execution capability, an abundance of highly skilled cheap labour, as well as high levels of political cohesion, public order and discipline in societal cultures (Moghalu 2014: 51). With the nemesis of dysfunctional colonial legacies, shortage of skilled labour, poor work ethics and fractionalized multi-party politics, it is evident that not many African countries are well placed to emulate and succeed in the Chinese model of state capitalism. To improve their chances of success, African countries attempting to copy the Chinese model need to implement the type of far-reaching economic and governance reforms that laid the foundation for the take-off of the Chinese economy under Premier Deng Xiaoping's regime (1978–1992) such as targeted opening up of the economy to highly developed countries that could stimulate industrialization through Foreign Direct Investments (FDI), massive investments in human capital development (especially quality education and healthcare), setting up of Special Economic Zones (SEZ), massive infrastructural development and strengthening state-owned companies in strategic sectors of the economy. Other measures include incentivizing small and medium scale enterprises and encouraging joint ventures with foreign capitalists, strengthening rule of law and indiscriminately punishing corruption in the public space, as well as promoting policy continuity based on long-term development planning. Under the prevailing conditions of short-term multi-party democracy in most African countries coupled with the imperatives of the sundry regional market integration arrangements in the continent, including the AfCFTA, the chances of implementing, sustaining and perpetuating these recommended reforms on individual country basis are practically not only tenuous but some of them may ultimately run counter to regional market integration objectives. The frequent policy changes tied to the short-term election cycles in liberal democracies which are often aimed at seducing the voters distract elected office holders from the job of addressing long-term policy challenges (Moyo 2018: 136–137).

Singapore arguably offers the best non-Communist ideology-oriented version of state capitalism (the democratic market economy model) in which the government owns a preponderant amount of the means of production and domestic assets, and controls a huge sovereign wealth funds through Temasek Holdings Private Limited with a 2020 net portfolio value of US$306 billion (*The Straits Times*, 21 July 2020). The Singaporean state controls 90% of the country's land (up from 31% in 1949), leads in real estate investments with over 80% of the population living in state constructed housing units under different tenancy arrangements and holds considerable equity and assets in diverse sectors of the domestic economy, as well as across Asia and the West to a lesser extent through Temasek (Bruenig 2018). Singapore has a small land mass—less than the size of the Nigerian Federal Capital Territory of Abuja, and with no natural resources but has a robust private sector driven by high-tech innovativeness and global competitiveness in key export-oriented manufacturing sectors (e.g., electronics, transport engineering, pharmaceuticals biomedical products, etc.), financial services and tourism. Singapore has a remarkably high level of infrastructural development, efficient transport and telecommunication systems and an advanced level of functional education and skills development which are altogether conducive to productive capitalist investments (local and foreign) and productivity. The country has a population of 5.85 million and the 2019 nominal per capita income is $63,987.10, one of the top 12 in the world (*Statistical Times* 2020).

8.2.3 Subdued Entrepreneurial Capitalism

According to Robert Price (n.d.) entrepreneurial capitalism is private capital, investing in private start-ups, with potential for a viable harvest, while entrepreneurialism could mean three things: starting your own business, finding new business opportunities and expansion at existing businesses.[9] The modern capitalism in Europe studied by Adam Smith in his 1776 classic, *An Inquiry into the Nature and Causes of the Wealth of Nations* is mainly centered on the productive and innovative power of division of labour in factory production and the overall capacity of the rational factory owners or entrepreneurs to drive the economy with the least interference of the government. According to Smith, the government should mainly restrict itself to the role of national defense against external aggression, administration of justice, as well as erecting and maintaining public institutions and those public works that will be advantageous to the larger society. Above all, the government should promote free trade and ensure an orderly framework for private investment, production and trade. Government interference in the economy which created undue monopolies and market distortion during the time of Smith, in his view, should give way to the "invisible hand" of the free market rooted in the enlightened self-interests of the economic man—the individual investors, producers, exporters, sellers and buyers. In accord with the Enlightenment philosophers of his time, Adam Smith had great faith in the goodness, innovative genius and rationality of man, and therefore reasoned that if equipped with the necessary economic freedom, these enlightened tendencies of the individual would produce the best results for the good of society—national wealth and prosperity for all.

Without any intention to promote or advocate the classical Smithian brand of entrepreneurial capitalism, it suffices to acknowledge that Adam Smith's economic philosophy of capitalism was one in which the "fair-playing" "free-market" entrepreneur is king. Innovativeness, creativity, productive risk-taking and above all, the availability of capital in its various forms are the hallmarks of entrepreneurial capitalism. For the potential of entrepreneurial capitalism to be unleashed, the engine of growth in an economy has to be powered by a large concentration of innovative small [and medium] enterprises engaged in manufacturing for the local and progressively external market. A vibrant manufacturing sector plays a unique role in boosting productivity throughout the economy by courtesy of its backward and forward linkages that fuel the development of other sectors, such as agriculture and services (Cilliers 2021: 12). From a basic input–output system's approach, backward linkages refer to the demand-side connections (e.g. raw materials) a firm has with other existing firms or producers in a region while forward linkages are concerned with the supply-side connections (e.g. services) of an industry with other existing firms in a region (Hefner and Guimaraes 1991: 229). Although manufacturing has for the most part been historically central to the development of entrepreneurial capitalism, its inter-industry linkages help to expand the frontiers of entrepreneurial capitalism to other sectors of the economy.

While manufacturing provides a strong fillip for entrepreneurial capitalism, it is pertinent to stress, however, that entrepreneurial capitalism could develop and flourish in other sectors of the economy independent of industrial manufacturing. This is the logic behind the growth of international tourism and the service sector in general in many emerging modern economies. The history of capitalism and industrialization in early modern Europe and the US is, among other things, strongly associated with entrepreneurial capitalism. The levers of entrepreneurial capitalism, especially productive capital and value-added manufacturing are practically subdued in Africa.

8.3 The Feasibility of Entrepreneurial Capitalism in Africa

As important as it is in today's global economy, entrepreneurial capitalism has its weakest regional expression in Africa, a region that on the contrary has perfected diverse forms of pseudo-capitalism. It is an essentially subdued form of capitalism in most African countries. Value-added manufacturing is still extremely low in Africa (the topmost producers being South Africa, Egypt, Nigeria and Morocco) while the entire continent accounts for only a meagre 1.5% of the global manufacturing outputs (Signe and Johnson 2018). A large number of the light manufacturing industries (e.g., textiles, leather and footwear, pharmaceuticals, beverages and food processing, building materials, automobile accessories, household utensils, pulp and paper, etc.) that were developing in Africa during the first 25 years of independence, many of them supported by the government's import-substitution industrialization programmes were destroyed by the economic crisis of the 1980–1990s, aggravated by the World Bank/IMF Structural Adjustment Programmes (SAP). In many African countries, these industries, including some of those that survived SAP but got liquidated later are yet to be rehabilitated. Their infrastructures largely remain moribund. The commodity boom windfall of the "Africa rising" years (2005–2015) was a potential opportunity to revive these industries and restore or create jobs. Hardly did any of the African states use their windfall revenues to rehabilitate or invigorate their light manufacturing sector and the embryonic home-grown industries, many of which are specialized in fabricating inferior local substitutes of imported goods. These are the sort of industries that need the support of any government that is serious with industrialization using soft credits, grants, tax breaks, technical assistance, quality assurance benchmarks and well-structured or smart protection from foreign competition. In making reference to import substitution, I do not recommend a replication of the profoundly flawed import-substitution industrialization strategies of the past but a purpose-driven selectivity and prioritization model that will delineate and resuscitate some of the highly needed but collapsed or under-performing industries that can add significant value to the local economy (see Sect. 5.1).

Instead of using the commodity boom windfall to set up or stimulate manufacturing industries, African countries—with a few exceptions—wasted the surplus revenues on non-productive expenditures; Ghana and Zambia, for instance, used profits from the commodity bonanza to solve short-term domestic problems, such as by increasing salaries for civil servants (Tafirenyika 2016). The Nigerian federal government shared most of their crude oil windfall revenues with the state governments ahead of the 2015 elections which they wasted in campaigning for office while many of the politicians pocketed a greater part of the money. At the inception of President Goodluck Jonathan's administration in 2010, the oil windfall account known as excess crude oil revenue account stood at $20 billion but by the time he left office in 2015, the money was depleted to about $2 billion (*Premium Times*, 17 July 2020). "Answering questions on an interview programme with Bloomberg TV, Jonathan blamed the state governors for regularly pressurizing the federal government to draw from the reserve fund 'to augment revenue allocations from the federation account'" (*Premium Times*, 17 July 2020). What an incredible defence! I cannot say more. This is liberal democracy Nigerianized by the politics of squanderation. The only practical strategy that most African governments have for industrialization is to wait for FDI without even investing significantly in providing the basic infrastructures that can help to attract FDI. Yet, they have many collapsed and under-performing or under-resourced local industries, public and private, they could start from.

Occasionally, we read in the news about African entrepreneurs and research institutions that have successfully manufactured different innovative products but in most cases the "breaking news" is the end of the story. Hardly are there follow-up investments towards products' improvement and commercialization. Some of the fascinating low- and high-tech products manufactured in Africa in recent years that would require massive commercialization investments and market promotion include *Mellowcabs*—a high-tech electric car manufactured in South Africa;

Cardiopad—a touch screen medical tablet for heart examinations manufactured in Cameroun; *Mubser*—a breakthrough navigational aid tool designed for visually impaired people manufactured in Egypt; *EZUGWU MRAP*—a Mine Resistant Ambush Protected armoured vehicle manufactured by the Nigerian Army Command Engineering Depot; a five-seater electric car produced by the Faculty of Engineering of the University of Nigeria Nsukka in 2019; hydroelectric generator—a water-powered electricity generator invented in 2019 in Nigeria by Emeka Nelson, as well as several local food cultivation and processing machines (Nseher 2014; Emergency Digest 2019). Remarkably, it is these sorts of unsung innovative products, which are largely at embryonic stages across the various African countries that are ideally the building blocks of entrepreneurial capitalism.

Targeted and deliberate state support is important for entrepreneurial capitalism to develop and gain strength, especially in the context of today's intensely competitive globalized economy in which mega-enterprises from powerful industrialized countries are dominant. State support could be in the forms of favourable access to start-up capital, regulation of competitive imports and massive infrastructural development (e.g., soft roads, railways, portable water, information technology and massive expansion in the capacity to generate, transmit and distribute electricity). Limited start-up capitals for Micro, Small and Medium Enterprises (MSMEs) represent the most distressing gap in the role of finance for economic transformation and the growth of entrepreneurial capitalism in contemporary Africa (see Moghalu 2014: 155). There is an evident scarcity of venture capitalists in Africa which is bad news for young entrepreneurs who may have a potentially viable business concept or product but in dire need of affordable credit for take-off or expansion. Even the available venture capitals disbursed in Africa are highly skewed in sectoral form in a way that ultimately undermines innovation, economic diversification and job creation. Data published by the London-based Africa Private Equity and Venture Capital Association (AVCA) indicate that between 2014 and 2019, the top-funded start-up sectors in Africa are as follows: consumer discretionary (28%), financials (23%), industrials (18%), utilities (17%), information technology (6%), communication services (3%), healthcare (3%) and consumer sales (1%) (Kazeem 2020). The nature of sectoral bias in the start-up's distribution is not healthy from the standpoint of invigorating entrepreneurial capitalism and inclusive growth. Sectors like industrials, information technology and healthcare deserve better funding. Furthermore, there is the need to develop or strengthen existing start-up laws to encourage indigenous entrepreneurs. Africa needs start-up laws that would provide tax breaks, intellectual property protections, funding access and other boasts to new businesses in which local entrepreneurs have the majority shares (Elliott 2020).

The double-digit interest rate charged by many commercial banks and their collateral requirements make their commercial credit facility prohibitive for most emerging entrepreneurs. Because of its high-risk probability, venture capital funding is unattractive to conventional banks and other commercial lenders, especially in infrastructurally weak and politically fragile developing countries. But given its immense long-term benefits for economic growth, development of entrepreneurial capitalism and sectoral diversification, venture capital needs to be made top priority by the state and development finance institutions, preferably in partnerships with the private sector. It has the advantage of not only providing the much-required cash-flow for emerging businesses but appropriately designed, also guarantees the infusion of the necessary expertise and mentorship through the equity and managerial participation of the venture fund. Venture capital can also provide the necessary opportunity for products diversification and access to new markets. A leveraged buy-out of the venture fund by the business owner or their natural exit after they have profitably recovered their money could happen as the business matures. In a joint venture fund comprising the state, development finance institutions and/or the private sector, the effective commitment of the fund to the long-term success of the business would be enhanced if the fund is steered and managed by the profit-driven private sector.[10] There is the need for the state to back up its prioritization of venture capital with sustained and sufficient investments in research and development, as well as technical and vocational education and training to increase growth in the medium and long term.

Interestingly, the knowledge-base for the expansion of entrepreneurial capitalism and economic transformation in Africa is resilient and growing by the day—thanks to the thriving business schools and engineering colleges in the continent, such as the famous Lagos Business School, Gordon Institute of Business Science in Johannesburg, American University in Cairo Business School, Makerere University Business School, as well as the colleges of engineering in the University of Cape Town, Stellenbosch University, Cairo University, University of KwaZulu Natal and the Ecole Superieure Polytechnique in Dakar, among others. There are also several hands-on ICT and innovation hubs and centres of excellence in Rwanda, Kenya, South Africa, Egypt, Senegal and Nigeria. The resilient and thriving university institute and knowledge-based economy centres are a vital part of the infrastructure required for growth and therefore need to be more vigorously supported and expanded.

Similarly, there is a burgeoning younger generation of high-tech savvy entrepreneurs in diverse productive sectors of the economy in many African countries that have demonstrated the drive and promise the likes of Jack Ma (the Alibaba business chain mogul) exhibited in the early years of the Chinese quantum leap. The American business magazine Forbes publishes an annually revised list of some of these successful entrepreneurs, most of whom have navigated the murky waters of dysfunctionality in their various states to set up multi-million dollars phenomenal businesses that create thousands of high-earning jobs for the growing African middle class, but also small jobs for the masses. This new generation of African entrepreneurs can be found in diverse sectors like mobile communication and technology, light manufacturing, financial services, media and film, food processing, fashion and design, solar energy, real estate and E-Commerce. With the rapid increase in mobile phone connectivity and mobile money in Africa, E-Commerce and digital economy have great potential but at the moment still face some uphill challenges, especially the problem of poor internet and allied infrastructures like electricity and soft roads, broadband market monopoly or domination by the state in some countries, market fragmentation tied to country-specific tariffs and regulations, as well as the wide digital divide within and between countries. Remarkably, some of these challenges are likely to be addressed under the AfCFTA framework with the plans underway to include e-commerce in the regional trade negotiation.

The International Trade Centre (ITC) working in partnership with the Amsterdam University of Applied Science have launched the Africa Marketplace Explorer to help address the lack of comprehensive information about online marketplaces in more than 50 African countries and at the time of writing the tool provides analysis of more than 630 business-to-consumer marketplaces in the continent (ITC New, 6 May 2020). Nigeria, South Africa, Kenya and Rwanda have some of the most thriving e-commerce in Africa while Kenya is the most advanced in mobile money. In Rwanda for instance the American firm Zipline launched the use of drones to deliver medical supplies in 2016 which was a creative remedy by the government for navigating the country's mountainous topography to save lives. The drone delivery model could help the expansion of e-commerce in Africa in the future.

Generally, with expanded venture capital incentive and supportive fiscal policy measures from the state, development finance institutions and other long-term financiers, there will likely be a stronger momentum for the ascendancy of entrepreneurial capitalism in many African countries in the long term. Expanding and strengthening women participation in the economy, especially in MSMEs is for instance a major area that can be specifically targeted and stimulated through efficient injection of micro-finance, venture start-ups and expertise. This is important for medium and long-term gender inclusivity and broad-based prosperity. By courtesy of the China—Africa business partnerships, several industrial centres have been constructed and jointly operated in a few African countries to enhance the development of local industries and entrepreneurs. The best examples could be found in Ethiopia. Governments should deliberately plan and encourage more female participation in the emerging industrial centre activities.

Having emerged as dominant players and beneficiaries in the globalized capitalist system (supported by the structures of WTO and the Bretton Wood institutions), there is predictably only a minimal limit to which the West would genuinely encourage the growth of autonomous entrepreneurial capitalism in Africa because that would ultimately be antithetical to their trade and investments interests. By Western default in outsourcing manufacturing and technology transfer to take advantage of cheap skilled labour, political stability and good infrastructures, however, a number of Asian countries with strong developmentalist policy drive have been able to develop a thriving and globally competitive industrial sector powered by entrepreneurial capitalism (e.g., China, Singapore, Malaysia, South Korea and, to a lesser extent India). The successful East Asian economies remarkably benefitted from the post-World War II growth in Japan, the latter itself massively aided by the USA. This history is not likely to be replicated by the West for Africa's benefit. Under the prevailing international circumstances, the African countries and regional economic blocs need a combination of home-grown strategies and constructive international economic engagements or diplomacy to boost industrialization and manufacturing, as well as to strengthen the prospects of intra-African investments and trade.

8.4 Further Thoughts on Prospects of Accelerated Capitalist Development in Africa

Thoughts on the prospects for accelerated capitalist development in Africa could be gleaned from many forward-thinking observations and proposals I have made in the preceding section and also in the various chapters of this book. In this section, I will try to weave some of the key interdependent proposals together.

1. ***Institutional Reforms and Infrastructural Development:*** To accelerate capitalist development in Africa, there is the need to uproot and sweep out the aberrant versions of capitalism pervasive in the continent. If the aberrant versions of capitalism that primarily serve the interests of a corrupt elite and their external allies, while conversely impoverishing the masses, continue to remain pre-eminent in Africa, the continent is likely to witness more popular revolts akin to the Arab Spring and further military coups despite the illegality of the latter. The combination of dysfunctional capitalism, pervasive corruption, insensitive governance, expanding youth bulge and high level of youth unemployment is a recipe for recycling of instability, perpetuation of "no-war no-peace" conditions and the ultimate unravelling of statehood as presently constituted. It will make perilous states like Mali, Central African Republic, South Sudan, Somalia, Zimbabwe and Sudan extremely hard to fix. Deeply divided countries like Nigeria and Cameroun especially, but also Burundi, Guinea, Kenya and Uganda to a lesser extent are likely to become more fractured and unstable if they continue to reinforce the dominance of dysfunctional capitalism and its governance dimensions. Deepening internal contestation of statehood with possibilities of implosive armed struggles may not be ruled out in some of the worst-case scenarios. As the Arab Spring and the successful secession of South Sudan and Eritrea have demonstrated, "people power revolution" and violent armed struggles do not necessarily solve underlying structural problems or guarantee better futures. This is why proactive institutional reforms to fix the foundations of capitalism and political governance are by far a preferred option.

In terms of priority areas for genuine capitalist development, this will require far-reaching institutional transformation in political, economic, corporate and security governance to strengthen investor confidence and make African economies more business friendly. Building strong, accountable and impersonal political and governance institutions are indispensable for sustainable growth and development, not least in the neoliberal trajectory that Africa has embraced. We should make no mistakes about it, the warped models of capitalism entrenched in many African countries are incapable of generating sustainable growth and inclusive development. Similarly, the anachronistic political institutions and patrimonial governance style promoted by fetish regimes exemplified by countries like Equatorial Guinea and Eswatini, among others, are unconscionably anti-capitalism, anti-people and anti-development. Without a strong commitment to genuine governance and macroecnomic reforms to mitigate dysfunctionality, commodity-exporting countries need to be wary that increased volatility in global markets is probably ahead and will as ever challenge their fiscal viability and stability (NIC 2012: 79).

Quality investments in infrastructure and human capital development are important to lay the necessary foundations for industrialization to take-off and be scaled up in many African countries and regions. This will include investments in power generation, link roads and rail-tracks, water and sanitation, healthcare facilities and practitioners, agriculture and food production, as well as technical education and employability skills training. The disproportionately high rate of budgetary imbalance between recurrent expenditure and capital expenditure among African countries which has seen many countries (e.g., Zimbabwe, Liberia, Nigeria, etc.) spending between 70 to 90% of their revenue inflows in recurrent expenditure with only a little left for major development infrastructures is unacceptable. Appallingly, a huge chunk of most states' recurrent budget is channelled into funding the bloated cost of governance.

2. ***Addressing the Orientation to Politics, Cost of Governance and Prebendal Corruption:*** The dominant orientation to political governance in several African countries is for wealth aggrandizement as opposed to public service, with the result that the perquisites of holding public offices in many African countries are by far more attractive than in most advanced countries of Europe and Asia. The mind-blowing perquisites of holding public office coupled with the high level of political corruption in countries like Nigeria, Kenya, Sudan, DRC, South Sudan, Angola, Equatorial Guinea, Eswatini, Burundi and Guinea-Bissau, among others, are a serious drain on public resources and an expression of blatant insensitivity to the plight of the impoverished majority in their countries. It is an act of officialized kleptocracy, which inadvertently makes the struggle and quest for political power extremely combative and deadly,

usually to the detriment of the poor masses who are made casualties of electoral and political violence. Recent research findings based on the self-generated African Peer Review Mechanism (APRM) reports submitted by many African countries have shown that one of the greatest and most widespread sources of violent conflicts in contemporary Africa is electoral violence associated with liberal democracies—multi-party election cycle and democratic transitions (cf. Gluhbegovic 2016; Omeje 2019). Multi-party politics in transitional societies characterized by ethnic, religious and cultural heterogeneity could under certain circumstances precipitate violent conflicts, not least when the contest is zero-sum in nature and access to political power is perceived as a mechanism for wealth aggrandisement and exclusion or persecution of opponents and adversarial groups (Omeje 2019). All these observations point towards the need to reform the orientation to public office and curtail the cost of governance in Africa, which is important to enhance sensitivity to the needs of the populace, as well as efficiency in resource allocation and service delivery. There are too many full-time and lifetime politicians in Africa—all living on fat salaries and spoils of office that are unhealthy for political and economic development. To cut down on the cost of governance, it suffices to recommend that most African states for instance do not have a need for bicameral legislatures, full-time parliamentarians, a prolific number of subnational states and counties, long motorcades for top government officials and state governors, outrageous retirement packages for politicians that have occupied diverse public offices (presidents, vice presidents, governors, deputy governors, etc.), office of the first lady at subnational government levels and a fully fledged diplomatic mission in countries where they have no serious affairs and in which their foreign embassies cannot generate enough funds to cover their operational cost without unduly extorting their own diaspora nationals in need of consular assistance. These are all insensitive devices of enriching the "political class" and their nepotic clients at the expense of citizens' well-being and the public good. Slimmer governments with part-time legislators that are paid only seating allowances will get the same job done and even more effectively. The emoluments of the different arms of government need to sensitively reflect the wage conditions and economic outlook of the country.

Furthermore, Africa needs a compelling recognition that pervasive corruption heavily rooted in the prebendal "eating" culture is a major impediment to growth and development and as such adopt an effective regional approach to the problem beyond the existing intergovernmental or stakeholders' voluntary mechanisms offered by APRM and the more global Extractive Industries Transparency Initiative (EITI). If the political will can be awakened, an effective regional anti-corruption framework is possible, a framework that can help strengthen the disparate national efforts. Tackling corruption effectively will among other things help to redirect more funds to worthy ventures like growth-oriented programmes, infrastructures, human capital development and poverty reduction, and further bolster investors' confidence in the economy. The dominant populist mode of fighting graft in most African countries devoid of solid institutional foundation calls for reformist attention. Every new government that comes to power in Africa is always noisy initially about fighting corruption and the approach is often centred on appointing an activist or public servant of repute to lead the anti-graft campaign, believing that based on his reputation and activism the anti-corruption Tzar will stamp out the malaise. Using a Pidgin English colloquialism, the Nigerian public Intellectual and professor of Political Science Jideofor Adibe describes this flawed approach as *gra gra* or grandstanding (Daily Trust, 8 July 2020). Major institutional and legal reforms, as well as systematic capacity-building in the area of prevention, whistle-blowing, investigation, prosecution and punishment of corruption are required to make effective and sustainable gains in the anti-corruption campaign. Equally important is the need to strengthen the capacity of public finance and revenue institutions at all levels of government (in terms of skills development, workplace facilities and new technology, conditions of service, etc.). As President Nana Akufo-Addo of Ghana observed: "The institution of transparent budget and expenditure management systems, that allocate resources wisely to agreed national priorities, and that ably monitor their implementation, is, therefore, of the utmost importance" (Daily Guide Network, 28 February 2020). The Nigerian federal government has had a convoluted experience in its fight against corruption within state institutions, the political space, business sector, social networks and quite ironically the anti-corruption agency (EFCC) itself from which some important lessons could be drawn. In July 2020, the Acting Chairman of EFCC Mr Ibrahim Magu was suspended by the federal government over allegations of official misconduct. Also suspended were the twelve directors of EFCC and the Commission's secretary. In contravention of the law, Mr Magu held the position of head of the government's anti-corruption agency EFCC (technically in an acting capacity) for five years, a position that requires parliamentary approval and which the Senate refused to grant on the two occasions that his nomination was submitted by the president. In July 2020, Magu was suspended and investigated over "weighty" allegations of misconduct by a presidential panel on corruption, which submitted its report to the President in November 2020. Magu denied all the charges against him as politically motivated and many of his sympathizers saw his removal from office as a case of "corruption fighting back." Regardless of the outcome of the inquiry into Mr Magu's stewardship, there are some issues that need to be fixed in the entire anti-corruption process in Africa based on the observed lapses in the Nigerian example.

Box 8.1 Relevant Institutional Reforms to Help Strengthen the Anti-Corruption Campaign in Africa

Based on the several lapses discernible in the highly beleaguered anti-corruption campaign carried out by the Nigerian federal government since the establishment of the EFCC in 2003, it is pertinent to propose the following reform measures to help strengthen the anti-corruption campaign in Africa in general.

1. The anti-corruption campaign must be held within a well-structured legal framework that clearly establishes the powers of all operating agencies and their officials, as well as the rights and obligations of suspects and convicted persons. The legal framework must also clearly delineate and delimit the powers and nature of relationships between the central government and sub-national governments in the overall campaign to avoid unnecessary structural contradictions and conflict.
2. The appointment and dismissal of the top officials of anti-corruption agencies need to be taken away from the executive and placed in the hands of an independent body working possibly in concert with a parliamentary committee. This will help to minimize political interference and manipulation. In fact, this procedure should be extended to the appointment of all other top officials of diverse agencies involved in the anti-corruption chain. An open and transparent service appointment, review and termination process is required and there is the need for an independent agency to coordinate the overall implementation of any such statutory mechanism. A relatively good

example of this process could be found in the present constitution that Kenya adopted in 2010, albeit the implementation of the process remains significantly challenged because of political pressure and the persisting culture of impunity in the realms of power.

3. The management of recovered funds and assets should be taken away from the anti-corruption agency and handled by another independent body. This will help to minimize the mismanagement and re-looting of recovered funds and also decongest the preoccupation of the anti-corruption agency.
4. The accounts of the anti-corruption body and the agency managing the recovered funds must be audited annually by independent external auditors and the outcome of the audit made public to enhance public confidence and transparency.
5. The anti-corruption agency and all other agencies associated with public revenues must be subjected to regular auditing and transparency standards in which independent external auditors need to be involved.
6. There is the need to ensure that all agencies involved in the anti-corruption fight operate in compliance with the law and promptly obey court orders. An independent judicial agency should handle this compliance process.
7. Corruption is a punishable crime in every country, but the punishment of the crime in most African states is lenient and, in some cases, hardly enforced. The punishment against corruption, especially the stealing, looting and misappropriation of public resources, must be tough, decisive and loud as a deterrence to all. A punishment that, among other measures, includes custodial sentence for convicted weighty offenders and stripping them of all the criminally acquired funds, assets and resources will be appropriate.

African governments have to encourage FDI by enunciating and effectively implementing anti-corruption and investment-friendly legislations, and furthermore, by systematically harmonizing national legislations backed with appropriate sanctions as the continent transitions to a regional market. To improve the quality of political representation and ruling making, there is the need for states to adopt laws that could permit civil servants and employees of the public and private sectors in general to stand for elective offices without having to resign or lose their jobs. This will help to inject more experienced participants in the political process and over time hopefully minimize the proportion of unemployed school leavers and career politicians in the political space.

3. ***Promoting Entrepreneurial Capitalism and the Productive Economy***: From the preceding sections of this chapter, and the exposé in Chapter 5, the feasibility (or otherwise) of the various types of capitalism practised in contemporary Africa is by now supposedly obvious. Among the least harmful and most productive models of capitalism prevalent in Africa today are mixed economy capitalism, state capitalism and entrepreneurial capitalism. Safari capitalism, which was not fully discussed in the preceding narratives is also a functional model which could stimulate the economy and create productive jobs if well cultivated and managed. Apparently, under the neoliberal development trajectory that Africa has embraced, strong emphasis must be placed on entrepreneurial capitalism, how to ensure that it takes centre-stage to drive growth and development, taking into account the peculiar sociological conditions and realities of the African people. With respect to adapting entrepreneurial capitalism to the existential conditions of the Africans, George Ayittey[11] presents an interesting analysis. He argues that given the peculiar history of the continent, the economy of the average African postcolonial state is divided into three sectors: the first is the elitist modern sector (the formal business sector) covering big businesses owned by expatriates and local tycoons, investors and middlemen; the second is the traditional sector which is based on agriculture and dominated by farmers and peasant cultivators and livestock breeders; the third is the informal sector comprising smallscale traders, artisans and micro-business enterprises. The vast majority of the African workforce and people are engaged in the traditional and informal sectors, but ironically these two sectors have been consistently neglected and disadvantaged by the states' development policies which have most disproportionately favoured the highly elitist modern sector. Too often, governments' economic development aid and incentives have been allocated to the modern sector because of the vested interests of powerful state officials. Ayittey argues that if African leaders are serious with inclusive development, then they have to prioritize incentivizing the traditional and informal sectors where the bulk of the African people work extraordinarily hard to merely eke out inadequate livelihood. Granting tax waivers to the wealthy modern sector will for instance have a much smaller multiplier effect on the economy compared to giving the same incentive and additional aid such as favourable access to credits, access to improved technologies and skills enhancement training to the

traditional and informal sectors. This will be a more sensitive and appropriate way to bolster entrepreneurial capitalism in the African context as opposed to imitating the tax-cuts system for mega-businesses and the wealthy capitalist class, which is a major policy drive immanent in the trickle-down economics favoured by the American Republican Party and many other neo-conservative parties in the West. The Western economies do not have similar structures as most African economies where the bulk of the working people are employed in the hardly incentivized traditional-peasant and informal micro-business sectors.

Making a solid case for the need for the state to build a healthy private sector by supporting small businesses, the World Bank writes as follows:

> An economy cannot thrive without a healthy private sector. When local businesses flourish, they create jobs and generate income that can be spent and invested domestically. Any rational government that cares about the economic well-being and advancement of its constituency pays special attention to laws and regulations affecting local small and medium size enterprises (SMEs). Effective business regulation affords micro and small firms the opportunity to grow, innovate and, when applicable, move from the informal to the formal sector of an economy. (World Bank 2019)

It suffices to argue that supporting the traditional and informal sectors, including Micro, Small and Medium Enterprises, with adequate liquidity in the African context should be seen as a cardinal part of building a healthy private sector. Adequately supported, the traditional and informal sectors in Africa have the potential to expand job creation, and stimulate innovation, home-grown technologies and export-oriented manufacturing.

Box 8.2 *Africapitalism* as a Model for Capitalist Production and Development

The Nigerian entrepreneur and philanthropist Tony Elumelu has advanced a strong case for an African brand of capitalism or capitalism with an African face, which he called "Africapitalism." In theory, Africapitalism is coterminous with community capitalism already discussed in this chapter. Africapitalism is an economic philosophy that advocates the need to unlock African entrepreneurship potential through long-term private investments in strategic sectors (agriculture, power, healthcare and finance) with the object of delivering financial returns to shareholders, as well as economic and social benefit to stakeholders, which may range from the immediate host community of the business investment to the larger national and regional contexts.[12] In a strategic sense, Africapitalism is a way of integrating the African collective-help tradition of wealth transfer and redistribution to the profit-motive inherent in capitalism. It is a philosophy that has the potential of empowering African growth and development but fundamentally only if it is deliberately embraced, executed and promoted by African governments, development banks and regional institutions (AU, ECOWAS, SADC, IGAD, ECCAS, COMESA, etc.). Through the Tony Elumelu Foundation established in 2010, the Nigerian philanthropist and proponent of Africapitalism has championed an exemplary advocacy by committing $100 million to train, mentor and financially support 100,000 young entrepreneurs in Africa over a 10-year span, a project that has attracted partnership support from the UNDP (Pedroncelli 2019).

As important as the export manufacturing-led industrialization and growth is, it certainly cannot be pursued at the expense of using necessary incentives to stimulate the rural agricultural sectors that still employs a greater percentage of the African labour force as already indicated. Other sectors such as the emerging service and tourism industries cannot also be neglected. To a reasonable extent, the fundamentals of the global economy and the political calculations driving it have undergone tremendous change and therefore the Asian economic "miracles" of the Cold War and early post-Cold War era may not be replicated in the same manner and scale. The 2001 Nobel Laureate in Economics Joseph Stiglitz was right in cautioning that the Asian economic miracle may not be repeated in the same way in Africa and that Africa needs an economic model that contains "elements of manufacturing, agriculture, resources and services" (Bloomberg 2018). To this end, a more holistic approach to growth and development tailored to suit the continent's sociocultural, demographic, and political realities while at the same time dealing effectively with the nemesis of prebendal graft and the institutional context of dysfunctionalities is required in contemporary Africa. More significantly, Africa does not need an industrialization model that will reproduce the flawed economic dualism of the past, a stagnant rural peasant economy and an industrial sector-inclined urban economy, both scarcely and minimally integrated to one another. Instead, what the continent requires are new viable models of industrialization by the organic integration of the rural and urban economies to maximize opportunities for symbiotic growth, development of appropriate technologies, technical skills and for expansive prosperity. The African peasant economy cannot be displaced but integrated more sustainably with the urban market and industrial economies. The integrated rural–urban economy also needs to be jointly integrated into the systems of knowledge production or "research and development" (R&D). Many developing countries serious about making an inroad into today's knowledge-based economy are systematically encouraging and scaling up investments in knowledge products (ICT softwares and databases, R&D, branding & design, etc.), what Jonathan Haskel and Stian Westlake in their book *Capitalism Without Capital* (2017) described as "the rise of the intangible economy." In the African scene, Rwanda is a shining example regarding investments in intangible assets. Across Africa, relevant government ministries and agencies need to be capacitated to plan and execute the important trilateral integration of rural economy, urban economy and intangible economy necessary for sustainable growth and development. Africa needs a capacitated, interventionist and regulatory state to drive economic planning and development in a manner that will be beneficial to the goal of "wealth creation from below," poverty reduction and "bridging the income inequality from above" as opposed to an economy driven by the whims of free-marketers in collaboration with corrupt state officials and "useful idiots" of all breed.

Regarding safari capitalism which has enormous potential to contribute more to economic growth and job creation in this age of advanced globalization, it suffices to say that the safari industry will benefit more from the multiplier effects of the state creating enabling conditions for and supporting entrepreneurial capitalism, as well as from direct policy interventions (e.g., ease of securing holiday visas, strengthening local security, improving destinations of touristic attraction, regulating and standardizing hotel services, professionalizing the government department or ministry in charge of tourism, targeted international marketing of holiday destinations, and so forth). Most countries in Eastern Africa, West Africa, North Africa and Southern Africa have the need to maximize the potential benefits of safari capitalism. In the North African economies of Tunisia and Egypt where tourism is a major source of revenue and employment generation, accounting for 11–16% of GDP, there is the need to improve security and the backstopping infrastructures of tourism.

4. ***Access to Favourable Long-Term Credits:*** Access to large long-term credits is crucial for any capitalist economy, not least a comparatively small and underdeveloped market as the African. It is a welcome development that many African countries have increasingly ventured to the international capital market for credits, especially countries that may not be eligible to access concessional long-term funds from IDA and other multilateral institutions. Even for countries that do qualify for IDA financing and related debt relief for Heavily Indebted Poor Countries (HIPCs), there is a recognition that reliance on IDA financing and aid resources alone is not sufficient to finance their huge development needs, including public infrastructure and poverty reduction (Ahouassou 2011). Hence, many African countries have over the years obtained credit ratings from reputable agencies like Standard & Poor's Global Ratings, Fitch Ratings Inc. and Moody's Investor Service. Among the direct and indirect benefits of obtaining credit ratings in the Western capital market include to help African states issue sovereign bonds, attract FDIs, stimulate the growth of the private sectors—further helping them gain access to the global market, as well as to enhance the development of the local capital markets. However, the sticking point for the African market bloc is that a "risk premium"[13] is attached to Africa. As President Akufo-Addo pointed out, credit rating agencies and lenders add an "African Risk Premium," which makes it expensive to raise sustainable and competitive long-term capital and this is despite the fact that many countries in the African region offer one of the highest returns on foreign direct investments (Daily Guide Network, 28 February 2020). African countries are borrowing from the financial market at significantly higher rates relative to most developing countries elsewhere that have not repeatedly defaulted in their international debt obligations. The removal of the so-called "Africa Risk Premium" and levelling of the international capital market playing field by credit agencies is an urgent necessity to help Africa source more investment funds and opportunities.

Moreover, there is the need to strengthen the existing structures of regional capital markets integration in Africa, notably "the two Francophone-driven regional stock exchanges"[14] and the more inclusive African Securities Exchanges Association (ASEA) to *inter alia* expand cross-listing, investor access and market capitalization. This is important to leverage the contributions of the capital markets to GDP growth. From the standpoint of raising the much-needed long-term private sector equity capital and debt securities, most of the African capital markets are still relatively underdeveloped. Greater capacity-building, market-friendly regulations, availability of market data and regional coordination of financial market opportunities using new technologies are required to enhance investor access and strengthen capital markets development and integration in Africa.[15]

5. ***Encouraging Smart Regulations:*** Smart regulation using multi-faceted policies is important for growth and development. The classical *laissez-faire* economics of Adam Smith characterized by the invisible hand of market forces is a utopian construct that can only be likened to the communist classless society of Karl Marx on the opposite end of the ideological spectrum. The post-Smithian rational market theory and trickle-down economics devoid of constructive interventionism by the state is a recipe for the worst expressions of human greed and covetousness. The World Bank and IMF aggravated the African economic crisis of the 1980s and 1990s by promoting outrageous versions of deregulation that have never been practised anywhere in the West, the bastion of modern capitalism. Attributing the Western financial crisis of 2007—2008 principally to the failure of regulation and also underscoring the importance of regulation, Angel Gurria ex-Secretary General of OECD admitted as follows:

> We failed as regulators, we failed as supervisors, we failed as corporate governance managers, we failed as risk managers, and we also failed in the allocation of roles and responsibilities for international economic organisations. Some international organisations saw the crisis coming. Some even managed to put out some warnings, but they did not co-ordinate their assessments, they did not speak with one strong voice. Thus, they were ignored in an atmosphere of great prosperity where everybody was making a lot of money and everybody thought that innovation was the name of the game - and by warning that something could go wrong, you would look like you were holding progress back. There was also the philosophy that markets needed to function with the least possible government intervention. But that did not mean that they could work without any intervention at all, nor did it necessarily mean that the intervention could be such a light touch that you were not able to identify risks. (BBC, 23 September 2011)

So, as Gurria implied, markets cannot work without any intervention at all, and the intervention does not necessarily have to be a light touch. Africa governments need to get the philosophy of state intervention to reform and regulate the markets right. State intervention in the economy and protectionism are on the rise even among the developed capitalist countries (Moyo 2018: xix). Smart market reforms, smart regulation and smart protectionism are all required in Africa to forestall the type of undue short-term profit maximization tendencies of financial capitalism principally behind the Wall Street crash of 2008, as well as to stimulate the "real economy," foster growth of local production and industries, bridge levels of inequality and create jobs. Smart regulation and protectionism are what all flourishing market economies and economic blocs do in various degrees both in the West and in the East and they would always argue their way through the WTO "non-discrimination" and "free trade" regulations to justify their policies and practices. There is an inbuilt paradox in the capitalist system, both local and international, which was well captured by Raghuram Rajan and Luigi Zingales in their stimulating book *Saving Capitalism from the Capitalists* (2003), which is the hypocrisy of "extolling the virtues of competitive markets with every breath while attempting to extinguish them with every action." Capitalist investors and financiers chant the ideology of free market to help them gain privileged access to new markets but once they get in, they become "incumbent" defenders of the status quo and enemies of free market, championing the course of protection against competition, and mobilizing political power to limit open access to capital market financing. This is part of the reasons why Rajan and Zingales espouse the idea of saving capitalism from the hypocritical capitalists by privileging strong competitive financial markets as opposed to entrusting more centralized decision-making powers to the state.

The idea of saving capitalism from the capitalists is a vital argument but the modality for doing it seems more debatable. In the case of Africa, capitalism needs to be saved not only from the capitalists (perhaps more accurately pseudo-capitalists and useful idiots), but more importantly from a parasitic "political class" that dominate most of the state systems—the political entrepreneurs. Having said that, it is pertinent to observe that some of the African countries already do have smart regulatory policies in place to protect or encourage local production but on a regional scale such measures are fragmented and need to be synchronized, especially as the continent heads towards regional trade and market integration. It is interesting that following the financial crisis in the West, all their governments were adopting measures to save capitalism from the capitalists—strengthening regulation using fiscal and monetary policies, and increasing state intervention in their economies—in other words, doing the diametrical opposite of what they recommended for Africa during the African economic crisis of the SAP years.

6. ***Strengthening the Tax Infrastructures***: In Chapter 4, I have discussed the issue of the weak taxation regulations, capacity and infrastructures in Africa which many TNCs take advantage of to perpetuate their diverse tax dodging devices. The chapter also discusses the role and responsibility of the developed countries regarding illicit financial flows from the continent. However, it is not only the foreign multinationals that take undue advantage of the weak tax infrastructures in the continent but also indigenous businesses in both the formal and informal economies. A greater proportion of the African workforce is concentrated in the informal economy. Except for personal income tax in the formal economy, the capacity and infrastructures for all other forms of taxation in most African countries are weak—corporate income tax, value-added tax, excise duty, capital gains tax, and so forth. Even the calibration systems of personal income tax in many countries are outmoded and problematic with the result that in diverse sectors high earners, including the political elites do not pay their fair share of taxes. A number of important publications have provided vital information about the fundamental problems with African tax systems and also proffered practicable reforms and strategies for overcoming them. One of such brilliant reports is the joint report by TJN-Africa and Christian Aid titled "Africa Rising? Inequalities and the essential role of fair taxation" published in 2014. The report among other things pinpoints constraints such as weak tax laws and regulations, weak tax authorities with limited expertise and resources to tackle tax abuse, undue reduction in corporate income tax for sundry reasons notably tax dodging, tax exemptions by governments that mistakenly believe that tax breaks will attract sustainable investment, and so forth.[16] In recent years, several African countries (e.g., Ethiopia, Kenya, Mauritius, Nigeria, Seychelles, Gambia, etc.) have taken advantage of digital technologies and available technical expertise and skills training opportunities to introduce measurable reforms in their tax systems to minimize under-reporting and improve efficiency in tax collection. In most of the countries, such reforms are however, not as comprehensive as they should be to produce optimal impact in macroeconomic performance. Constructive reforms to address the identified problems need to be introduced and implemented across all sectors of the economy and spanning the various levels of government, supported with the necessary digital technology-driven capacity-building. The challenges of digitalization are of course enormous, being linked to

the overall poor state of public infrastructures discussed in this book. As such, the implementation of any well-crafted reforms can be streamlined and time-lined in phases. Reforming and strengthening the public tax infrastructures are important not only for the purpose of improving the revenue base of governments but also to help provide the funds required for essential services like education and public health, as well as to ensure that the proceeds of growth are appropriately taxed to address and mitigate the high levels of inequality in most countries. Furthermore, there is the need to integrate regional dimensions to reforming the tax systems in Africa, especially in the context of the emerging regional markets and the contiguous but porous land borders between states to avoid foreign investors and importers taking undue advantage of areas of low or zero taxation.

7. ***Mitigating Illegal Capital Outflow and Repatriation of Looted Funds:*** The obligation of the "international community" or the developed market economies to help Africa in mitigating illegal capital outflow, repatriate stolen wealth stashed away in their commercial banks and confiscate related assets, such as properties acquired with resources looted from the various African countries for the benefit of the latter cannot be over-emphasized. Extreme intolerables such as economic collapse, brutal repression and war anywhere, not only in Africa, can trigger or accentuate avoidable humanitarian crisis whose resonance could impact many other countries, near and far. The developed countries have a moral and political responsibility to cooperate with African governments and regional multilateral institutions like the African Development Bank to help Africa recover looted funds, mitigate money laundering from the continent and also develop transparent frameworks for the use of recovered funds to improve the delivery of essential services in areas such as education, health, smallscale agriculture and poverty reduction.

On another note, there is an incredibly enormous volume of Africa's wealth (both the ill-gotten and legitimate) stashed abroad in foreign banks which are not beneficial to the continent. Proactive legislations, policy measures and sensitization campaigns are required from African governments and national and regional institutions that should aim to encourage wealth repatriation and investment in the continent. An amnesty regime for the repatriation and investing of irrecoverable "looted funds" to help create jobs might be worthwhile. The African diaspora community should also be encouraged to invest more in the continent.

Intra-African investments across national boundaries need to be more vigorously encouraged and promoted.

8. ***Strategic Mobilization of International Finance and Development Assistance:*** Finally, there are levels of capitalist economic transactions and relations—local, regional and international. The strategic and mobilizing importance of the international level of capitalism for Africa's economic prosperity at the national and regional levels cannot be over-emphasized. The epicentres of big bang transformation that I adumbrated in Sect. 2.4 can hardly happen without significant international support, albeit not the traditional nuisance model of foreign aid that Dambisa Moyo already dissected and repudiated in her epic publication, *Dead Aid* (2009).[17] I will not revisit the issue of failed aid in this book. The nature of international support required by Africa is the type of financial market support and FDI infusion that post-war Japan received from the USA and the rest of the successful Asian economies later received from Japan and the West, especially the USA. If history is anything to go by, I imagine that Africa is less likely to receive the required quantum of foreign capital and technical support for a tectonic economic shift from the big economies of the West than from China. I wish and do hope that I will be proved wrong on this assumption. Until recently, China was a Third World country and still diplomatically claims to be Third World even though they are no longer. However, because of their lived experience, the Chinese political leadership seems to have a better understanding of what it means to be Third World. The West on the other hand is largely governed by a hegemonic ensemble that has inherited and perpetuated global entitlement, a mentality that the world is theirs to run. Over the years, this mentality has often produced contradictions of parlous insensitivity and patronizing tokenism towards the developing world. With respect to Africa in particular, the Western superiority complex has frequently resulted in what President Paul Kagame of Rwanda described as the infantile characterization of African states as toddler states that require "adult supervision." Speaking at the fifth meeting of the high-level group of personalities on Europe—Africa relations convened by Mo Ibrahim and Etienne Davignon in December 2020, President Kagame further remarked that: "There cannot be a mutually respectful partnership premised on the unspoken assumption that one party (*i.e. Africa*) lacks values or has defective values, while the other party (*Europe*) is a fully formed moral agent" (Bizimungu 2020).

If we juxtapose the centuries of Africa—West economic relations with Africa—China relations I am persuaded to imagine that the big economies of the West do not have the mindset and goodwill to genuinely support Africa's economic transformation as much as China has demonstrated. If such a mentality or goodwill exists anywhere in the West, it is certainly not among the big economies. It will probably be found among the comparatively smaller social welfare economies of the Scandinavian that do not have any imperial or neocolonial baggage in Africa—Norway, Denmark and Finland. Having said that, the large market space and economic opportunities that the West has lost to China in Africa in recent years is something that could ultimately work to Africa's advantage by generating a need- and envy-fuelled demand in the West to recover their dented economic influence in Africa. For instance, in August 2018 when ex-Prime Minister Theresa May undertook a business visit to Africa covering South Africa, Nigeria and Kenya, the UK government announced a new ambition for the UK to be the largest G7 investor in Africa by 2022. In the context of BREXIT, the UK government is in search of new markets, which could work to Africa's advantage. On 20 January 2020, the UK prime minister, Boris Johnson, hosted the UK–Africa Investment Summit in London which announced billions of Pounds of new commercial deals and agreed on new lasting partnerships between the UK and African countries to deliver more investment, jobs and growth (UK Government, 2020). The ongoing development of the mammoth export-oriented $20 billion Liquified Natural Gas (LNG) project in Mozambique has received an unprecedented synergy between the West, the East and African partners. The USA, Japan, UK, Italy, Netherlands, South Africa and Vietnam are putting public money towards a $14.9 billion package of loans for the project while the African Development Bank (AfDB) and 19 commercial lenders are also contributing (Darby 2020). AfDB has approved a loan of $400 million for the LNG project. The French oil major Total is leading the project after buying out US Anadarko's shareholding in September 2019, and the other project partners include Japanese Mitsui, Mozambique state energy company ENH, Thailand's Public Company Limited and 3 Indian energy firms—Oil and Natural Gas Company (ONGC), Bharat Petroleum Resources and Oil India (Darby 2020; Zawadzki 2020; Thompson 2020). The massive international investments in Mozambique's LNG project is not an act of charity, but an indication of investors' confidence in the long-term viability of the project. So, does Africa still need the West? Absolutely Yes! Africa needs the West for favourable

FDI, and technical assistance and it is apparent that the challenge of wresting some markets from China or preventing them from taking more could work in Africa's favour. The Chinese are giving the West a tough competition in Africa, even outcompeting them in many respects, and ultimately this may well precipitate the necessary change in the way the West perceives and relates to Africa. Furthermore, Africa needs to continue to engage Western-based multilateral institutions for necessary opportunities, especially aid to backstop MSMEs, promoting participation in international trade and to negotiate better "fair trade" deals. As President Kagame has aptly pointed out, Africa needs to strengthen strategic and mutually beneficial partnerships with the West in areas of trade, peace and security, migration and climate change (Bizimungu 2020).

In connection with tapping external relations and opportunities to bolster growth and development, Africa needs to be free to forge political, trade and economic relations with any countries and regions of the world mindful of its own strategic regional interests. I am not sure of how united contemporary African states are around whatever they have conceived as their strategic regional economic interests. In terms of thinking and action about regional strategic interests, the gaps I see today in Africa are clearly similar to the unpreparedness in 1980 when the defunct OAU adopted the forward-looking *Lagos Plan of Action for the Economic Development of Africa (1980–2000)*, but without any serious commitment and political will to implement it. The World Bank capitalized on Africa's lack of preparation and political will for implementing the *Lagos Plan of Action* to literally impose on Africa their commissioned 1981 counter-Plan known as the Elliot Berg Report on "Accelerated Development in Sub-Saharan Africa: A Plan for Action." Many African political economists and avid students of the subject may still remember the famous Berg Report which was behind SAP. The development of Sub-Saharan Africa was not accelerated but instead deaccelerated and ruined by SAP. As is well known, the West was complicit in the imposition and execution of SAP. Incalculable damage was done. A few lessons probably learned. Africa has moved on!

States and regional trading blocs, no matter how wealthy, do not venture into the international economic arena with the object of altruism and charity towards the less privileged states and blocs. The best they can render is a win–win. But a win–win outcome is hardly 50-50. Mathematically, it can be very far from it. The allocative share of what each party gets in the win–win outcome is politically determined. Africa must learn to play the required politics, and they need to learn fast. For any foreign powers to strongly identify with Africa's strategic regional interests with the object of pursuing a win–win agenda that could be optimally beneficial to Africa, the present generation of African leaders and states need to get their act together. More serious policy re-engineering work needs to be done regarding the African Union's AfCFTA agreement signed by African countries and which entered into force on 30 May 2019. In signing up to the AfCFTA, individual member states have committed to remove tariffs on about 90% of goods at the initial stages, and gradually phase off the remaining 10% over time (Signe 2018). Non-tariff barriers to trade in the continent such as fragmented protectionist regulations and customs procedures, as well as logistical aspects like poor transport, seaport, aviation, power and digital connectivity infrastructures are expected to be addressed under the AfCFTA regime using regional frameworks. This presents an opportunity for the African bloc to work towards an effective operationalization of the WTO Trade Facilitation Agreement (TFA) of 2014 (which entered into force in February 2017) that aims to ease bureaucratic bottlenecks on external trade in developing and least developed countries "by the simplification, modernization and harmonization of export and import processes" (WTO 2020). The TFA contains provisions for expediting the movement, release and clearance of goods, including goods in transit and also sets out measures for effective cooperation between customs and other appropriate authorities on trade facilitation and customs compliance issues (WTO 2020). It is believed that promoting intra-African free trade will help to create economies of scale for investors and make Africa more competitive in global trade and value chains (World Economic Forum 2019). It is quite lamentable that Africa currently has the lowest percentage of intra-regional trade in the world valued at 18%, compared to 70% in Europe, 55% in North America, 45% in Asia and 35% in Latin America (World Economic Forum 2019). The implementation plan for AfCFTA, originally scheduled to start on 1 July 2020 but practically rendered infeasible by the Covid-19 pandemic crisis, seems perfunctory in my view. A new implementation date of 1 January 2021 was set. There is the need for a comprehensive review and streamlining of the too many trade and/or investment agreements that different African states and regional and subregional blocs have signed with the more developed market economies such as USA, UK, Canada and the EU (individually and as trading blocs) which in the context of the weak regulatory institutions throughout the continent could potentially undermine AfCFTA. The most prolific of the trade agreements is the

Economic Partnership Agreements (EPAs) concluded or negotiated with the EU. In Africa, the EU has: "an EPA with Madagascar, Mauritius, Seychelles and Zimbabwe in Eastern and Southern Africa (ESA); an EPA with Cameroon in Central Africa; an EPA with the SADC EPA group; and in West Africa an EPA with Côte d'Ivoire and one with Ghana. In two regions, EPA negotiations have been concluded and the adoption process is ongoing: the West African region covering 16 countries; and the East African Community (EAC) covering 5 countries" (European Commission 2018). The review, coordination and streamlining process for these EPAs and all similar external trade and economic cooperation agreements if properly done would necessitate some of the Africa states and regional and subregional blocs having to ultimately withdraw from or renegotiate a number of them for the collective good of Africa and AfCFTA. This will help to prevent the EU and indeed other non-African trading blocs and states from enjoying undue trade preferences and taking advantage of the tariff removal benefits that continental trade liberalization will confer on AfCFTA members thereby, leading to significant loss of tax revenues. Robust practical strategies are required to expand the capacity for accelerated value chains in industrial development as a means to improve regional trade because there isn't much for African countries to trade among themselves at the moment.

Summary Points

1. From a neo-Weberian standpoint, there is "a spirit of capitalism," and different societies have different spirits of capitalism or social economy. Put in another way, there is no universal spirit or episteme of capitalism. The spirit of capitalism in any society cannot be disconnected from the dominant religious or philosophical worldview of the people.
2. There are discernible nuances within Western capitalism, as well as in any other regional capitalist bloc.
3. The driving spirit of capitalism in contemporary Asia cannot be disconnected from their religious and philosophical foundations of Confucianism, Buddhism and in the case of India, Hinduism.
4. The chequered colonial and postcolonial experiences of Africa have essentially impeded the emergence of a constructive spirit of capitalism in the continent despite the African rich heritage and

worldview founded on Christianity, Islam and various indigenous faith systems.

5. Many productive models of capitalism are taught in African business schools, most of them having foreign origins. These models include Fordism, managerial capitalism, shareholder capitalism, customer service capitalism, social market capitalism, neo-corporatism and community capitalism. The impact of these various models on the wider macroeconomic spectrum is extremely minimal.
6. There are a few relatively marginalized but sublime models of capitalism in postcolonial Africa that may form the basis for future transformation, and these are mixed economy capitalism, embryonic state capitalism and most importantly entrepreneurial capitalism which for the most part remains practically subdued in contemporary Africa.
7. Targeted and deliberate state support is important for entrepreneurial capitalism to develop and gain strength. State support could be in the forms of favourable access to start-up capital, regulation of competitive imports and massive infrastructural development (e.g., soft roads, railways, portable water, information technology and massive expansion in the capacity to generate, transmit and distribute electricity).
8. The dominant orientation to political governance in several African countries needs constructive reformation to tackle the deep-rooted problems of institutional dysfunction and prebendal squanderation.
9. The "international community," notably the developed market economies need to step up in their obligation to help Africa mitigate illegal capital outflow, repatriate stolen wealth stashed away in their commercial banks and confiscate related assets, such as properties acquired with resources looted from the various African countries for the benefit of the citizens concerned.
10. African governments and regional institutions need to strengthen strategic engagements with external actors, wealthy states, trading blocs and multilateral institutions for necessary economic and technical opportunities, especially aid to backstop MSMEs, promote participation in international trade negotiate better "fair trade" deals, etc.

Discussion Questions

1. What do you understand by the Weberian terminology, "the spirit of capitalism"?
2. Does the term "spirit of capitalism" have any analytical relevance in the study of capitalist economies today?
3. How is the capitalism practised across most countries of Western Europe different from American capitalism?
4. What are the major differences between the nature of capitalism practised in China and the West?
5. What do you understand by the term financial capitalism?
6. Is financial capitalism a counter-productive model?
7. Is state capitalism feasible in the liberal democratic states of Africa?
8. What are the challenges facing entrepreneurial capitalism in Africa?
9. Discuss five important reform measures that could help African countries in the fight against corruption in political and economic governance?
10. Is the "*African Continental Free Trade Area*" (AfCFTA) the key to accelerated economic development and industrialization in Africa? Explain in detail.

Notes

1. See: Sociology Group (n.d.) "Protestant Ethic and the Spirit of Capitalism: Summary", https://www.sociologygroup.com/protestant-ethic-spirit-capitalism-summary/.
2. Max Weber (1992; written in 1905 but first published in 1930) *The Protestant Ethics and the Spirit of Capitalism.* Translated by Talcott Parsons with "Introduction" by Anthony Giddens. London: Routledge, pp. x–xiii. Available at: https://is.muni.cz/el/1423/podzim2013/SOC571E/um/_Routledge_Classics___Max_Weber-The_Protestant_Ethic_and_the_Spirit_of_Capitalism__Routledge_Classics_-Routledge__2001_.pdf.
3. Max Weber (1992; first published 1930) Ibid., reference to note 2.
4. See: Dambisa Moyo (2011) *How the West Was Lost: Fifty Years of Economic Folly and the Stark Choices Ahead.* New York: Penguin Books. Jeffrey Friedman and Wladimir Kraus (2011) *Engineering the Financial Crisis:*

Systemic Risk and the Failure of Regulation. Philadelphia: University of Pennsylvania Press.

5. Taken from the serialization of: Adam Smith's book *An Inquiry into the Nature and Causes of the Wealth of Nations* (1776) in the following website: http://historymuse.net/readings/smithwealthofnations.html; For more elaborate reading of Adam Smith, see the following websites for 2 volumes of *An Inquiry into the Nature and Causes of the Wealth of Nations* edited by Edwin Cannan: https://oll.libertyfund.org/titles/smith-an-inquiry-into-the-nature-and-causes-of-the-wealth-of-nations-cannan-ed-vol-1; https://oll.libertyfund.org/titles/smith-an-inquiry-into-the-nature-and-causes-of-the-wealth-of-nations-cannan-ed-vol-2.
6. The emphasis in italics is mine. Financial capitalism (also known as financialization) is the type of capitalism that has grown in the USA and many Western countries since the 1970s, especially since the President Ronald Reagan's market deregulation that unduly empowered the Wall Street and its unproductive risk model of short-term profit maximization in the highly speculative global financial market. According to the renowned economic sociologist Paul Windolf (2008: 3), financial capitalism is a system of institutions in which traditional bank loans are not the dominant financing instruments but shares and the relations between the financial markets and real economies are characterized by the mechanisms of the global financial markets. "Gerald A. Epstein has presented a most encompassing definition of financialization, which for him means the increasing role of financial motives, financial markets, financial actors and financial institutions in the operation of the domestic and international economies" (cited in Alexander Engel 2015). According to Rana Foroohar (2016) financial capitalism "includes everything from the growth in size and scope of finance and financial activity in the economy; to the rise of debt-fuelled speculation over productive lending; to the ascendancy of shareholder value as the sole model for corporate governance; to the proliferation of risky, selfish thinking in both the private and public sectors; to the increasing political power of financiers and the CEOs they enrich; to the way in which a 'markets know best' ideology remains the status quo."
7. For further detail on [neo]corporatism in continental Europe, see Molina (2007).
8. Definition of welfare capitalism is adapted from the online Merriam Webster Dictionary available at: https://www.merriam-webster.com/dictionary/welfare%20capitalism.
9. In the indicated definition of entrepreneurialism Robert Price quoted Carl Voigt, Dean of the Marshall School of Business at the University of Southern California.
10. This observation in partly in line with the view expressed by experts like Moghalu (2014: 155–157).

11. Professor George Ayittey's views were extrapolated from his Calvin University's interview on "African Solutions to African Problems", 7 April 2012, available at: https://www.bing.com/videos/search?q=George+Ayittey+African+Solution+for+African+Problems&&view=detail&mid=3E4950D2FD3333F154AE3E4950D2FD3333F154AE&&FORM=VRDGAR.
12. The definition is extrapolated from the Concept Note title: "What is Africapitalism?" published in the website of The Tony Elumelu Foundation, 24 June 2019; see: https://www.tonyelumelufoundation.org/news/what-is-africapitalism.
13. "Risk premium refers to the difference between the expected return on a portfolio or investment and the certain return on a risk-free security or portfolio. It is the additional return that an investor requires to hold a risky asset rather than one that is risk free. Underlying the term *risk premium* is the idea that there should be a higher expected return – a premium for bearing risk." See: Market Business News (n.d.) What Is Risk Premium?", https://marketbusinessnews.com/financial-glossary/risk-premium-definition-meaning/.
14. The two Francophone-driven stock exchange markets are the Bourse Régionale des Valeurs Mobilières (BRVM) based in Abidjan, Cote d'Ivoire principally serving the WAEMU members states and the Bourse Régionale des Valeurs Mobilières d'Afrique Centrale (BVMAC) based in Libreville, Gabon that serves the CEMAC member states. See Chapter 3 for more detail on WAEMU and CEMAC.
15. The indicated factors are partly based on a survey of 50 African asset-managers for the African Exchanges Linkage Project (AELP) posted on 30 July 2020 by the African Securities Exchanges Association (ASEA) Secretariat in their website and discussed in the briefing titled: "African Fund Managers Look for Governance in New Markets," see: https://african-exchanges.org/. For additional relevant information, see also: Murinde (2006) and Kapingura et al. (2014).
16. The joint TJN-Africa and Christian Aid report has been brilliantly summarised by Nick Shaxson of Tax Justice Network (TJN) in a piece published in TJN website titled "New Report: Growth in Africa Fails to Curb Soaring Inequality", 24 February 2014, https://www.taxjustice.net/2014/02/24/new-report-growth-africa-fails-curb-soaring-inequality/.
17. Dambisa Moyo (2009) makes a strong case in favour of fair trade as against development assistance, arguing that foreign aid has aggravated the syndromes of dependency, corruption, consumerism, clientelism and tokenism in postcolonial Africa. Furthermore, development aid is too

often diverted to military security purposes to foster authoritarian crackdown or prosecute armed conflicts, a phenomenon widely known as the fungibility of aid in development economics.

References

Afrobarometer. 2016. World Development Information Day: China's Growing Presence in Africa Wins Positive Popular Reviews, October 24. http://afrobarometer.org/press/world-development-information-day-chinas-growing-presence-africa-wins-positive-popular-reviews.

Ahouassou, Aristide. 2011. African Countries Credit Ratings: Key for Effective Resource Mobilization on International Capital Markets. Africa Development Bank, May 24. https://www.afdb.org/en/news-and-events/african-countries-credit-ratings-key-for-effective-resource-mobilization-on-international-capital-markets-8023.

Ayittey, George. 2018. Indigenous African Free-Market Liberalism, September. https://yafopportunities.org/pdf/INDIGENOUS-AFRICAN-FREE.pdf.

Barton, Dominic. 2011. Capitalism for the Long-Term. *Harvard Business Review*, March. https://hbr.org/2011/03/capitalism-for-the-long-term.

Baumann, Chris, Hume Winzar, and Doris Viengkham. 2019. *Confucianism, Discipline, and Competitiveness*. New York: Routledge.

BBC. 2011. Has Western Capitalism Failed, September 23. https://www.bbc.co.uk/news/business-14972015.

Bizimungu, Julius. 2020. Let's Not Ask What Can Be Done for Africa, Kagame Tells Europe. *The New Times*, December 3, 2020. https://www.newtimes.co.rw/news/lets-not-ask-what-can-be-done-africa-kagame-tells-europe.

Brookings. 1997. Community Capitalism: Rediscovering the Markets of America's Urban Neighborhoods. Brookings Report, April 1. https://www.brookings.edu/research/community-capitalism-rediscovering-the-markets-of-americas-urban-neighborhoods/.

Bruenig, Matt. 2018. How Capitalist Is Singapore Really? March 9. People's Policy Project. https://www.peoplespolicyproject.org/2018/03/09/how-capitalist-is-singapore-really/.

Calabrese, John. 2020. Towering Ambitions: Egypt and China Building for the Future, October 6. Middle East Institute. https://www.mei.edu/publications/towering-ambitions-egypt-and-china-building-future.

Cilliers, Jakkie. 2021. *The Future of Africa: Challenges and Opportunities*. Cham, Switzerland: Palgrave Macmillan.

Daily Guide Network. 2020. Remove 'Africa Risk Premium' From the Credit Rating Structure, February 28. https://dailyguidenetwork.com/remove-africa-risk-premium-from-the-credit-rating-structure-akufo-addo-to-capital-markets/.

Daily Trust. 2020. The Suspension of Magu, July 8. https://www.dailytrust.com.ng/the-suspension-of-magu.html.

Darby, Megan. 2020. Seven Countries Back Africa's Biggest Investment, a $20 Billion Gas Project. Climate Home News, July 20. https://www.climatechangenews.com/2020/07/20/seven-countries-back-africas-biggest-investment-20-billion-gas-project/.

David, Kumar. 2017. Oligarchic Capitalism and Party – State Structure: Same or Different? November 19. https://www.colombotelegraph.com/index.php/oligarchic-capitalism-party-state-structure-same-or-different/.

Bloomberg. 2018. Stiglitz Warns Against Expecting Africa to Repeat Asian Miracle, September 15. https://www.bloomberg.com/news/articles/2018-09-15/stiglitz-warns-against-expecting-africa-to-repeat-asian-miracle.

Elliott, Vittoria. 2020. African Governments Rushed to Protect Local Start-ups. *Rest to World*, December 22. https://restofworld.org/2020/for-africa-by-africa/.

Emergency Digest. 2019. Nigerian Army to Launch Armoured Vehicle Named Ezugwu MRAP, October 25. https://emergencydigest.com/2019/10/25/nigerian-army-armored-vehicle/.

Engel, Alexander. 2015. The Bang after the Boom: Understanding Financialization. *Studies in Contemporary History* 12 (3). https://zeithistorische-forschungen.de/3-2015/5278#:~:text=Sociologist%20Paul%20Windolf%20defines%20financial%20market%20capitalism%20as,production%20in%20the%20so-called%20%E2%80%BAreal%20economy%E2%80%B9%20is%20governed.

European Commission. 2018. Economic Partnership Agreements (EPAs), September. https://trade.ec.europa.eu/doclib/docs/2017/february/tradoc_155300.pdf.

Foroohar, Rana. 2016. American Capitalism's Great Crisis. *Time*, May 12. https://time.com/4327419/american-capitalisms-great-crisis/.

Giddens, Anthony. 1992. "Introduction" to Max Weber's book, *The Protestant Ethics and the Spirit of Capitalism*. First published 1930 and trans. Talcott Parsons. London: Routledge.

Gluhbegovic, Rebeka. 2016. Types of Conflict in Africa: How Do the APRM Reports Address Conflicts? EISA Occasional Paper AP8, September. https://www.eisa.org.za/pdf/aprm2015aps8.pdf.

Haskel, Jonathan, and Stian Westlake. 2017. *Capitalism Without Capital: The Rise of the Intangible Economy*. Princeton, NJ: Princeton University Press.

Hefner, L. Frank, and Guimaraes P. Paulo. 1991. Backward and Forward Linkages in Manufacturing Location: Decisions Reconsidered. https://rrs.scholasticahq.com/article/9069-backward-and-forward-linkages-in-manufacturing-location-decisions-reconsidered.

ITC News. 2020. New Africa Marketplace Explorer Enables Small Businesses to Understand Africa's Nascent E-Commerce Sites, May 6. https://www.int

racen.org/news/New-Africa-Marketplace-Explorer-enables-small-businesses-to-understand-Africas-nascent-e-commerce-sites/.

Jahan, Sarwat, and Ahmed Saber Mahmud. 2015. What Is Capitalism? *Finance and Development* 52 (2) (June). https://www.imf.org/external/pubs/ft/fandd/2015/06/basics.htm.

Kapingura, Mingiri Forget, et al. 2014. Integration of African Stock Markets to the Global Market: Case Study of South Africa. *Mediterranean Journal of Social Sciences* 5 (2): 619–628.

Kazeem, Yomi. 2020. African Venture Funding Is Expected to Slow but Impact Investors Are Boosting Health and Agri-tech Startups. *Quartz Africa*, June 26. https://qz.com/africa/1869334/covid-19-impact-investors-eye-african-agriculture-health-startups/.

Kuo, Lily. 2016. China's Model of Economic Development Is Becoming More Popular in Africa than America's, October 28. *Quartz Africa*. https://qz.com/africa/820841/chinas-model-of-economic-development-is-becoming-more-popular-in-africa-than-americas/.

Moghalu, C. Kingsley. 2014. *Emerging Africa: How Global Economy's 'Last Frontier' Can Prosper and Matter*. London: Penguin Books.

Molina, Oscar. 2007. Trade Union Strategies and Change in Neo-corporatist Concertation: A New Century of Political Exchange? *West European Politics* 29 (4): 640–664.

Moyo, Dambisa. 2009. *Dead Aid: Why Aid Is Not Working and How There Is Another Way for Africa*. London: Penguin.

Moyo, Dambisa. 2012. *Winner Take All: China's Race for Resources and What It Means for Us*. London: Penguin.

Moyo, Dambisa. 2018. *Edge of Chaos: Why Democracy Is Failing to Deliver Economic Growth and How to Fix It*. London: Little, Brown.

Murinde, Victor. 2006. Capital Markets: Roles and Challenges. https://www.afdb.org/fileadmin/uploads/afdb/Documents/Knowledge/09484315-EN-CAPITAL-MARKETS-ROLES-CHALLENGES-DRAFT1.PDF.

NIC. 2012. *Global Trends 2030: Alternative Worlds.* A publication of the US National Intelligence Council (NIC), December. https://www.dni.gov/files/documents/GlobalTrends_2030.pdf.

Nseher, Mfonobong. 2014. Seven Innovative Products from Africa you Should Know, February 13. https://www.forbes.com/sites/mfonobongnsehe/2014/02/13/seven-innovative-products-from-africa-you-should-know/#6747bddb7f1c.

Omeje, Kenneth. 2019. Peacebuilding in Contemporary Africa. In *Peacebuilding in Contemporary Africa: In Search of Alternative Strategies*, ed. K. Omeje, 3–19. London: Routledge.

Pedroncelli, Peter. 2019. Tony Elumelu Partners with United Nations to Empower 100,000 African Entrepreneurs. *The Moguldom Nation*, July

22. https://moguldom.com/214084/tony-elumelu-partners-with-united-nations-to-empower-100000-african-entrepreneurs/.

Premium Times. 2020. How We Were Pressured to Squander $18bn Excess Crude Saving — Jonathan, July 17. https://www.premiumtimesng.com/news/headlines/204809-pressured-squander-18bn-excess-crude-saving-jonathan.html.

Price, J. Robert. n.d. Entrepreneurial Capitalism. https://robertwprice.com/entrepreneurial-capitalism/#:~:text=%20Entrepreneurial%20Capitalism%20%201%20Entrepreneurs%2C%20Low%20Taxes%2C,to%20look%20back%20to%20the%20early...%20More%20.

Rajan, Raghuram, and Luigi Zingales. 2003. *Saving Capitalism from the Capitalists: Unleashing the Power of Financial Markets to Create Wealth & Spread Opportunity*. New York: Crown Business.

Sally, Razeen. 2015. What Is a Social Market Economy? *Daily FT* October 7. http://www.ft.lk/article/479813/What-is-a-Social-Market-Economy.

Schuman, Michael. 2012. Can Asian-Style Capitalism Save the West? *Business Time*, March 25. https://business.time.com/2012/03/25/can-asian-style-capitalism-save-the-west/.

Signe, Landry. 2018. Africa's Big New Free Trade Agreement Explained. *The Washington Post*, March 29.

Signe, Landry, and Chelsea Johnson. 2018. The Potential of Manufacturing and Industrialization in Africa: Trends, Opportunities, and Strategies. Africa Growth Initiative at Brookings. https://www.brookings.edu/wp-content/uploads/2018/09/Manufacturing-and-Industrialization-in-Africa-Signe-20180921.pdf.

Sociology Group. n.d. Protestant Ethic and the Spirit of Capitalism: Summary. https://www.sociologygroup.com/protestant-ethic-spirit-capitalism-summary/.

Statistical Times. 2020. List of Asian Countries by GDP Per Capita, February 29. http://statisticstimes.com/economy/asian-countries-by-gdp-per-capita.php.

Stubbs, Richard. 2018. *Rethinking Asia's Economic Miracles: The Political Economy of War, Prosperity and Crisis*, 2nd ed. London: Palgrave.

Tafirenyika, Masimba. 2016. Why Has Africa Failed to Industrialize? Africa Renewal, August–November. https://www.un.org/africarenewal/magazine/august-2016/why-has-africa-failed-industrialize.

The SDG Centre for Africa. 2019. 2019 Africa SDG Index and Dashboards Report, June. https://s3.amazonaws.com/sustainabledevelopment.report/2019/2019_africa_index_and_dashboards.pdf.

The Straits Times. 2020. Temasek Portfolio Value Dips 2.2% to $306 Billion Amid Covid-19: Preliminary Data, July 21. https://www.straitstimes.com/business/economy/temasek-reports-preliminary-portfolio-value-of-306-billion-slightly-lower-than.

Thompson, Felix. 2020. Total Secures ECA-backed Deal for Major Mozambique LNG Project. *Global Trade Review*, July 22. https://www.gtreview.com/news/africa/total-secures-eca-backed-deal-for-major-mozambique-lng-project/.

UK Government. 2020. UK Government Statement on the UK-Africa Investment Summit. UK Government Policy Paper, January 20. https://www.gov.uk/government/publications/uk-government-statement-on-the-uk-africa-investment-summit.

UNDP. 2019 *Human Development Report 2019*. UNDP. http://hdr.undp.org/en/content/human-development-index-hdi.

Windolf, Paul. 2008. What Is Financial-Market Capitalism. Department of Sociology, University of Trier, D- 54286 Trier, Germany. https://www.uni-trier.de/fileadmin/fb4/prof/SOZ/APO/FinancialMarketCapitalism.pdf.

World Bank. 2019. Doing Business 2019. The World Bank, Washington, DC. https://www.doingbusiness.org/content/dam/doingBusiness/media/Annual-Reports/English/DB19-Chapters/DB19-Overview.pdf.

World Economic Forum. 2019. How Africa Can Secure Its Long-Term Economic Growth, September 4. https://www.weforum.org/agenda/2019/09/how-africa-can-secure-its-long-term-economic-growth/.

WTO. 2020. Trade Facilitation. World Trade Organisation, https://www.wto.org/english/tratop_e/tradfa_e/tradfa_e.htm.

Zawadzki, Sabina. 2020. Anadarko Approves $20 Billion LNG Export Project in Mozambique. *Business News*, June 18, 2019. https://www.reuters.com/article/us-mozambique-anadarko-lng-idUSKCN1TJ2DI.

CHAPTER 9

Postscript on Covid-19 in Africa

All the members of human society stand in need of each other's assistance and are likewise exposed to mutual injuries.[1]—Adam Smith, eighteenth-century Scottish economist and philosopher of capitalism.

9.1 The Covid-19 Pandemic

The need to pay attention to our complex interconnectedness as a global community, which proponents of globalization have stressed and theorized for many years has been vindicated by the Covid-19 pandemic. The rapidity and extensity with which Covid-19 spread within three months of its detection in Wuhan in China in December 2019 to literally affect every part of the globe is an indication that our contemporary world is in the words of neoliberal globalists "a cobweb of highly interactive global society" (Mcgrew 2010). International trade, Internet technology, and immigration are arguably the greatest drivers of globalization.

Remarkably, Covid-19 is also known as Severe Acute Respiratory Syndrome (SARS-Cov-2), a name designed to distinguish it from an earlier similar infection known as Severe Acute Respiratory Syndrome (SARS-Cov-1 or SARS for short). Earlier in November 2002, some 17 years before the detection of Covid-19, Severe Acute Respiratory Syndrome (SARS), caused by a slightly different strain of coronavirus was detected in Foshan in Guangdong province of China. This led to

K. Omeje, *The Failure and Feasibility of Capitalism in Africa*, International Political Economy Series,
https://doi.org/10.1007/978-3-030-75170-8_9

an extensive epidemic that affected some 32 countries, resulting in about 8,422 cases of infection, with 919 recorded deaths by July 2003 (Yang et al. 2020). South Africa was the only country affected by SARS in Africa. SARS was quickly contained in less than two years and no new cases have been reported worldwide since 2004.

Early COVID-19 infections were linked to a live animal market in Wuhan, China, suggesting that the virus was arguably transmitted from animals being sold as exotic food to humans, a transmission phenomenon known as zoonosis (Yang et al. 2020; Chen 2020). Zoonoses[2] are simply infectious diseases—caused by bacteria, viruses, fungi or parasites—that spread from animals to humans (Walzer 2020). Too often, the zoonotic pathogens do not affect the animals in which they reside, but they can represent an enormous risk to humans who have no natural immunity to them (Walzer 2020). There are many examples of zoonotic diseases that have spilled over from animals or wildlife to humans and they include SARS, MERS (Middle East Respiratory Syndrome), Avian Influenza, Ebola and arguably HIV. Covid-19 is arguably the latest addition in the long list of zoonotic diseases. In terms of transmission methods:

> COVID-19 is mainly spread from person to person through airborne droplets that are coughed or sneezed out by an infected person. People may also get a COVID-19 infection by touching something that has the virus on it and then touching their own mouth, nose, or eyes. The virus is usually transmitted by a person with symptoms of the disorder, but it can be transmitted by people before they exhibit symptoms and even by people who are infected but never develop symptoms. The symptoms of Covid-19 include fever, cough, shortness of breath or difficulty in breathing, chills or repeated shaking with chills, fatigue, muscle pain, headache, sore throat, new loss of smell or taste, nausea, vomiting, and diarrhea. (Tesini 2020)

Symptoms usually manifest within 14 days of one's infection. Most people who contract the virus only exhibit mild symptoms, but the infection fatality rate is significantly low—a fatality rate of below 2% of infected people in high-income countries and below 1% in low-income countries (Ellis 2020). Research and empirical evidence suggest that elderly people (especially those above the age of 85) and those with disabilities and pre-existing health symptoms that weaken the respiratory or immune system (e.g., heart disease, hypertension, asthma and diabetes) are the most at risk of dying from Covid-19. Since the outbreak of the pandemic, new and seemingly easily transmissible variants of coronavirus with different mutations have been separately reported, notably in the UK, South Africa, Brazil and India.

There are disputed claims among frontline medical doctors and the scientific community about the efficacy of the long-standing anti-malaria medication hydroxychloroquine in treating, preventing and mitigating the effects of Covid-19 based on results from various clinical trials in different parts of the world. There are conflicting results from the outcomes of the various trials on diverse categories of patients, some pointing to a high success rate and others pointing to a high rate of failure and uncomfortable potential side effects.

A research breakthrough from the Oxford University in the UK in June 2020 showed that the low-cost steroid dexamethasone, anti-inflammatory steroid commonly used to treat rheumatoid arthritis and asthma, is the first drug to significantly reduce the risk of death among severe COVID-19 cases (*The Guardian*, 16 June 2020). From the trail results among those with severe Covid-19 cases who could only breathe with the help of a ventilator, dexamethasone reduced deaths by one third (*The Guardian*, 16 June 2020). The steroid is not suitable for patients with milder cases of Covid-19. In July 2020 it was announced that preliminary trial results from a potential coronavirus vaccine developed by AstraZeneca and Oxford University and tested on 1,077 people reveal that the vaccine candidate induces a strong immune response and appears to be safe (*Independent*, 20 July 2020). The trail vaccine reportedly induces the immune system to produce antibodies and white blood cells capable of fighting the microscopic virus. Overall results from phase three of the Oxford AstraZeneca trial show the vaccine is 70.4% effective on average but when administered at a half dose and then a full dose of the vaccine can be up to 90% effective (Gartner et al., 2 December 2020). Russia announced its new Sputnik V vaccine in August 2020, which offers 95% protection against the coronavirus (Rainsford 2020).

Two additional major vaccine trial breakthroughs were announced in November 2020. The first is the vaccine candidate produced by the US pharmaceutical company Pfizer and German biotech firm BioNTech which the manufacturers said is 95% effective in preventing Covid-19 and has passed its safety checks, with no severe side effects beyond fatigue that affected 3.7% of participants (Gartner et al., 2 December 2020). The second is a vaccine candidate produced by the US biotechnology company Moderna, reported by the multinational to have an overall efficacy of about 94.1% against the virus with no serious safety concerns identified yet (Gartner et al., 2 December 2020). Available evidence suggests that the developed vaccines might work on the new variants of coronavirus detected in the UK and South Africa, and indeed could most likely develop a strong immune response to act against a broad mutation and variation in the virus (Wood, 23 December 2020).

The additional authorized and prominent Covid-19 vaccines that have entered the global market include Sinopharm (China), Sinovac (China), Janssen (Johnson & Johnson, USA), Bharat Biotech (India) and Covishield (India). Most authorized vaccines have been approved by either the WHO or the relevant national medicines and healthcare regulatory agencies, and in the case of the European Union authorization has to be given by the European Medicines Agency (EMA). Many governments around the world have ordered large stocks of Covid-19 vaccines and commenced largescale vaccination campaign to combat the pandemic, an indication that the end of the crisis is in sight. As expected, and for obvious reasons of disproportionalities in global wealth distribution, the developed countries are ahead of most developing countries in the vaccination campaign. National access to Covid-19 vaccines is further affected by the basic norms of free market competition amidst incongruence in demand and supply, leading to concerns about "vaccine nationalism" and "questionable forms of vaccine diplomacy." Vaccine nationalism is a tendency towards capturing the vaccine distribution market whereby some governments or their agencies sign agreements with vaccine manufacturers (in most cases those within their national jurisdiction) or compel the manufacturers by fiat to first deliver large supplies to them before making the vaccines available to other countries, thereby limiting the access of national populations elsewhere to Covid vaccines. In the questionable forms of vaccine diplomacy, some influential countries are disbursing their national vaccines in a patronizing way to curry favours, strengthen imperial hegemony and make political statements in different parts of the world. The online progress review published by Gavi, the global Vaccine Alliance, indicates that there are dozens of other promising vaccine candidates in countries like USA, Germany, China, Italy, Cuba, UK, Canada, Taiwan and Australia that are at advanced trail phases at the time of writing (Gavi, 2 December 2020).

9.2 Predictions and Economic Impact

When the spread of Covid-19 increased in early 2020 extending to the different parts of the globe, many experts predicted a public health catastrophe in Africa because of the weak infrastructures, financial resources and technical capacities of most African states. In one of such apocalyptic predictions, Melinda Gates, the famous American philanthropist and co-chair of the Bill and Melinda Gates Foundation, warned in an interview with CNN on 10th April 2020 that in countries in Africa the impending scale of the Covid-19 crisis would result in "dead bodies being put out across the streets" as was already happening in Ecuador, according to her.[3] What an exaggeration, if not pure scaremongering, but apparently with no malicious intent.

With limited funding and technical capacity to tackle pre-existing epidemiological diseases and public health problems, most African governments, experts predicted, would not be in a strong position to tackle the Covid-19 health crisis without significant international support. So far, the prediction about a public health catastrophe has not happened in Africa and available indications do not suggest it is likely to occur. Analysing why Covid-19 has not taken a heavy toll on Africa as earlier predicted, the Oxford's Leverhulme Centre for Demographic Science in collaboration with the African Research Network in a study published in June 2020 offered a twofold explanation: First is that the low number of severe cases could be partially attributed to the younger demographic, with only 3% of the population in Sub-Saharan Africa over the age of 65. A second "plausible theory" for the lower morbidity rate in African countries could be climate—temperature and humidity are known factors in the transmissions of other coronaviruses (Nature Medicine 2020). "Africa's total population accounts for 17% of the world's population, but confirmed cases account for only 3% of the world's total" (Teller Report, 21 June 2020). An additional point worth noting is that the demographic and health data in Africa are sketchy, under-reported and in many circumstances, unreliable. The actual proportion and numbers of Covid-19 cases are likely to be significantly higher than reported due to limited testing centres and facilities in the continent. However, the bulk of the reported Covid-19 cases are in Europe, America, India and Brazil. In the World Economic Outlook report released by the World Bank in June 2020, the economy of Sub-Saharan Africa was predicted and expected to shrink by 2.8% in 2020 (Teller Report, 21 June 2020).

Covid-19 has not only battered people's physical health and lives globally, but it has also adversely affected global, regional and national economies. The global lockdown and quarantine measures have shot down many businesses in various sectors of the economy and created rising levels of unanticipated unemployment and a time of furlough that has occasioned much privation for many hardworking individuals and households. For most surviving businesses, the Covid-19 safety guideline imperatives of limited person-to-person interaction, 2 weeks self-isolation to observe some unduly exposed persons for symptoms of coronavirus, and the 2 metres social distancing have imposed restrictions on their capacities to effectively utilize personnel and resources for optimal production or service delivery. This has set in motion a far-reaching crisis of underproduction across global economies. In the prevailing circumstances, many distressed businesses, big and small, have increasingly made demands for government bailout while growing numbers of individuals and households are in need of state welfare support. Most governments are overwhelmed by the disastrous impact of the Covid-19 crisis on people's lives and their economies. Africa is not an exception.

Despite Africa having one of the least regional incidents of Covid-19, the economic impact of the pandemic on the continent has been enormous. African countries are faced with the continent's worst economic crisis in a quarter of a century. Most African economies depend heavily on primary commodity exports, tourism and to a lesser extent, remittances from their diaspora populations. Export commodity prices, tourism and remittances have been battered by the Covid-19 crisis. Prior to the Covid-19 crisis, Africa had 7 out of 10 of the fasted growing economies in the world. In April 2020, the United Nations Economic Commission for Africa (UNECA) reviewed its earlier economic growth projection for Africa, stating that the growth will at least drop from 3.2 to 1.8%, and maybe more (Vanguard, 7 April 2020). Some of the African economies slipped into recession due to the economic impact of Covid-19, and for a country like South Africa that was already in its second recession in two years before the pandemic crisis, the impact is even more devastating.

The fledgling indigenous private sectors in Africa have been severely battered by the Covid-19 pandemic and unlike their counterparts in the developed countries that have received massive stimulus packages from their governments, in Africa the resource capacity and political will to stimulate the indigenous private sector are to say the least weak.

Pat Utomi,[4] Chair of the Pan-African Private Sector Trade and Investment Committee (PAFRAC) and an ex-presidential candidate in Nigeria coalesces the differential fate suffered by the private sectors in the developed countries and the developing countries of Africa under the Covid-19 battered business environment as follows:

> We have seen during this pandemic, companies in the industrialised world have received massive bailouts, tax incentives, not to mention government contracts and fiscal stimuli. Companies in Africa were not so fortunate and will have to deal with a world where trade will be depressed because of the post-Covid environment. As such, a fairer global trade environment and trading system is more urgent today than ever. (APO Group, 10 September 2020)

Who will deliver the fairer trade environment advocated by Utomi, which many African countries, NGOs and trade policy intellectuals have demanded for decades? One could easily reason that "the WTO will deliver it," being the multilateral institution in charge of promoting global trade and fair trade. But such an answer would be extremely naïve and wishful. International trade is an extension of international politics in which hegemonic interests are pivotal and dominant. That is essentially why multilateralism and the WTO framework have not been able to deliver on the fairer trade deals which developing countries have frantically campaigned for over the years.

9.3 Approach, Intervention and Support

The approach to Covid-19 pandemic has been mixed in Africa. Countries like Tanzania and Burundi have downplayed it. Others like Cameroun and Somalia have only paid lip service to it with no serious action. Countries like Nigeria, Rwanda, South Africa, Ethiopia, Uganda, Madagascar and the vast majority of African countries have adopted varied levels of serious measures. On 8 June 2020 Burundi's President Pierre Nkurunziza was reported dead after suffering a cardiac arrest, aged 55. It was reported in the news media that the president and his wife had tested positive for Covid-19. The first lady was flown to next door Kenya where she was successfully treated.

In early June 2020, the WHO expressed concern over the Tanzanian government's apparent trivialization and their suspension of the publishing of data on the disease. The late Tanzanian President John Magufuli declared an early victory over Covid-19 to the irritation of WHO and, among other things, criticized the national laboratory for exaggerating the number of infections before suspending the publication of national data on the virus. Based on the last official data published on 29 April 2020, Tanzania reported 509 cases of coronavirus, with 21 deaths (BBC News, 2 June 2020). President Magufuli not only trivialized the Covid-19 pandemic but also reproached the corresponding vaccines produced by the developed countries to combat the pandemic. This extremist approach is rather surprising considering that President Magufuli held a Ph.D. degree in Chemistry and most likely could not have been a novice on the scientific understanding of the pandemic. Unexpectedly, President Magufuli took ill in early 2021 (an illness that unconfirmed media reports attributed to Covid-19) and died about a month later. The Tanzanian government which was secretive about the President's health condition until his passing announced that the 61-year-old leader died of heart complications at a hospital in the capital city of Dar es Salaam. Despite his Covid-19 policy foibles, President Magufuli was ostensibly a selfless patriot widely beloved by the people he served most passionately, the Tanzanian masses. Renowned Tanzanian Professor of Law, Issa Shivji, however, characterized Magufuli as a populist leader that exemplified the messianic variant of civilian Bonapartism, who ruled by personal fiat often legitimized not only by material measures in the interest of the down-trodden or oppressed, but also by metaphysical appeals derived from the Catholic faith he zealously professed (Shivji 2021: 4). Critics like Anthony Squazzin (2020) are of the view that President Magufuli ostensibly adopted populist postures to Covid-19 to please the electorate ahead of the country's national elections in October 2020 by allowing them to go about their normal businesses to make a living, disregarding the WHO safety guidelines and the lockdown protocol (see also Squazzin 2020). It suffices to remark that many African countries announced the early lifting of lockdowns for two major reasons. The first is the low infection rate witnessed in Africa compared to other regions of the world. The second is the practical unsustainability of prolonged lockdowns from an economic point of view given the fact that an overwhelming size of the African workforce is employed in the informal sector, with most of them living on their daily earnings. Data from the International Labour Organization (ILO) global report on informal economies reveals that in Africa, 85.8% of employment is in the informal sector; the proportion is 68.2%

in Asia and the Pacific, 68.6% in the Arab States, 40.0% in the Americas and 25.1% in Europe and Central Asia (ILO 2018). Evidently, freezing public movements and economic activities by a prolonged lockdown will practically shut down the livelihood of too many people in Africa, and worsen the level of extreme poverty and even poverty-related deaths.

In March 2020, the Indian Ocean island of Madagascar launched its home-made herbal "remedy" for Covid-19 known as Covid-Organics or CVO for short. The launching of CVO was greeted with excitement in the country, giving many of its citizens the hope that they are protected from the pandemic crisis. For a considerable part of 2020, Madagascar's President Andry Rajoelina promoted CVO as mainly a preventive (and remotely curative) medicine, claiming that it is so safe that even school children could take it (Baker 2020). Following its official launch, many African countries, as well as Haiti, placed an order for shipment of the herbal tonic. While stating that CVO was not yet available for export, Rajoelina acquiesced by sending samples for free (Baker 2020). Madagascar despatched cargos of CVO to several African countries including Comoros, Guinea-Bissau, Equatorial Guinea, the Democratic Republic of Congo, Liberia, Niger, Tanzania, Nigeria, Senegal and Chad. In May 2020 WHO announced that it had offered to support the design of a study to look into Madagascar's herbal product [Covid-Organics] to scientifically verify its efficacity. In early July 2020, Madagascar reimposed full lockdown in its central region, which includes its capital city of Antananarivo, some two months after lockdown had earlier been lifted. The measure was taken to control and combat the resurgence of the virus. Many saw the reimposition of lockdown as a possible proof that Covid-Organics is inefficacious.

Cameroun has shown the most horrendous example of how not to fight Covid-19 in Africa or indeed anywhere else for that matter. With no reliable statistics of the spread of the virus or a robust plan to contain it, the government does not want to fight the virus, and in the name of politics, is fighting anybody that shows commitment to fight the virus. The Human Rights Watch has documented the following scandalous timeline of how the Camerounian government has fought the virus:

1. On 11 May 2020, 6 volunteers from the "Survival Initiative," a fundraising initiative launched by opposition leader Maurice Kamto to respond to the health emergency, were arrested while handing out protective masks and sanitizing gel for free to people in Yaoundé, the

capital.—The volunteers are faced with charges of rebellion and—if found guilty, they could face up to 4 years in prison.

2. Earlier in May 2020, the health minister rejected a donation by Kamto's initiative of 16,000 protective and surgical masks and 950 Covid-19 screening and testing kits, claiming the initiative had not been legally established.
3. On 7 April 2020, the Minister of Territorial Administration Paul Atanga Nji told anyone fundraising to fight Covid-19 to stop and urged citizens instead to make contributions to the "Special Fund of National Solidarity" created by Cameroon's president, Paul Biya.
4. On 9 April 2020, Territorial Administration Minister Mr Nji ordered accounts belonging to Kamto's initiative to be closed and its money frozen, and later called for an investigation into the "Survival Initiative." He also instructed communication companies to close mobile accounts opened to support the fund (HRW 14 May 2020).

The Camerounian government's response is to say the least scandalous. Kenya has been rocked by scandals over massive impropriety in the procurement of Covid-19 supplies and looting of donated Personal Protective Equipment (PPE) for frontline medical personnel and most of the stolen medical supplies have been reportedly sold to underground agents in neighbouring Tanzania. The Kenyan media have exposed how the government medical procurement officers handpicked companies that were given multi-million Dollar irregular contracts for Covid-19 supplies leading to embezzlement of funds and the supply of substandard PPE; also exposed is the criminal diversion of some of the equipment which had been donated by individuals and international agencies (SABC News, 27 August 2020). In response to public protests, the Kenyan government instituted an inquiry into the scandalous theft and impropriety. Months later in 2021, sections of the social media-savvy Kenyan public launched an online petition demanding that the IMF cancels a $2.34 billion loan it had recently approved for the Kenyan government to support the country's Covid-19 response programme. The over 160,000 petitioners based their protest on the looting of public treasury by state officials, mismanagement of previous loans and the country's growing external debt burden. To many readers, these Covid-19-related stories from Cameroun and Kenya might seem embarrassing. But it suffices to say that politicians and state officials from the two Sub-Saharan African countries have thick skins and strong shock-absorbers when it comes to international embarrassments of this nature. There are countries in Africa and elsewhere around the world where the proverbial deterrence of "name and shame" does not work, at least for now.

Some positive trends for managing Covid-19 and its effects have emerged elsewhere in Africa. For instance, a team of young engineering students in Senegal's Ecole Superieure Polytechnique (ESP) based in Dakar developed a small robot dubbed "Dr Car" which is able to measure patients' blood pressure and temperature, thereby helping to reduce the workload of frontline healthcare personnel in the fight against Covid-19 (France24, 13 May 2020). Moreover, researchers in a Senegalese laboratory used their experience in combating HIV/AIDS and Ebola to develop a rapid immune-based testing kit for Covid-19, commercially available for the equivalent of one US Dollar.

In April 2020, the Ghanaian government introduced the use of drones to convey the Covid-19 test samples from more than a thousand remote villages to diagnostic laboratories based in towns and cities. The new drone measure, the first in Africa, was introduced by the Ghanaian Ministry of Health in partnership with an American firm Zipline to increase the number and speed of testing.

Box 9.1 Fighting Covid-19 in Africa: The Outstanding Example of Rwanda

Rwanda's preparedness and response to the COVID-19 pandemic were robust and rapid, ranging from strengthening health systems to mitigating socio-economic impact (WHO Rwanda, 13 November 2020). The Rwandan government's response has three intervention components[5]:

1. Strengthen the health system to contain COVID-19 spread:
2. Safeguard economic resilience against COVID-19 shocks:
3. Mitigate the impact of COVID-19 on the vulnerable, through expanding social protection coverage (Terry 2020).

It is pertinent to mention that "Rwanda was in the middle of an economic boom prior to the COVID-19 pandemic with a real economic growth of 9.4 percent in 2019, driven mostly by large public investments for implementation of the National Strategy of Transformation" (UN Rwanda 2020). The pandemic adversely affected the growth momentum as the services sector which accounts for over half of Rwanda's gross domestic product received a devastating hit amid disruption in international trade and travel (UN Rwanda 2020).

To contain the spread of Covid-19, the Rwandan government implemented a range of measures with effect from March 2020, including all WHO Covid-19 safety protocols (social distancing, handwashing, etc.), suspension of domestic and international travels, mass screening and testing of the population, mandatory wearing of masks in public, teleworking, closure of all learning institutions and a total lockdown of the country from 21/03/2020 to 04/05/2020 (AfDB, 18 December 2020). These early measures were highly successful in preventing the virus from spreading.

With a population of about 12 million people, 2019 GDP of $10.21 billion and per capita of $824.90,[6] the Rwandan government spent about $73 million in the fight against the COVID-19 pandemic in the first six month of the pandemic (March–September 2020), and an additional budget of $11 million dollars was earmarked for the period running up to December 2020 (WHO Rwanda, 13 November 2020; Xinhua Net, 3 October 2020).

In May 2020, Rwanda, Africa's leading ICT and high-tech innovation hub, exhibited its five new multifunctional medical robots designed to improve the fight against Covid-19. The high-tech robots have the capacity to, among other things, screen 50 to 150 people per minute, monitor patients' status, deliver food and medication to patients' rooms, capture data, keep medical records and notify officers on duty about detected abnormalities (*The Guardian*, 20 May 2020). Rwanda's humanoid robots were designed to help minimize the contact between medical staff and patients which is critical in mitigating the spread of Covid-19. In addition, Rwanda also deploys conventional drones for the delivery of medicine, as well as some unique drones equipped with loudspeakers that fly above city streets to broadcast virus-fighting measures, a strategy pioneered by China to fight Covid-19 (Butera and Sguazzin 2020). Another important strategy devised by the Rwandan Ministry of Health to fight Covid-19 is the effective use of home-based care to treat infested patients, which turns out to be significantly more cost-efficient relative to those treated in the government's quarantine centres and hospitals. The severe cases that may require Intensive Care Unit (ICU) special attention are referred to hospitals. The patients eligible for home-based care include those who are asymptomatic and must be below 65 years old, without other long-lasting health complications and must have a suitable accommodation with own bedroom at home (Xinhua Net, 3 October 2020).

Overall, with the efficient intervention measures of President Kagame's government, Rwanda has had one of the least cases of Covid-19 infections and death in Africa and indeed globally. Official figures published on 19 December 2020 reveal that since the pandemic began, Rwanda has recorded a total of 7,105 coronavirus infections, 57 deaths and 6,089 recovered cases (Reuters, 19 December 2020).[7]

Africa has experienced tremendous international goodwill and support in the fight against Covid-19, most of which have come from the WHO, EU, China, big businesses and independent charities such as the Jack Ma Foundation owned by the Chinese E-Commerce billionaire Mr Jack Ma. African-based non-state actors such as religious and business organizations, and wealthy individuals have also made donations to support the efforts of the state in the forms of money, ventilators, medicines and Personal Protective Equipment (PPE), ambulances and foodstuffs.

In terms of support to African economies, the World Bank Group in early February 2020 approved a raft of emergency support operations for developing countries in general to backstop their Covid-19 response capacities. Under the measures the World Bank Group plans to deploy up to $160 billion over the next 15 months to support COVID-19 measures ($55 billion of which was earmarked for Africa) that will help countries respond to immediate health consequences of the pandemic and bolster economic recovery (World Bank 2020a). The Bank's plan to help bolster economic recovery include, supporting the poverty reduction policies of states, and capital infusion that can benefit small and medium enterprises and help to create conditions for growth. Private creditor support to Africa in 2020 was estimated at $13 billion but Africa needs an estimated $114 billion in 2020 in its fight against COVID-19, leaving a financing gap of around $44 to $46 billion (World Bank 2020a).

Table 9.1 shows an initial set of Covid-19 emergency response projects funding announced by the World Bank for developing countries. Of the 25 beneficiary countries, 11 are in Africa.

By far, the largest set of allocations ($100 million and above) were made to Asian countries—India, Pakistan, Sri Lanka and Afghanistan.

Table 9.1 Initial set of Covid-19 emergency response projects funded under the fast-track facility[a]

Country	*$USD (Mil)*	*Country*	*$USD (Mil)*
Afghanistan	100.4	Maldives	7.3
Argentina	35.0	Mauritania	5.2
Cabo Verde	5.0	Mongolia	26.9
Cambodia	20.0	Pakistan	200.0
DRC	47.2	Paraguay	20.0
Djibouti	5.0	São Tomé & Principe	2.5
Ecuador	20.0	Senegal	20.0
Ethiopia	82.6	Sierra Leone	7.5
Ghana	35.0	Sri Lanka	128.6
Haiti	20.0	Tajikistan	11.3
India	1,000.0	The Gambia	10.0
Kenya	50.0	Yemen	26.9
Kyrgyz Republic	12.5		

[a]Total project shows the full amount of the operation, FTF financing as well as IDA18, IBRD, Trust Funds or front-loaded IDA19
Source World Bank (2020b)

Africa's three largest beneficiaries are Ethiopia ($82.6 million), Kenya ($50 million) and Ghana ($35 million).

On 17 April 2020, the World Bank Group and IMF convened a virtual conference of African leaders, bilateral partners and multilateral institutions to deliberate on Covid-19 response in Africa and the meeting among other things restated an earlier agreement announced by the G20 countries to temporarily suspend debt payments to IDA and least developed countries with effect from 1 May 2020. A range of financing options and policy tools were discussed at the conference to help mitigate the medium and long-term impact of the pandemic on African economies.

Speaking to journalists after his farewell address to the WTO General Council, the organization's highest decision-making body in Geneva on 23 July 2020, outgoing WTO Director General Roberto Azevedo remarked that: "There are big variables" in addressing the Covid-19 pandemic: "We don't know how long it's going to last. We don't know how effective we are going to be in fighting it. We don't know how quickly it will spread or be controlled" (Turkish Press, 23 July 2020). The "big variables" that Azevedo pointed to are important "unknowns" that have far-reaching implications for economic recovery and growth, not least in weak developing regions like Africa. Diverse helps have been pledged and/or provided to support Africa's recovery from the Covid-19 crisis and also to mitigate the medium and long-term impact on the economies of states. Ultimately, African leaders have a responsibility to effectively mobilize and deploy all available external opportunities, as well as the human and material resources within their jurisdictions to ensure speedy economic recovery and protect the health and livelihoods of their people. It is remarkable that virtually all the African governments have already promulgated post-Covid-19 stabilization and revitalization programmes that can help their economies absorb the pandemic-related shocks in the short run and hopefully bounce back on a growth trajectory.

Summary Points

1. Covid-19 was first detected in Wuhan in China in December 2019. Within three months of its detection, the virus had practically spread to every part of the world due to the forces of globalization.
2. "COVID-19 is mainly spread from person to person through airborne droplets that are coughed or sneezed out by an infected person. People may also get a COVID-19 infection by touching something that has the virus on it and then touching their own mouth, nose, or eyes" (Tesini 2020). Symptoms usually manifest within 14 days of one's infection.
3. As at the time of writing, a number of vaccines have been developed and are being utilized for the containment and prevention of Covid-19, which has come as a welcome relief after about one year of devastating global impact by the virus.
4. Contrary to all the earlier predictions pointing to a public health catastrophe in Africa because of the weak infrastructures, financial resources and technical capacities of most African states, the continent has been the least affected region by the Covid-19 pandemic.
5. The most severe toll of the virus has occurred in the more developed countries (notably USA and Europe), as well as India and Brazil.
6. Covid-19 has not only battered people's physical health and lives globally, but it has also adversely affected global, regional and national economies.

7. The approach to Covid-19 pandemic has been mixed in Africa. While some countries have downplayed the severity of the virus, others have only paid lip service to it with no serious action. There are yet other countries that have responded effectively to the pandemic using all the necessary medical technologies and following all the WHO safety guidelines.
8. Most African countries have received substantial international support to help control the spread of Covid-19 and manage its health and socio-economic impact.

Discussion Questions

1. What is the meaning of the term zoonosis and how is it related to Covid-19?
2. Why has Africa been the least affected region by the Covid-19 pandemic?
3. In what ways has the Covid-19 pandemic affected global, regional and national economies?
4. How has Covid-19 more severely affected the fledgling indigenous private sector in Africa in comparison to their counterparts in the developed countries?
5. In what specific ways has Africa been assisted by development partners and external state and non-state actors to cope with Covid-19 and its adverse socio-economic impact?

Notes

1. See Dominic Barton (2011) "Capitalism for the Long-Term", *Harvard Business Review*, March, https://hbr.org/2011/03/capitalism-for-the-long-term.
2. Zoonoses is the plural form of zoonosis.
3. Taken from an Arise News podcast (by Courtesy of CNN), "#MelindaGates - Africa Will Have Dead Bodies On The Streets. #Covid19 - Trending with @OjyOkpe", 14 April 2020, https://www.youtube.com/watch?v=MPFXsJokaHM.

4. I have previously referenced Pat Utomi in Chapter 5 as a public intellectual and professor of political economy.
5. The Rwandan government's response is partly funded from a concessional loan of $97.675 million approved by the African Development Bank (AfDB) to support the Rwandan Government's multi-sectoral Covid-19 Crisis Response Budget Support Programme (see Terry 2020).
6. Statistical Times (24 February 2020) "List African Countries by GDP", http://statisticstimes.com/economy/african-countries-by-gdp.php; See also: Statistical Times (29 February 2020) "List of African Countries by GDP Per Capita", http://statisticstimes.com/economy/african-countries-by-gdp-per-capita.php.
7. Reuters (19 December 2020) "Covid-19 Tracker – Rwanda", Reuters News, https://graphics.reuters.com/world-coronavirus-tracker-and-maps/countries-and-territories/rwanda/; Worldmeter (19 December 2020) "Total Coronavirus Cases in Rwanda", Worldmeter, https://www.worldometers.info/coronavirus/country/rwanda/.

References

AfDB. 2020. Rwanda – Covid-19 Crisis Response Budget Support Program (RCRBS), December 18. https://projectsportal.afdb.org/dataportal/VProject/show/P-RW-K00-013.

APO Group. 2020. African Private Sector Upbeat about the Future but Demands Fairer and more Transparent Global Trading System, September 10. https://www.africa-newsroom.com/press/african-private-sector-upbeat-about-the-future-but-demands-fairer-and-more-transparent-global-trading-system.

Baker, Aryn. 2020. Could It Work as a Cure? Maybe! A Herbal Remedy for Coronavirus Is a Hit in Africa, But Experts Have Their Doubts, May 22. https://time.com/5840148/coronavirus-cure-covid-organic-madagascar/.

BBC News. 2020. Coronavirus: John Magufuli Declares Tanzania free of Covid-19, June 2. https://www.bbc.co.uk/news/world-africa-52966016.

Butera, Saul, and Antony Sguazzin. 2020. Robots Deployed to Fight Coronavirus in Rwanda. Bloomberg, May 20. https://www.bloomberg.com/news/articles/2020-05-20/robot-says-we-will-prevail-in-rwanda-s-fight-against-virus.

Chen, Zigi. 2020. COVID-19 and Emerging Viral Diseases: The Journey from Animals to Humans, April. Harvard University: The Graduate School of Arts and Science. http://sitn.hms.harvard.edu/flash/2020/covid-19-emerging-viral-diseases-journey-animals-humans/.

Ellis, Ralph. 2020. COVID-19 Infection Fatality Ratio is About 1.15 Percent, October 30. https://www.webmd.com/lung/news/20201030/covid-19-infection-fatality-ratio-is-about-one-point-15-percent.

France24. 2020. Senegal's Engineering Students Design Machines to Fight Covid-19, May 13. https://www.france24.com/en/20200513-senegal-s-engineering-students-design-machines-to-fight-covid-19.

Gartner, Annelies, et al. 2020. Covid-19 Vaccine: Latest Updates on Oxford, Moderna and Pfizer Breakthroughs - And Who Will Get It First? *The Telegraph*, December 2. https://www.telegraph.co.uk/global-health/science-and-disease/covid-19-vaccine-moderna-oxford-latest-pfizer-when-coronavirus/.

Gavi. 2020. The Covid-19 Vaccine Race. Gavi - The Vaccine Alliance, December 2. https://www.gavi.org/vaccineswork/covid-19-vaccine-race.

HRW. 2020. Covid-19 Brings Out Government's Ugly Side in Cameroon, May 14. https://www.hrw.org/news/2020/05/14/covid-19-brings-out-governments-ugly-side-cameroon.

ILO. 2018. *Women and Men in the Informal Economy: A Statistical Picture*, 3rd ed., April. https://www.ilo.org/wcmsp5/groups/public/—dgreports/—dcomm/documents/publication/wcms_626831.pdf.

Independent. 2020. Coronavirus Vaccine: Oxford Trial Is 'Safe' and Produces Immune Reaction, First Study Results Show, July 20. https://www.independent.co.uk/news/health/coronavirus-vaccine-oxford-university-study-trial-result-covid-19-safe-a9628491.html.

Mcgrew, Anthony. 2010. Globalization and World Politics. In *The Globalization of World Politics: An Introduction to International Relations*, ed. John Baylis, Steven Smith, and Patricia Owens, 1st American ed., 15–33 New York: Oxford University Press.

Nature Medicine. 2020. African Countries Battle-Ready to Take on COVID-19, June 11. http://www.ox.ac.uk/news/2020-06-11-african-countries-battle-ready-take-covid-19.

Rainsford, Sarah. 2020. Coronavirus: Sputnik V Vaccine Rushed Out to Wary Russians. BBC News, December 8. https://www.bbc.co.uk/news/world-europe-55221785.

SABC News. 2020. Kenya's President Orders Investigations into Alleged Theft of COVID-19 Funds, August 27. https://www.sabcnews.com/sabcnews/kenyas-president-orders-investigations-into-alleged-theft-of-covid-19-funds/.

Shivji, Issa. 2021. The Dialectics of Maguphilia and Maguphobia. *CODESRIA Bulletin Online*, No. 13. http://www.codesria.org/IMG/pdf/13-_shivji_codbul_online_21.pdf.

Squazzin, Anthony. 2020. John Magufuli Declares Victory Over the Virus Despite No Health Data Being Released, June 19. https://www.businesslive.

co.za/bd/world/africa/2020-06-19-tanzania-president-downplays-covid-19-ahead-of-elections/.

Teller Report. 2020. China-Africa Special Summit: Why Was It Held at this Time? June 21. https://www.tellerreport.com/news/2020-06-21-china-africa-special-summit–why-was-it-held-at-this-time-.H1wieaP3a8.html.

Terry, Olufemi. 2020. Rwanda: African Development Bank Commits $98 Million for Multisector COVID-19 Response. AfDB, July 24. https://www.afdb.org/en/news-and-events/press-releases/rwanda-african-development-bank-commits-98-million-multisector-covid-19-response-37032.

Tesini, L. Brenda. 2020. Coronaviruses and Acute Respiratory Syndromes (COVID-19, MERS, and SARS). University of Rochester School of Medicine and Dentistry, May. https://www.msdmanuals.com/home/infections/respiratory-viruses/coronaviruses-and-acute-respiratory-syndromes-covid-19,-mers,-and-sars.

The Guardian. 2020. Rwanda Deploys Robots to Fight COVID-19, May 20. https://guardian.ng/news/rwanda-deploys-robots-to-fight-covid-19/.

The Guardian. 2020. Dexamethasone: Low-cost Drug Helps Prevent Deaths of Sickest Coronavirus Patients, June 16. https://www.theguardian.com/world/2020/jun/16/steroid-found-to-help-prevent-deaths-of-sickest-coronavirus-patients.

Turkish Press. 2020. Prepare for Another COVID-like Crisis: WTO Chief, July 23. https://turkishpress.com/prepare-for-another-covid-like-crisis-wto-chief/.

UN Rwanda. 2020. The Socio-Economic Impact of Covid-19 in Rwanda. *UNDP*, June. https://www.greengrowthknowledge.org/sites/default/files/downloads/resource/UNDP-rba-COVID-assessment-Rwanda.pdf.

UNDP Rwanda. 2020. UNDP Rwanda: Support to the National Response to Contain the Impact of COVID-19. *UNDP Rwanda*, April. https://www.undp.org/content/dam/rba/docs/COVID-19-CO-Response/undp-rba-covid-rwanda-apr2020.pdf.

Vanguard. 2020. COVID-19: What Nigeria, Africa must do to Mitigate Damaging Effects, April 7. https://www.vanguardngr.com/2020/04/covid-19-what-nigeria-africa-must-do-to-mitigate-damaging-effects/.

Xinhua Net. 2020. Rwanda Lowers Costs of Fighting COVID-19 Through Home-based Care: Official, October 3. http://www.xinhuanet.com/english/2020-10/03/c_139416538.htm.

Wood, Vincent. 2020. Covid: Another New Variant Found in UK from South Africa. *The Independent*, December 23. https://www.independent.co.uk/news/uk/home-news/covid-variant-uk-south-africa-coronavirus-update-b1778225.html.

Walzer, Christian. 2020. The COVID-19 Pandemic Has Introduced Us to a New Word: Zoonosis (Op-Ed), April 1. https://www.livescience.com/dangers-of-zoonoses-pandemics.html.
World Bank. 2020a. World Bank Group and IMF Mobilize Partners in the Fight Against COVID-19 in Africa, April 17. https://www.worldbank.org/en/news/press-release/2020/04/17/world-bank-group-and-imf-mobilize-partners-in-the-fight-against-covid-19-in-africa.
World Bank. 2020b. World Bank Group Launches First Operations for COVID-19 (Coronavirus) Emergency Health Support, Strengthening Developing Country Responses, April 2. https://www.worldbank.org/en/news/press-release/2020/04/02/world-bank-group-launches-first-operations-for-covid-19-coronavirus-emergency-health-support-strengthening-developing-country-responses.
WHO Rwanda. 2020. UN Rwanda: Frw19.6 Billion and Counting as the Fight against COVID-19 Continues, November 13. WHO Rwandan Office. https://www.afro.who.int/news/un-rwanda-frw196-billion-and-counting-fight-against-covid-19-continues.
Yang, Yongshi, et al. 2020. The Deadly Coronaviruses: The 2003 SARS Pandemic and the 2020 Novel Coronavirus Epidemic in China, May. https://www.ncbi.nlm.nih.gov/pmc/articles/PMC7126544/.

Index

K. Omeje, *The Failure and Feasibility of Capitalism in Africa*, International Political Economy Series,
https://doi.org/10.1007/978-3-030-75170-8

The manufacturer's authorised representative in the EU is Springer
Nature Customer Service Centre GmbH, Europaplatz 3, 69115 Heidelberg,
Germany. If you have any concerns regarding our products, please
contact ProductSafety@springernature.com

Printed and bound by CPI Group (UK) Ltd, Croydon, CR0 4YY
06/10/2026
02228468-0005